SELF AS NATION

THE SCHUSTERMAN SERIES IN ISRAEL STUDIES

Editors: S. Ilan Troen, Jehuda Reinharz, and Sylvia Fuks Fried

The Schusterman Series in Israel Studies publishes original scholarship of exceptional significance on the history of Zionism and the State of Israel. It draws on disciplines across the academy, from anthropology, sociology, political science and international relations to the arts, history and literature. It seeks to further an understanding of Israel within the context of the modern Middle East and the modern Jewish experience. There is special interest in developing publications that enrich the university curriculum and enlighten the public at large. The series is published under the auspices of the Schusterman Center for Israel Studies at Brandeis University.

For a complete list of books in this series, please see www.upne.com

SELF AS NATION

CONTEMPORARY HEBREW AUTOBIOGRAPHY

TAMAR S. HESS

Brandeis University Press | Waltham, Massachusetts

Brandeis University Press
An imprint of University Press of New England
www.upne.com
© 2016 Brandeis University
All rights reserved
Manufactured in the United States of America
Designed by April Leidig
Typeset in Whitman by Copperline Book Services

This book was published with the generous support of
Mandel Scholion: Interdisciplinary Research Center in the
Humanities and Jewish Studies, the Mandel Institute of
Jewish Studies, and the Faculty of Humanities at the
Hebrew University of Jerusalem.

Special thanks to the Kaniuk Estate and David Tartakover
for permission to reproduce *Matchbooks* on the jacket.

Page 201 constitutes a continuation of this copyright page.

Library of Congress Cataloging-in-Publication Data
Names: Hess, Tamar, 1966– author.
Title: Self as nation : contemporary Hebrew autobiography / Tamar S. Hess.
Description: Waltham, Massachusetts : Brandeis University Press, [2016] | Series:
The Schusterman series in Israel studies | Includes bibliographical references and index.
Identifiers: LCCN 2016004945 (print) | LCCN 2016015895 (ebook) |
ISBN 9781611688795 (cloth: alk. paper) | ISBN 9781611688801 (pbk.: alk. paper) |
ISBN 9781611689662 (epub, mobi & pdf)
Subjects: LCSH: Autobiography—Israeli authors. | Israeli literature—History and
criticism. | Authors, Israeli—Biography—History and criticism. | Hebrew literature,
Modern—History and criticism. | Autobiography in literature. | Autobiography—
Women authors.
Classification: LCC PJ5033.5 .H48 2016 (print) | LCC PJ5033.5 (ebook) |
DDC 892.48/703—dc23
LC record available at https://lccn.loc.gov/2016004945

5 4 3 2 1

In loving memory of my father

John Harris Hess (z"l)

1932–2011

CONTENTS

ACKNOWLEDGMENTS

AS I PART WITH THIS BOOK and send it to print, Jerusalem is gripped with fear, violence, hate, racism, and despair. In the fall semester of 2015, I returned to some of the autobiographies discussed here with my students at the Department of Hebrew Literature at the Hebrew University of Jerusalem. The Mount Scopus campus has always been an enclave. My students arrive in class after a tense ride on public transportation. The sting of tear-gas the wind has carried from neighboring Isawiya may greet them outside. But inside the campus is calm and alive with diversity. Hijab-adorned young women sit in the cafeteria by Orthodox Jewish students with head coverings that range from elaborate creations to minimal headbands. Jewish secular students share notes with ultra-Orthodox. In my class students from settlements outside Jerusalem prepare class presentations with students from kibbutzim. It is a small group of fifteen. When we speak of trauma, narrative, and memory, reading the autobiographies of Yoram Kaniuk or Netiva Ben-Yehuda, discussion becomes openly personal. Two mothers in this graduate class have lost their children to terror attacks. Opposing and controversial opinions are not left outside the room. Our discussion carries them. We listen to each other and weave our voices together in profound respect for close interpretation of Hebrew culture and texts. Every meeting with my students, our ability to critically study Hebrew literature is a privilege that fills me with hope. I hope the readings of Hebrew autobiography presented in this book carry some of this spirit and the love of Hebrew literature that permeates our discussions.

I first contemplated this book in spring 2001 when, still a graduate student, I taught a class on Hebrew autobiography. The students in that seminar and those who followed over the years have been an endless source of probing questions and provocative ideas. I am grateful to them and to my academic home, the Hebrew University. I first conceptualized the ideas that were to become this book as a Mandel Postdoctoral Fellow at the Scholion Interdisciplinary Research Center in the Humanities and Jewish Studies, a nurturing haven for academic endeavors and thought. An early version of this book's last chapter was first published during my years there in *Prooftexts* (27, no. 1, 2007). An ISF grant helped me map out the terrain of Hebrew autobiography in the twentieth century with the aid of research assistants Yael Tamir, Kineret Rubinstein, and Lee Maman. The Faculty of Humanities and the Mandel Institute of Jewish Studies at the Hebrew University both contributed funds toward the publication. I thank Carrie Friedman, Merav Yaacobi, Varda Schwartz, and Marina Shusterman for smoothing administrative hurdles with constant and friendly efficiency. Elena Birman and Tsippy Rabinovitch at the School of Literature provided daily backup.

My dear colleagues and friends in the Department of Hebrew Literature provide the perfect supportive setting for research. I am especially indebted to Matti Huss, Hannan Hever, Galit Hasan-Rokem, and Shimrit Peled. I can't imagine having written this book without your vast scholarship, encouragement, critique, and generous insights. Nancy K. Miller has been an inspiring mentor and guide. Conversations with colleagues in the field of Hebrew literature—Alan Mintz, Nili Gold, Barbara Mann, Mikhal Dekel, Yigal Schwartz, and Ruth Ginsburg—have all contributed to this project. I am grateful to Katja Sarkowsky for opening concepts of theory of autobiography, and a stimulating continuing exchange, and to the German Humboldt Foundation for initiating our collaboration. Special thanks to Menachem Brinker for his timely intervention.

Brandeis University Press and Phyllis Deutsch at UPNE have been inconceivably patient in nudging this book to completion. My annual meetings with Sylvia Fuks Fried, the director of Brandeis University Press, at AJS conferences have offered crystallizing directions of thought, as well as great pleasure. Marilyn Lidor, Karen Maron, and Nir Erron edited earlier versions of the manuscript; Jason Warshof's final editing of the book was an exquisite demonstration of perfect editorial craftsmanship.

The families Hess and Segman have put their hearts and days on end into this book, in countless ways. Ronnen, Rachel, and Ayelet will all celebrate it finally moving out of the house. I would not want to write anything without you.

SELF AS NATION

Hebrew Autobiography—
Nation, Relation, and Narration

I SRAELI AUTOBIOGRAPHY has been instrumental in the shaping of contemporary national Israeli selves and, in turn, is influenced by concepts
of selfhood in Israeli culture. A key literary genre in modern Hebrew
letters, autobiography grapples with the dilemmas of modern Jewish and national Israeli being. The Israeli self finds and articulates its voice within this
genre. The study of autobiography, therefore, offers keys to understanding
the shifting spirit and soul of Jewish and Israeli nationality and allows for
a revitalized look at the Hebrew canon. Moreover, by reading Israeli autobiography at the convergence of the individual, universal representation,
and national specificity, this volume joins wider discussions of autobiography outside Hebrew literature, and also enables a meeting of two critical
fields of discourse: autobiography and nationalism.

Autobiography, as the term *auto* indicates, pertains to individual self-
narrated lives. However, as has often been noted, autobiographical selves
do not germinate in seclusion. They may relate to other individuals, and
more often than not, they relate to communities.[1] Following Benedict Anderson, nations can be thought of as collectives under continuous creation
that necessitate cultural construction, rather than as fixed or given enti-
ties.[2] Autobiography in a national context often negotiates the individual's
relationship to the community, whether imagined or not, and in doing so
defines the conditions enabling its being. The act of narrating singular lives
allows the narrator to map out his or her contacts with the collective. These
contacts or contracts constitute the making of the culture within which
they are practiced.

Autobiographical writing harbors a basic tension between memory and the forgotten. It necessarily shifts between the reconstruction of a specific past and the denial of evasive qualities from that past, and between varying levels of recognition of memory's limits. This, as Ernest Renan famously wrote, is also characteristic of nations, which are necessarily founded on forgetting as well as on remembrance, which is more than mere remembering—forgetting the violent acts on which they were constituted, monumentalizing common achievements and sacrifices.[3]

In national literatures the individual self is generally defined as both particular and universally representative. In autobiography individual selves are traditionally perceived as representatives of larger collectives, while simultaneously representing their singularity. The relationship between the self as representative and as private is political. As Leigh Gilmore has put it, "The interface of singular and shareable goes to the issue of political representation, for the autobiographical self who is cut off from others, even as it stands for them, is a metaphor for the citizen."[4] The political is ingrained in the Western canon of autobiography, beginning with Saint Augustine's *Confessions* (397–400 AD), widely considered the formative text of Western autobiography and rooted in the author's journey toward conversion and persuasion of his readers to follow his path.[5]

I read Israeli autobiography as part of a continuum with Hebrew autobiography, which began in the mid-nineteenth century. Indeed, modern Hebrew narrative fiction was born of autobiography. In Eastern Europe, Hebrew Enlightenment (*Haskalah*) literature offered two major models for modern Hebrew literature: the idyllic, neoclassical, neobiblical narrative introduced and perfected by Abraham Mapu (1808–1867), exemplified in his 1853 novel, *Ahavat zion* (The Love of Zion), and the critical, angry, embittered, and exposed narrative introduced by Mordechai Aharon Guenzberg (1795–1846), whose *Aviezer* was published in full posthumously, in 1863.[6]

Chroniclers of modern Hebrew literature repeatedly point to *Ahavat zion*, with its handsome heroes, eventful plot, and happy ending, as the starting point for modern Hebrew fiction. The actual literary terrain, however, points to *Aviezer* and other classic autobiographies, such as Solomon Maimon's 1792 work written in German and Moshe Leib Lilienblum's (Malal)

Hatot neurim (1876), as the stronger influences on major Hebrew modernists such as Michah Yosef Berdichevsky, Yosef Haim Brenner, and Uri Nissan Gnessin. The birth of modern Hebrew fiction entailed a fictionalization of the autobiographical story that *maskilic* literature had introduced.[7] Hebrew modernists repeatedly acknowledged their debt to autobiographies written by Haskalah authors. Malal (1843–1910) set the standard for this continuity when he wrote *Hatot neurim*. He relied on his reader's familiarity with Guenzberg's *Aviezer*, announcing that he would pick up where his predecessor's memoir had left off, joining the two lives in a linear, collective autobiography that they and their followers adopted as representative of the identity and experience of a generation of men from a specific background and class.[8]

Autobiography also offered a linguistic model different from Mapu's linguistic purism consisting of biblical language, idioms, and images. The language and form of autobiography were disrupted, broken and cracked, inclusive and hybrid. Hebrew mixed with other languages; biblical parables, interpretation, and traditional discourse appeared alongside philosophical essays, social parodies, and confession. Malal's autobiography, for example, included documents, letters, manifestos and public declarations, summaries of his essays, as well as narratives of memoir and confession. The flexible language of Hebrew autobiography differed greatly from the polished and stylized "code," or *nusah*, that Shalom Ya'akov Abramovitch (Mendele Mocher Sforim; 1836–1917) forged, and which had a formative imprint on modern Hebrew fiction.[9] While the *nusah* style left its mark on authors such as Haim Nachman Bialik in his short stories and Yitzhak Dov Berkovitch, the master of short fiction, it was the language of autobiography that filtered into modernist psychological realism and attempts at stream of consciousness. Likewise, while other literary models laid the foundation for modern Hebrew fiction—hasidic literature, Yiddish literature, major European literatures, traditional Hebrew legal literature and written debates, chronicles, letters—the predominant model that set this literature's course was autobiography.

Although written within a literary community that privileged the making of an imagined national community over any other collective endeavor, Hebrew autobiography cannot be considered separate from its prenational beginnings in Haskalah literature. When authors who had no direct personal connection tied themselves to one another and related their lives through their contemporaries and predecessors, they created an imagined community. (Such connections continued into the twentieth and twenty-first centuries, as I will try to show in linking Yoram Kaniuk's work with predecessors such as Solomon Maimon.) Zionism read Haskalah literature as an overture or a bridge to nationalism. Malal's advocacy of Zionism in "Derekh tshuva" (Road of Return), the conclusion to *Hatot neurim*, the major autobiographical work of the Haskalah period, seems to corroborate this view. Thus, although it was not committed to Jewish nationalism as an exclusive cause, Haskalah was read in retrospect as the prefiguration of national collectivity.[10]

Ernest Renan's seminal essay "What Is a Nation?" (1882) famously states: "Where national memories are concerned, griefs are of more value than triumphs, for they impose duties, and require a common effort."[11] This same sentiment is apparent in Lilienblum's 1881 essay "Al yisrael ve-al artso" (On Israel and Its Land), in which he declares that the year's assaults on Russian Jews would yield the positive outcome of halting assimilation and reconnecting Jews to their historic experience of victimhood.[12] In line with Renan's dictum, where Hebrew autobiography is concerned, "griefs are of more value than triumphs." Failure, frustration, humiliation, and desolation are the mainstays of early modern Hebrew autobiography specifically, and of modern Hebrew narrative fiction as a whole. Solomon Maimon, who is justifiably credited with importing Rousseau's autobiographical model into Jewish literature, and Guenzberg and Lilienblum, who introduced the model into Hebrew, all harnessed their personal pain toward a collective project. While they enlisted the community they were trying to relate to, they offered in return self-exposure, or the satisfaction of their readers' voyeurism, by revealing an enticing personal story.[13] Each could have narrated a counterimage embodying success—Maimon achieved prominence in the culture to which he immigrated with nothing but his personal competence, determination, devotion, and extraordinary intelligence; Guenzberg was an esteemed author and historian; and Lilienblum became the spiritual leader of a generation.[14] For his part Maimon is indeed proud of his achievements, but his followers find their own experience of failure to override any successes.

When, in the later nineteenth century, Hebrew literature eventually became intertwined with the territorial national project and with aspirations of sovereignty, the national modern Hebrew autobiography had already been formed, and was adopted as such by subsequent generations of authors. We need not determine whether Mordechai Aharon Guenzberg can be identified as a proto-Zionist to accept his self-portrait, cast after Maimon's, as that which shaped relations between the collective and the individual in modern Hebrew literature.[15]

As Dan Miron has pointed out, a unified biography was the essential element needed to fuse individuals into an imagined national community.[16] Lilienblum, for his part, carried his autobiographical self through the hopes of the Enlightenment until he embraced the Zionist cause. His narrative was to become the paradigm adopted by Zionist historians as encompassing the rise of Zionism and modern Jewish national experience. It was a narrative that until very recently overshadowed any alternative. Long into the 1950s, the powerful impact of this masculine Hebrew model was palpable. Lilienblum fashioned his autobiographical self on this model, and Brenner in turn positions his fictional character-narrator as the last in the line of autobiographers.[17] Shmuel Yosef Agnon revisited the story of *Aviezer* in *Sipur pashut* (A Simple Story).[18] And Shlomo Tsemah (1886–1974), an agronomist, educator, and author, returned to these narratives in his 1952 memoir, *Shana rishona* (First Year), in order to characterize the Second Aliya—referring to Jewish immigrants to Ottoman Palestine in the decade before World War I—and himself as their representative.

By the time statehood was achieved in 1948, the nineteenth-century autobiographical strands of pressing despair encompassed by *Aviezer*, morphing into the active national politics of the next century, had become a safe nostalgic space in which to nestle. Although the nation was young, these were the tales of old men.[19]

AUTOBIOGRAPHY LOST its canonical status in Hebrew literature in the early twentieth century, absorbed by narrative fiction, which would become the central literary genre of Hebrew modernity for most of the century, pioneered by Hebrew writers such as Berdichevsky, Brenner, Baron, and others. Yet autobiographical writings were continuously produced.

Looking back to the latter part of the previous century, personal narratives had been geared toward an audience abroad. Just as generations of Holy Land pilgrims had done before them, immigrants and travelers published their Hebrew memoirs in order to document their visits to or settlement in Palestine, but even more so to entice others to join them.[20] But now Zionism lent Hebrew autobiography a triumphant tone. In late Ottoman and Mandatory Palestine, autobiographical writings replaced an ethos of defeat with immigrant stories celebrating victorious settlement in a new home. In line with its Eastern European origins, the settler autobiography is deeply rooted in collective national life, with the individual virtually attempting to merge with the collective and present his or her own life story as an emblem of national success.[21]

A clear gender divide exists in writings of this period. Namely, against a common story line of triumph from men, the many women immigrants to Palestine who wrote their memoirs did so in a conciliatory tone, projecting pride in achievement despite obstacles but very seldom trumpeting victory. Their stories often tell of disillusionment and disappointment, at times intermingled with a sense of betrayal at the hands of their male fellow settlers.[22]

Elements from the Zionist labor movement, influenced by Russian revolutionary norms of self-documentation, have provided us with numerous memoirs, many left unpublished in archives. These works represent attempts by the authors to free themselves from obscurity.[23] Many of the immigrant memoirs are collections of short narratives published in anthologies aimed at commemorating and consolidating the writers' achievements and identity as part of a founding group. Examples of such texts include *Sefer ha-aliya ha-shniya* (The Second Aliya Book), *Divrei po'alot* (The Plough Woman), *Sefer ha-Shomer* (The Watchman Book), and *Sefer ha-Palmach* (The Palmach Book).[24] Perhaps even more such texts were written by individuals who wished to secure their place on the State of Israel's wall of founders, or to correct a picture they felt had been distorted.[25]

The twentieth-century emergence of fiction as a preferred mode of expression has left autobiographical writings often marginalized and disregarded. Despite, or perhaps because of, its minor position within Hebrew literature, autobiography has also become a venue for expression by marginalized voices, such as women, Holocaust survivors, immigrants, settlers, and Others more broadly. The predominance of founding narratives in Hebrew autobiography has also marked its marginalization as a genre. As Hebrew autobiographical writing became synonymous with institutionalized ideology, it was regulated and produced at the margins of the Hebrew literary landscape, with major cultural voices preferring fiction.

In recent years Israeli autobiographical writing has surged. Over the past two decades, autobiographical works by diverse authors such as Amos Oz, former chief rabbi Meir Lau, and Yoram Kaniuk have dominated the bestseller lists.[26] Three autobiographical works have won Israel's Sapir Prize— Dan Tsalka's *Sefer ha-aleph-bet* (Alphabet Book; 2004), Alona Frankel's *Yalda* (Girl; 2005), and Yoram Kaniuk's *Tashah*, or *1948* (2010).[27] These works exhibit a wide range of techniques and material, and have gained high visibility, some as popular literature and some as entrants to the canon.[28]

The Israeli autobiographical work to attract perhaps most attention, both domestically and internationally, is Amos Oz's *A Tale of Love and Darkness*.[29] In a study based on approximately four hundred readers' letters sent to Oz after the memoir's publication, Yigal Schwartz showed that the book elicited an especially passionate response from a very specific group of readers, consisting of those born in Israel whose parents emigrated from either Poland or Russia between the two World Wars.[30] Between ages forty-five and sixty-five when the study was conducted, these readers tended to be either kibbutz members or residents of well-established towns. Most were secular and professional—that is, part of what is considered the Israeli elite.[31] According to Schwartz it was the vulnerable, painful, and exposed nature of Oz's story that enabled the readers to connect to its suggested collective story. This group's members have found in Oz's narrative a depiction of themselves as fragile and vulnerable, rather than as part of a ruling—or, as they have been cast more recently, dethroned—hegemony. In other words, Oz has legitimized their "rightful" place in Israeli society as the salt of the earth, clearing them of whatever collective blame they might have carried in the formation of the State of Israel, and its cultural, financial, and social components.[32]

One of the letters Oz received was from Yehudit Kafri, whose own distinctly different memoir is of interest to this discussion (and is discussed in chapter 4).[33] In her letter Kafri marks the death of Oz's mother as the narrative's watershed moment, when Oz will reclaim it as his own from the sphere of the collective—a past in which Kafri is no longer able to read herself. Kafri formulates this moment as a shift from light to darkness, paralleling the time of day, sunset, she devotes to reading the book. It is noteworthy that in the Hebrew edition of *Sipur*, the page Kafri refers to as the turning point (565) comes immediately after the book's only photograph, of Oz as a child with his parents, again giving concrete specificity to his story. Kafri's letter begins as follows:[34]

September 5, 2002
Rosh Hashanah

Greetings to you, Amos Oz,
I am on page 565 of your story of love and darkness, and am finally writing you the letter about reading it, the letter that I have been writing in my head as I read along day after day for several months.

What made me realize that I could not postpone writing you any longer was the knowledge that in the very next pages I will probably be reading about your mother's death, and it will sadden me so—so that if I write you then, I will be unable to convey to you the feeling that has accompanied me all these months that I have been reading the book. Sorrow will dampen it, and it is such an illuminated feeling.

I've instituted a reading ritual, and every evening around 7 p.m., at dusk, I sit on the easy chair on our balcony that looks westward, to the darkening light summer sky, and read a few small chapters of your book, and save the rest for days to come. Now that I have got a little more than twenty pages left, I am sorry in advance toward the end.

Chapter 5, which is conspicuously omitted from the book's English translation, is a brief manifesto presenting the author's vision of his autobiographical project, and directing his reader toward the "correct" way to consume it.[35] Here Oz differentiates between "bad readers" and "good readers." Bad readers are motivated by voyeurism and gossip, and will search for a "subversive" political "bottom line." Bad readers will hold the author responsible for his text—for example, accusing Nabokov of pedophilia or Dostoevsky of a tendency toward murder. While Oz parodies concrete readings of fiction, he positions himself alongside authors of the great Western tradition. He also insists that he will never confide in us: "Everything is autobiographical: If I ever write a story about a love affair between Mother Teresa and Abba Eban it would certainly be an autobiographical story, although it would not be a confession. Every story I have ever written is autobiographical, and not a single one is confession."[36] Oz invites the "good reader" to look for himself rather than for the author in the text: "Do not ask: Are these really facts? Is this what goes on in this author's mind? Ask yourself about yourself. And you may keep the answer to yourself."[37]

As Oz encourages his reader to find himself in the text, he also casts his story, in the tradition of male Western autobiography, as representative and universal.[38] The role of the individual male author in representing the collective and spirit of the nation, with its goals, triumphs, losses, and pains, has been widely documented.[39] As an individual representative of the nation, Oz attempted to carry the torch of traditional Hebrew autobiography, and his attempt could not have been more successful. As Oz himself said, "I was digging in my own backyard, and I must have touched an underground cable; suddenly, the lights in all of the windows began to flash."[40] Innumerable readers lit up along with Oz's best-selling book.

Hannan Hever has observed that texts of national literature are commonly described, within national and liberal thought and practice, as representing the imagined community out of which and for which they are produced. But in Hebrew literature this representation, he continues, is enacted through a clash between the author and the imagined community, a confrontation perceived as aesthetic but that is at once a moral and a political difference between the writer and his or her readers.[41] The national author's traditional position here echoes that of the prophet figure. From this privileged position the author represents the moral national demands to which the community is entreated to respond. Hever contends that a substantial part of Israeli canonical fiction today dodges the conflict between the national elite and the readers of these texts. This avoidance results not only in an apparent lack of moral conflict in Israeli literature, but correlatively in an eradication of the complex aesthetic mode that is the counterpart and backdrop of this moral conflict. This dynamic may explain the popularization prevalent in Israeli literature. Indeed, according to Hever, major Israeli fiction today is produced as popular literature, catering to the collective palate, approving and affirming its values and refraining from an attempt to restore the tensions of the past. I would suggest, in response, that in Israeli autobiography this tension and criticism are maintained.

Israeli autobiography has become a zone where silenced and marginalized voices can confront the center, rewriting and renegotiating their relationship with it. It has become an arena of vivid friction with hegemonic Israeli ideology, where transparent realities are brought to light. These characteristics connect Israeli autobiography to its mid-nineteenth century roots as a genre of stinging social critique.[42] As at its inception, Israeli autobiography written today takes critical moral stands that challenge the Israeli collective, while still asserting a deep and very personal commitment to that collective. Israeli autobiographers are refiguring models of plot and expression as they expose the reference frames that mainstream literature has learned to conceal.

BY TAKING ADVANTAGE of the subversive position of the autobiography form, Oz, in *A Tale of Love and Darkness*, probes the marginalized experience of those deeply rooted in Israeli culture, a deep-rootedness attested to by the book's warm reception. Indeed, those unchallenged or unthreatened by the work considered it a balm. Put another way, Oz's memoir is a sophisticated manipulation of the Israeli autobiographical mode in a popular work (which affirms its readers' worldview, or refrains from challenging it).[43]

More broadly, contemporary Israeli autobiography ties Israeli-born authors and immigrants to their non-Israeli past. It revives their connection to other countries, cultures, languages, and places. This ethnically conscious writing does not align itself with the national Zionist impulse—espoused with particular vigor in the early decades of statehood—identified as "negation of the diaspora." Immigration can be viewed, according to this alternative view, as a point of innovation.[44]

If autobiography is viewed not as narrating a finite and formed past, but as a narrative event in and of the present, as Eakin has described it, then narration is itself the autobiographical event.[45] If we align this conclusion with the national role of Israeli autobiography, then the need emerges to constantly define specific countries or ethnicities of origin against nationality and national identity. Thus Kaniuk, Oz, Aharon Appelfeld, and other authors must also continuously define their ethnic, gendered, or familial identities against their nationality. As they attempt to distance themselves from nationality, they reveal its fundamental instability and need for support, as opposed to their ethnicity. A negation of Zionist identity, therefore, creates instability, which paradoxically fortifies nationalism by creating a platform from which it must be constantly reaffirmed and consolidated. Perhaps this is the case because ethnic identities tend to overrun Jewish nationalism.

Thus, while producing marginal subjects, the autobiographical writings to be analyzed here simultaneously fortify the need of the "imagined community" to be maintained, "reimagined," and recreated. Like other autobiographers in different times and places, Israeli autobiographers write against erasure. They write to sustain, maintain, reveal, and define their being. In many ways Israeli autobiographers are influenced by the "age of memoir" still sweeping American and Western European cultures—even as this surge in popularity hasn't always granted the form critical recognition. Language provides another lens, with "I-narratives" in Israel published in multiple languages. Despite this variety, the texts covered here are all written in Hebrew, and this book highlights how these writings are specifically Israeli; how their authors identify as Israelis and articulate the experience of being Israeli. Against the political and historical grounding of contemporary Israeli autobiographical discourse, the potential of universalizing specific personal stories becomes a tool in the autobiographer's hands to carve out a space in the national agora, or public space.[46] Israeli selves are not only inseparably amalgamated in national selves—they are first and foremost national selves.[47]

Israeli national selves are written in continuous friction and competition with one another. Writers advocate for the acceptance of their personal self as national self and, implicitly, as the privileged national self that marginalizes others. They strive to define the Israeli self as their own and, conversely, attempt to crack the cultural movement that would form a unified homogeneous Israeli self that might threaten their own specific identity. This culture of colliding identities, which has been thriving in Israeli literature in recent decades, is laden with pain, humiliation, and political strife. Our discussion of the works of Ballas, Appelfeld, Be'er, and Kafri, for example—each from a distinct background—will reveal some of these collisions.

THE AUTOBIOGRAPHIES DISCUSSED in the following chapters reconstruct a past, but more important, they exhibit the reliving of the past; they showcase the moment of remembrance, or of narrating an autobiography, that dictates how the story will be told and what it will contain.[48] As such, these works present a group portrait of Israeli identities in the making, and of the tensions, conflicts, and desires that conduct and structure them. I believe they provide a concise and multivoiced portrait of Jewish Israeli society and culture today.[49]

CHAPTER ONE

"To Be a Jew among Jews"

The Reluctant Israeli Native in Yoram Kaniuk

YORAM KANIUK, who was born in Tel Aviv in 1930, published fiction prolifically beginning in the early 1960s but did not achieve critical recognition until three decades later, with the postmodern turn in Israeli fiction.[1] In his final years his popularity rose to its greatest heights, with academic conferences devoted to his work and tributes offered by young authors.[2] His last memoir, *Tashah, or 1948* (2010), was awarded the Sapir Prize and remained on the best-seller list for months. His public declarations became front-page news, and his works have been adapted for theater, film, and a television series.[3]

Kaniuk was always somewhat of a misfit in Israeli literature. Biographically he could be counted among writers of the Palmach generation, but he began publishing alongside the "generation of the state," including slightly younger authors such as A. B. Yehoshua (b. 1936) and Amos Oz (b. 1939).[4] Poetically his writing diverged from the general characteristics of both generations. He adopted neither the stylized realism of the Palmach generation nor the symbolic-naturalist writing of the state generation. For his part, Kaniuk described himself as a compulsive outsider. In his 2007 work *Al ha-haim ve-al ha-mavet* (Of Life and Death) he wrote of himself: "I have never managed to make the art that I should. . . . When I was young I wanted to be like everyone else. I could not do it. . . . I wrote as others did not wish to write, I did not know how to write as they did, as was demanded. I have always been controversial because I was a man of his own, a writer of my specific sort, and that is not good."[5]

In 1961 Kaniuk published his first novel, *The Acrophile*, translated into English, followed by the Hebrew version (*Ha-yored lemata*) two years later. Its English title aptly describes the whole of Kaniuk's literary project. *Acro* is the Greek word for "tip," "extreme," "peak," or "summit"—and Kaniuk is indeed a lover of edges and extremes. His poetics oscillate between opposites and avoid compromise and equilibrium. While carrying his narratives to extremes, however, he never does so to one extreme; his worldview contains polar opposites, and contradictions are never resolved but rather maximized, highlighted, and further ignited. Kaniuk's poetics are violent, often grotesque and fantastic. Fittingly Gershon Shaked (1929–2006), the first to devote comprehensive critical attention to Kaniuk's work, described Kaniuk's poetics as expressionistic, and characterized by intensely expressed emotion and stark, often bracing imagery.[6]

Since Kaniuk's fiction is closely related to his autobiographical work, I will briefly review some central points in the critical reception of his fiction. Hanna Soker-Schwager has suggested that Kaniuk's marginal position within Israeli literature may be better understood if his fiction is recognized as "camp," defined by Susan Sontag in her classic 1964 essay as a "love of the unnatural: of artifice and exaggeration."[7] This accurate description of Kaniuk's fiction is also helpful in reading his autobiography. Nevertheless, and despite the similarity between the two modes, fiction and autobiography, with Kaniuk often blurring the difference between them, "camp" cannot aptly describe Kaniuk's autobiographical work.

Whereas viewing Kaniuk through the lens of camp is illuminating with respect to his hyperbolic contradictory tone, it understates his deep engagement with Jewish nationalism and the importance he places on confrontation and pathos. Camp puts everything in parentheses, whereas Kaniuk is more often than not earnest. Also, where camp emphasizes style at the expense of content—"It goes without saying that the Camp sensibility is disengaged, depoliticized—or at least apolitical"—Kaniuk's writing is anything but apolitical.[8] Camp, cast as "playful, anti-serious [but allowing one to be] serious about the frivolous, frivolous about the serious," also "neutralizes moral indignation. . . ."[9] Yet Kaniuk's writing often loudly projects moral indignation.[10]

Dvir Zur's 2009 afterword to Kaniuk's novel *The Last Jew* (1981), his major fictional work alongside *Adam Resurrected* (1969), relates to broad themes of Jewish history, such as the Shoah and Jewish identity, and their representation in Jewish and Israeli culture, all handled in a manner distinct from camp. If the novel, as Zur views it, draws from words "the meaning of life," it is wholly un-camp-like. Zur singles out Kaniuk in his generation for refusing to abide by the Zionist divisions between "old Jew" and New Hebrew, between immigrant and native.[11] As Zur reads Kaniuk, the history of Israeli Jews cannot diverge from that of Jews the world over.[12] But of course this also reflects the hegemonic Israeli view—that the history of world Jewry is subject to and intertwined with that of the Israeli. Here, the wish to see Israelis as Jews also holds the opposite, possibly condescending attitude.

According to Soker-Schwager we find in Kaniuk's fiction "not a representation of the [Zionist] vision but a 'representation' of the stereotypes we have about it."[13] Uzi Weill, who wrote the book's preface, and Zur would read it as a straightforward representation of the same Zionist vision. Whereas Soker-Schwager reads *The Last Jew* as a novel in which the hyperbolic writing tears the "I" apart, and prevents its reconstruction, Weill and Zur read the self in it as multiple and shifting, but not as dismembered. My own reading adopts Soker-Schwager's description of the self in Kaniuk's work as ripped apart—not a playful or an empowered tear, but a searing, painful, shattering one.

Such an assessment demonstrates the inadequacy of camp as a prism through which to view Kaniuk's work. Camp, namely, does not account for the direct aggressiveness in Kaniuk's writing—whereas Shaked's "expressionistic" description does. In addition, the writer's extravagant performativity may exhibit an affinity to camp, but his avoidance of frivolity does not. What is serious remains serious. This suggests why many readers experience his work as pornography of violence, and also as sanctified core experiences in Jewish and Israeli history—such as the Shoah and 1948—rather than as a source of amusement. This also explains why he was rejected from the Israeli canon for more than three decades.

Whatever the differences in these critical views, they share attention to the formation of the self or of subjectivity in Kaniuk's work. Indeed, one major vein in Kaniuk's autobiographical writings involves the concern with the making of his subjectivity. Beginning with *Post Mortem* (1992), which has not yet been translated to English, Kaniuk cast himself as the product of parents whose identity—or, rather, lack of a defined identity—was a performance act.[14] The inquiry into the making of an identity is a staple of autobiographical writing and central to Kaniuk's life writings. However, in Kaniuk's case it becomes a study of a nonidentity, perpetually lost, in a continuous process, or the incapacity to construct a recognizable identity. That is, Kaniuk's work always eludes the point of balance or self-containment, though the "I-voice" is perpetually seeking this point. His starting point is that of a vacancy, the contours of which he continuously traces, marks, and highlights but never fills.

"It Isn't Entirely Incorrect to Call This Book a Work of Fiction"

Yoram Kaniuk's autobiographical project, like his fiction, is founded on two formative experiences. The first is the trauma he endured during Israel's War of Independence in 1948, as a young soldier in the Harel Brigade of the Palmach. Kaniuk served in an area near Jerusalem that his peers named "the butcher's arena," referring to the many casualties suffered there. The second is a trauma that he did not experience personally—the Shoah. In *Of Life and Death*, however, Kaniuk relates that as an adolescent, he adopted his neighbor's loss of her parents, who were murdered during the Shoah: "I would nestle in her pain which I almost understood, I absorbed it and it stayed in me as a guest who never leaves" (11). In *Ha-berlina'i ha-aharon* (The Last Berliner; German 2001, Hebrew, 2004) Kaniuk describes how after the publication of *Adam Resurrected* he was invited to meet a group of readers who were survivors of the Nazi camps. They questioned the authority of his writing, and when he corrected a woman's memory regarding the number of the Auschwitz block in which she was imprisoned, he was accepted as one of their own.[15]

Even though I have described Kaniuk—and he has described himself—as a "poetic misfit," he belongs biographically to Israeli cultural hegemony and its core social, political, and cultural elite. Along these lines I will try to show that although his writing clashes critically with major Zionist narratives, it does so to affirm Zionism and its causes, as well as his significant personal contribution to it. This critical "affirmative clash" is in essence, as this book will repeatedly suggest, the traditional canonical stand of Hebrew authors.[16]

Kaniuk's mother, Sarah Braverman, was a child when she came to Palestine from Ukraine in 1909, considered the peak year of Second Aliya immigration.[17] When her father, Simha, a Hebrew teacher, died in 1918 in young Tel Aviv, Sarah's mother supported the family by turning their home into a guesthouse. Thanks to a generous loan from a British guest, Sarah was able to study education at Oxford. She returned to Palestine in 1926 and found a teaching job in Haifa, where she met Kaniuk's father, Moshe, a recent emigrant from Germany who was earning a living by giving voice lessons. As for the meeting, Kaniuk writes in *Post Mortem*:[18] "The moment of their meeting held everything that would mark their lives. He did not know who she really was, and never bothered to find out. And she despite her attempts did not know who he was. As soon as they met, they had to invent themselves for one another and that is how they could cope with each other, because they were hidden from their own eyes, forged, fictionalized" (36).

Kaniuk's father, Moshe, the son of a baker, was born in Tarnopol, Galicia, and fought for Austria during World War I. He studied in Heidelberg and Berlin from 1918 to 1927 and later worked odd jobs, including as a stock trader and a musician during screenings of silent films. According to *Post Mortem*, Moshe "was educated, charming, aloof and a snob" (59). He was a friend of Zionist national poet Haim Nachman Bialik, who was the future writer's godfather and gave him his name (117; 15). Such details, including the "Mayflower" status of Second Aliya members, marked Kaniuk as belonging to the social, cultural, and political Jewish elite.[19]

As Kaniuk remarks in *Post Mortem*, "Moshe was not born in Berlin. True German Jews are born in Eastern Europe, not in Berlin" (42). Thus, "Moshe brought with him from Galicia his great love for Germany and its culture. . . . He wasn't born into it, he bore himself into it" (44). "His love for Germany," according to Kaniuk, "was poisonous, painful and funny. He told his friends that his parents were dead, and that he was an only son"

(45–46). Although suspicions held that Moshe left for Palestine to escape a soured love affair, this was never confirmed: "The truth is probably hiding in a fantasy zone in which I must play a bit with my imagination" (54).

Moshe and Sarah were married in 1927, and two years later Sarah traveled to Berlin to recover from malaria. Moshe eventually joined her and they toured Germany together. According to family lore Yoram was conceived on this journey. During this visit Moshe also gathered his former friends and beseeched them to immigrate to Palestine. Although they would be unhappy and unfulfilled in Palestine, they would be out of danger. Moshe repeated this manifesto decades later to Mira, Kaniuk's younger sister by seven years, in New York, in perfect German, after he had suffered a severe stroke. As articulated in *Post Mortem*, this was his first and last speech (64). Two essences remained in Moshe after his stroke—Zionism as an inevitable necessity and the adoration of German poetry, which he could recite. What remained was the veneration of Germany and German culture, and practical Herzlian Zionism, which despite his distaste for Jewish society in Palestine was a formative part of his identity.[20]

While still a younger man, meanwhile, Moshe was hired in 1931 to serve as first secretary to Tel Aviv's first mayor, Meir Dizengoff, as well as secretary of the Tel Aviv Museum, which the two men cofounded (155). Moshe served in the latter position for forty years, stretching decades beyond Dizengoff's death in 1936. His tenure encompassed much argumentation within the Israeli art community over the museum's direction. For her part Sarah taught elementary school, trained and educated teachers, and wrote textbooks.

In 1939 the Kaniuk family moved to 129 Ben Yehuda Street, in the heart of Tel Aviv. This was the apartment where the family lived until the 1960s, their trash cans, as Kaniuk never fails to sardonically mention, rubbing against those of Golda Meir. Irony aside, Sarah and Moshe were both engaged in public activities, and contributed to the development of Israeli society and culture.[21] It is precisely this public contribution, however, that Yoram later labeled as a disability, a façade, and an escape from familial responsibility, from intimacy, from parenting, and from love. In *Post Mortem*, community work signals the failure to love and be loved:

Each, in his way, did something important. They did something important because they did not have something unimportant to do, that is, just
live, make an art out of living, and really nurture a family. They could
not live the normal life of a couple. The children were brought up by
great housekeepers, but housekeepers. She believed she was raising her
son because once in a while she gave him a lecture, made a lousy omelet
or spanked him. . . . Moshe and Sarah had to find something to do with
themselves so that they would not have to meet each other excessively. . . .
Basic estrangement flowed in my veins. . . . Strangeness is not longing, in
longing there is hope. (96)

Kaniuk was seventeen years old when he joined the Palmach. From winter 1947 through spring 1948, Jewish parts of Jerusalem were under siege,
and the Harel Brigade, to which Kaniuk belonged, was facilitating passage
for supply convoys to these neighborhoods, which needed supplies of water,
food, and ammunition. In protecting these convoys, beset by Palestinian
sniper fire, the Harel fighters enshrined themselves in a chapter of Israeli
history still glorified today. The remains of burned-out armored vehicles,
preserved as monuments alongside the Tel Aviv–Jerusalem road and cloaked
every Memorial Day with flags and flowers, attest to this status.[22]

Kaniuk recounts several battles from the war in his fiction and life writing. The short story "Eytim" (Vultures), first published in 1977, refers to
the miserable end of the failed Palmach attempt to conquer Nebi Samuel,
a Palestinian village north of Jerusalem, on the night of April 22–23, 1948.
Kaniuk was part of a backup unit caught under fire. The unit's commander
deserted, and Kaniuk and others who had survived lay in the field, feigning
death until escaping to a nearby kibbutz, Ma'ale Ha-Hamisha. The wounded
and the dead were left on the battlefield, their mutilated bodies later re-
trieved with the aid of a British escort. This traumatic event surfaces in most
of Kaniuk's work, fiction and nonfiction.[23] In chapter 15 of *Tashah*, or *1948*,
he notes: "I once wrote a story about it, and I don't want to repeat it."[24] His
friend Menachem, whom he had known since childhood, bled to death next
to him. The scene in which he tells Menachem's parents of the tragedy is
recounted in his major novel *The Last Jew*, in which Menachem's father and

his garden serve as main protagonists, as well as in *Of Life and Death* and *1948*.[25] In each of these works Menachem's mother asks why it hadn't been Yoram to die instead of her son.

In the third week of May 1948, Kaniuk was shot and wounded in the battle over the Jewish quarter of East Jerusalem on Mount Zion, evidently by a British volunteer with the Arab Legion. The terror of lying wounded on the ground, in clear view of his shooter, awaiting the fatal next shot that never comes, resurfaces in many of his works.[26]

Although this analysis focuses mainly on *Post Mortem*, regarding the other works as orbiting and gravitating to it, Kaniuk's autobiographical project expanded continuously, the other works being *Haim al niyar zkhukhit* (*Life on Sandpaper*, 2003), *The Last Berliner*, *Of Life and Death*, and *1948*.[27]

Kaniuk's life writings involve both repetition and fragmentedness. Some segments are significant because he experienced them directly, and some because he helplessly witnessed them—such as the death of the most handsome boy in his elementary school, who dove into a tide pool that turned out to be too shallow.[28] The emphasis of the repeated scenes is not identical— in *Post Mortem* Sarah's reaction to the boy's death is the focus, a rare instance in which she does not fail her son, but rather is supportive and understanding; in *Of Life and Death*, the boy's death parallels the onset of Kaniuk's cancer and his own near-death experience. Often, in Kaniuk's autobiographical writing, witnessing is regarded as equal in importance to directly experiencing, a stance with implications to be discussed later.

Much of Kaniuk's autobiographical writing echoes his fictional writing. Notably scenes from his formative story "Vultures" and *The Last Jew* are narrated as autobiographical in his life writing.[29] This creates an unclear and sometimes diffuse relationship between documentary and fictional details in his work. Yet even as Kaniuk's writing meshes fiction and autobiography, the five works just outlined are clearly autobiographical.[30] In *Post Mortem*, a book prompted by his mother's death and focusing on both parents, central themes include Kaniuk's loaded relationship with Germany and the trauma of combat in 1948. *Life on Sandpaper* foregrounds 1948 and Kaniuk's years in New York, where he moved after working aboard ships bringing immigrant survivors from Europe to Palestine. He returned permanently to Israel in the early 1960s. *The Last Berliner* revisits the author's relationship with Germany. *Of Life and Death*, written as an ailing man's farewell, recounts Kaniuk's recovery from a near-death experience after surgery and concludes with burial instructions. Nevertheless, Kaniuk survived, and three years later he published *1948*. In this book, which he dedicated to his Palmach peers, Kaniuk again spotlights his experiences during the 1948 war.

Whereas Kaniuk includes scenes and material from his life in his fiction, he does not, in his autobiographical work, employ what Shaked calls "fantastic" or mythical materials that could cast doubt on its nonfictional status. Even as *Of Life and Death* abounds with hallucinations, they are clearly framed as such, and the line between the real and the fantastic is never blurred.[31] All the same, Kaniuk's anecdotes are often extreme and far-fetched, and ask to be read as tall tales.[32] Possibly this is what prompted the "Author's Note" added to the English translation of *Life on Sandpaper*, freeing the text from the implications of being a memoir, as it was labeled in Hebrew. The note reads: "It isn't entirely incorrect to call this book a work of fiction, despite its being an account of my memories from a certain period in my life, and despite the fact that many of its characters might also appear in history books concerning those same years."

The evasive "It isn't entirely incorrect" construction begs the question of whether it would be "entirely incorrect" to call the book autobiography —and whether Kaniuk might be somehow justifying evasions of the truth.[33] On this count Philippe Lejeune's 1973 definition of autobiography still provides the basic premise for most discussions: "retrospective prose narrative written by a real person concerning his own existence, where the focus is his individual life, in particular the story of his personality."[34] As established in this definition, the identity of the main subject, the narrator, and the author's name on the book cover bear weighty consequences. In declaring this identity authors sign what Lejeune has coined as the "autobiographical pact," dictating the mode in which readers will approach the text. Authorial intention, that sticky concept exposed and rejected in the twentieth century as the "intentional fallacy," becomes a legal and ethical commitment. The autobiographical pact demands a declaration of honest intent, and so allows readers to judge the hero-author and his or her motives. This judgment, despite the caution with which theorists of autobiography have handled concepts such as "truth," "intent," and "honesty," has led to expanding debates on ethics and a constant examination of the moral standing of the narrating subject and its limits.[35]

Although Paul de Man declared the line between fiction and autobiography an insolvable, dull, and redundant impasse, it has continuously engaged readers both popular and scholarly.[36] Cases such as Binjamin Wilkomirski's fabricated survival of concentration camps, James Frey's turbulent rehabilitation from alcoholism and drug abuse, which was exposed as a partial fiction on prime-time television, and the autobiography of 1992 Nobel Peace Prize winner Rigoberta Menchu, which was challenged as untrue, are just a few well-known examples.[37] The debate is not of a generic nature, but clearly a moral one. Readers of autobiography expect honesty from authors who have signed the "autobiographical pact" discussed earlier. This identity fusing the narrator with the name on the book cover, according to Lejeune, creates a bond that readers perceive as a commitment of honest intent. This does not mean readers of autobiography cannot accept contradictions and conflicting versions of single events. As Eakin writes in his influential *Fictions in Autobiography*, readers accept that "autobiographical truth is not a fixed but an evolving content in an intricate process of self-discovery and self-creation, and further, that the self that is the center of all autobiographical narrative is necessarily a fictive structure."[38] However, authors of autobiography are judged morally, and when their writing is evaluated, they themselves are being judged at the same time.[39] The heat and immediacy of this demand for authorial responsibility have not diminished after half a century of posthumanist theory.[40] That is, even readers reared on concepts of the self as performative do not forgo the demand for honest intent implied by Lejeune's invocation of a legal pact.[41]

An anthology edited by Paul John Eakin attests to the liveliness of the debate on the relationship between autobiography and truth, even as fiction, whether autobiographical or not, has been recognized as essential to the act of narrating.[42] Issues covered in the collection include how much we may reveal about our relations, and where we cross ethical lines; and when we tell more than others care to know.[43] These discussions mark a return of authorial intent as a dominant mode of reading autobiography, many decades after the term was rejected by literary discourse as a "fallacy."[44] This is possibly because, although readers recognize that the evolving story is indeed the essence of autobiography, they still perceive the form to reflect the telling of a sealed and finite past that exists independent of its narrative. As Eakin has put it, we "take for granted this expectation that autobiography is devoted to the recovery of the past."[45]

Even though I choose, in my reading of Kaniuk, not to enter the revolving door between fiction and autobiography—or to elicit a finite version of the events Kaniuk relates—I nonetheless recognize, as Leigh Gilmore and others have pointed out and as Lejeune's definition explicates, the material, ID-holding, taxpaying person outside the text whom we hold responsible.[46] Still, my reading does not focus on that man, but rather on his different self-representations, and what end these representations serve in constructing his identity as an Israeli, a Jew, an artist, a writer, a son, and a lover.

With those terms established, *Post Mortem* brutally exposes the Kaniuk family. The author's portrait of his parents often lacks empathy and is charged with rage and contempt. In its mellowest expression it views Sarah and Moshe Kaniuk with irony, but hardly ever with forgiveness. Sarah, for her part, is introduced at the end of her life, during a physical crisis before her final trip to the hospital. She is cast in Kaniuk's imagery even here as repulsive and entirely unworthy of empathy. When Sarah collapses in her apartment, Kaniuk describes her "as a murdered rose which had its water taken away from it," an image propagating kitsch conventions about collapse and decay; he then describes "her transparence, worn out like a half burnt sheet of paper, her body was gaunt and one could see her decayed flesh through the nightgown which wrapped air more than woman." As she hemorrhages on the floor, "her old thin skin was purple, and looked like the scales of a fried, scorched fish" (10). Her body is "old, gnashed, split open," and "she lay and clung to life like a hideous bleeding leach in her exposed nudity." Once at the hospital, Kaniuk must return to her home and fetch Sarah's false teeth, "wrapped in a pinkish gumlike material," another image that communicates repugnance rather than pity. When he last sees her in the hospital, "she lay like a carcass" (10).[47] Overexposure becomes a vision of contempt.

In these images Kaniuk strips his mother of her dignity. In describing her resentment of old age, he uses more animal imagery, depriving her position of legitimacy, not to mention possible displays of fortitude or character: "Sarah, against all illnesses and dangers and dramas, crept to the age of eighty-six with the devotion and tricks of a terrified old domesticated dog" (7). Later in the text he writes: "She battled old age not as a lioness but as a worm which had been cut but still writhes and does not die, clings to life. . . . Squatted in her old age she deloused her fabulous defeat, as if age were a nasty, unnatural vengefulness, directed expressly at her" (146). Kaniuk shows no greater forgiveness when he gazes harshly at his paralyzed father (97). The aggression Kaniuk directs at his parents must be justified by a story of parental failure, which indeed *Post Mortem* provides.

In what follows I probe Kaniuk's possible narratives of his self, the nation, the individual, and universal family narratives, and I study the tensions and dependencies with which he invests them. I will claim that Kaniuk's narration of the war as both personal and collective trauma—as that of an injured individual who also represents his immediate peers and his generation—consolidates his profile as a perpetual victim. As a witness, he refuses to frame his peers or accuse them of murder. Yet because Kaniuk avoids the level of detail that would make his narrative a testimony, the overall war scene's weight shifts from the revelation of the horrible facts to their influence on Kaniuk. The victims become marginal as the scene reaches its climax, emphasizing instead how Kaniuk functioned, how he responded, and how the scene affected the rest of his life.

Kaniuk emerges as a victim from scenes in which he is clearly on the aggressor's side—such as chapter 12 of *1948*, when he accidentally shoots and kills a Palestinian boy and witnesses the child's mother stabbed and his grandmother battered to death by his peers. The narrative focuses more on his helplessness among his friends and their ridicule of him because of his moral qualms and hesitations, and less on the crimes committed against the Palestinian family. When he describes the Palestinian child's murder, he does not name the village or the man who initiated the act allegedly as revenge for the mutilation of the body of their comrade, who also remains unnamed, in the battle over the village. These omissions are made supposedly in defense of a beloved friend. Kaniuk's attempts to stop his friends—whom he insists all along that he loves dearly—and his drive to bring them to trial or punishment constitute the focus of the story. His helplessness is cast as a greater trauma than the actual death and beating of unarmed and young or elderly civilians.

The climactic chapter 10 in *Post Mortem* exhibits these points clearly. Given that this chapter encapsulates most of the different identities that constitute Kaniuk's autobiographical self, and because it has not been translated to English, I will quote much of it:[48]

In 1938, together with all the students in my class, I wrote to children whose names were given to us by the Jewish Agency: "Dear Jewish child: Hitler will kill you. Come to Eretz Yisrael. If you do not make aliya you shall die. Yours . . . ," and everyone signed his name. The letters were collected in sacks and sent to Germany, which I already loved by then, and which bad people had robbed me of. . . . I was sorry that these poor children had to leave Germany. I was the only sabra [native-born Israeli] around who envied them, who preferred spinach to compote, and they used to laugh that I like to eat green shit. . . .

That was when the refugee children arrived. They brought wonderful toys and beautiful clothes with leather suspenders and Tyrolean hats . . . they had names like Robert, Peter, and Herbert, and I decided to be born in Germany. I knew the streets of my town through *Emil and the Detectives*.[49] Father's friends had arrived as refugees with shame and used to speak to me; through them I could drink coffee at Kempinski's. Berlin was part of the fantasy that was real life more than the *khamsin*. I felt sympathy for the refugees because I too had been expelled from Germany.

In order to be born in Germany I taught myself to shout *ow* when I was beaten instead of *ay* like the native-born children. Moshe liked that, it reminded him of something deep and painful in him. For a week Moshe and I practiced saying *ow* instead of *ay*. It was a painful game. I made him hit me. After a while he seemed to enjoy it. I would say, go ahead, punch. And he would wrinkle his face a bit, a dim and mean light would emanate from his perpetually warm eyes, and he would hit. The game was serious and Sarah used to stand by weeping and say, Moshe, leave the boy alone, but he had rediscovered me, it happened to him every so many years, and he enjoyed watching me be a German child; when I groaned in pain from the blows and mumbled *ow*, he recited poems by Hölderlin or Heine to me and strummed his guitar. He would stand me on the balcony, step back, and turn his back and call: Who are you, boy? And I would shout: Robert! Peter! And he looked enthusiastic. I hated him for the way he gave me up with ease to the other country, and the children in class hit me to see what I would yell. I shouted *ow*. I internalized a shallow German in my veins to satisfy Moshe's thirst to be who he was not. *So that we both turned out to be people who are not genuinely who they are.*" (38–39, my emphasis)

Here the native smugness of Jewish children in Mandatory Palestine is countered by his peers' overreaction and repulsion to the spinach, associated with the "Yekkim" (German émigrés to Israel), and by the young Kaniuk's admiration for material German culture—clothes, food, toys. Rather than imagine Germany as a hell to be escaped, Yoram adopts the nostalgic Germany his father's friends lost, and the Germany of Erich Kästner's children's books.

This scene overturns norms of domestic bliss and parenting. Father, mother, and child share a game that is transgressive, and unusual for the Kaniuk family in that it portrays Sarah weeping and Moshe playing with his son—but it is a game of erasure. Moshe's blatant general lack of interest in his son is captured in Yoram's description of him returning home from work and inquiring, "Did anyone ask for me?" Implicit here is Moshe's failure to ask about *them*, his family. So to gain his father's attention, Yoram in the game identifies, in an extreme way, with the aggressor. Another game, described later in the book, portrays a younger Yoram, at age three, who has learned to attract his parents' and their friends' attention by memorizing and reciting details about classical music. Here he would place a record on the gramophone and, perched on the sideboard, announce the name of the piece, the composer, and the performers: "Some of the records had the famous picture of the dog stamped on them, listening to music, to 'his master's voice.' At 3 Mendele Street in Tel Aviv, that was me" (79).

Kaniuk describes himself as a child trained to perform. When interest in his performance dwindled, he tried to run away from home. Kaniuk's maternal grandmother died when Sarah was pregnant with his sister, Mira. Sarah had had one miscarriage and was afraid and cried at nights: "I sat beside her and held her hand, and shocked and petrified, I recited the names of all the concerts that I knew, and she covered my mouth with her hand and shouted, enough, don't perform anymore, you are not your father's parrot!" . . . She did not understand from what depth within me I played the despised puppy for her" (87).

Performance marks one extreme in the book's treatment of culture and music, which oscillates between artificial and superficial, on the one hand, and existential and essential, on the other. Appreciation of music compels Sarah to fall in love again with Moshe, end a love affair, and thus remain in her stifling marriage. These conflicting views—of superficiality and intimacy or existential need—converge in a scene that is also repeated in Kaniuk's various writings.

In 1948, when Kaniuk had already endured his devastating experience during the war, lost all his friends, and been assigned to a different military unit because his no longer existed, he met a recent widow whose husband, a Shoah survivor, had died in battle. The woman took him to her room at Kibbutz Kiryat Anavim, where the Harel Brigade was stationed during the war, and explained that she knew his parents, having taken a teachers' seminar led by his mother and having attended concerts arranged by his father. She then gave him a recording of Bach's "Little" Fugue, which he listened to repeatedly on the gramophone that he and his friends had looted from a Palestinian village, until one day his tent partners destroyed the record in exasperation.[50]

This anecdote, like many related by Kaniuk, is tinged with tragicomedy, a heavily symbolic melodrama verging on "camp," given that the record is a relic rescued by a Shoah survivor from his former European life and carried through camps and crowded refugee ships, only to be smashed by Israeli Palmach troops. After committing the act, the troops sit silently in the dining hall, under their commander's supervision, and listen to the radio broadcast of civilians sending regards to their family members in combat. Yoram's parents send him greetings, and request that the station play Bach's Little Fugue in honor of his eighteenth birthday. In *Post Mortem* Kaniuk describes the experience of listening to the piece: "All of my life perhaps I had never loved Moshe and Sarah as I did that day in the blinding light which came through a crack in the tent when I sat there with the gramophone and the Little Fugue, which had never been played in a place stranger to it" (153). He reflects shortly thereafter: "To the dismay of my friends, facing their stifled shout, I heard with pleasure, which was never again repeated in my life to the sound of a musical piece, the most personal love letter from my parents, which had been written by Johann Sebastian Bach" (154).

It is fitting that Kaniuk's most intimate experience with his parents is mediated by both the public radio broadcast and Bach's position in the cultural canon. The family shares a love of the Western tradition of music, literature, and art, but Moshe and Sarah cannot express their parental love directly. On another level this common affinity for Western culture, and the broadcast to the army unit, separates Yoram from his peers. Yoram's ties with his parents, however, are themselves challenged when he tells them of hearing the piece—even as it might surprise that, in such a detached family, he would share the experience in the first place. His mother finds the pleasure he took in hearing the piece distasteful, and his father is "more insulted than angry": "He was insulted for Johann Sebastian. He thought it was 'sabra chutzpah' to say that Bach wrote me a love letter" (154).

In the German *ow/ay* game and the Little Fugue, German low and high culture are thus internalized as the father's language, and as home: a home that kept Yoram the child at a distance.[51] But there are circumstances under which Moshe draws his son near, countering Sarah's failed embrace and defending his son's experience. Kaniuk describes such an instance in chapter 10 of *Post Mortem*:

One day I went with friends to what was then known as an American bar in London Square. They sold ice cream specials in that bar. It was 1947. Shots were heard across the street, and then shouts. We paid no attention, we ate the "specials," we were used to it. Suddenly a group of people chasing a man appeared. One could see he was bleeding even from where we were standing. He fell under a street lamp on the corner of Allenby and Ha-Yarkon, and a pool of blood spread around him. His sudden collapse seemed to spoil the chase for his persecutors and they looked disappointed, stood bewildered, and did not know what to do. They looked at each other in search of affirmation for what they were doing because evidently they wanted revenge to be just, and they resumed hitting him, but the blows were already dampened and they searched for the anger.

The young Kaniuk begs a nearby Jewish policeman for help:

When my nagging got on his nerves, he said: look, you sweet little mama's boy, look, you Arab ass-lickin' *tzuker*, that one over there is dead anyway, so one more blow or less won't make a difference.

　[. . .]

I climbed through the dunes and came home. Sarah noticed my fallen face as soon as I walked in and asked what happened. I did not answer. I went to the toilet, threw up and came back to the room. She gave me her suspicious look, and asked why I was pale and what had happened to me. I said I'd seen Jews lynching. Sarah rose, alarmed, and asked if I had been hurt. I won't get any sleep tonight, she said in her punitive voice. She spoke in her tragic misery octave. I was tired and her words hurt me, the tears that had been in me . . . surfaced in my eyes. I shouted at her, but she kept on going, she did not understand what I was going through. She did not want to, she was irritated over her son's well-being being endangered, she said, you should not have gone there! I said, how dare you, what kind of a person are you, a dead man lay there, they kicked his teeth, a woman spat in his mouth! And Sarah said, I saw a row of bodies twice in my life, don't you preach to me, bad things happen, why weren't you considerate of others? You could have been hurt?

Suddenly Moshe, this introverted man huddled in his scheme of habits, rose, approached, and touched me. It was an intimate gesture I was unfamiliar with. He said, people don't do such things! . . . It is a disgrace, Sarah! Bastards! He turned pale, as if artificially, partially ironic, partially devastated, and stared through me until his gaze reached the dead Arab left within me, and he turned to Sarah and said, he is a grown boy, and he has seen a disaster.

During the war, after my friends died next to me, the commander decided to send me home for a day. An armored vehicle was sent to Tel Aviv to get someone, there was a blockade, and cars and buses did not get through. . . . Moshe and Sarah were amazed to see me. I sat in a chair for twenty-four hours. I did not eat, my clothes were bloodstained, I sat silent and staring. Sarah said, Moshe, he must talk, make him talk! And my father raised his voice and bellowed, he will speak when he has something to say! He came nearer, stood over me and with the sudden generosity that Sarah's words stirred in him, more in defiance of her than in support of me, only I didn't care, he said, be quiet as long as you like! And poor Sarah asked if I am angry at her and don't I love her any longer and don't I know what terrible nights she has been going through. I looked at her, I remember I did not know exactly who she was and why she was bothering me. I did not budge. I was an outcast and dazed and she sat opposite me and tried to elicit words, and I pursed my lips and kept silent. In her pain she didn't exactly know what shock was. She had been cast in iron and stale bread, and I in beeswax. After twenty-four hours I left for the central bus station. The armored car was waiting for me and we took off.[52] (39–40)

These events are revisited in several of Kaniuk's works. The lynching scene is retold, for example, in 1948, in which the event is set at a specific time, October 1947, a month before the UN decision to end the British Mandate for Palestine and establish two independent nation-states. In Post Mortem, by comparison, the event is simply identified as occurring "one day" in 1947. Also, in 1948, unlike in Post Mortem, Kaniuk and his friend are themselves shot at while eating ice cream. In 1948, the policeman shouts, "This is the *Arabush* who fired!"[53] More than a passive-aggressive bystander in this version, the policeman also slaps Kaniuk and yells at him. Here, too, distinct from *Post Mortem*, Kaniuk comes into direct contact with the victim:

> I wanted to help him. He pleaded and cried and said in Hebrew that it was not he who had fired the shots, and that he got caught there by accident. I believed him. He looked wretched, confused, and miserable, but they didn't want to believe him. A real enemy had fallen into their hands.[54]

In this version, when Kaniuk spots the victim, he lies on top of him to protect him from his attackers, led by a woman already in the establishment, along with bystanders who drop their ice creams to join in the assault. These attackers use the vicious words used by the policeman in *Post Mortem* to ridicule Kaniuk. The author, who returns home "insulted" and dripping with the victim's blood, encounters parents who play very different roles from those in *Post Mortem*: "My mother, Sarah, took care of me and pitied me, and my father, Moshe, said, it is wild here, this is how *Palestina* is."[55] Here they are united in support of their son, attentive to his needs, whereas in *Post Mortem* Sarah's portrayal is one of maternal failure. In 1948 the lynching is framed as the event that prompts the young Kaniuk to join the Hashomer Hatza'ir youth movement because of its support for a binational state.[56] In *Post Mortem* it holds no such connection.

Notably Kaniuk was nearly twenty years older when he described the lynching in 1948, as compared to the writing of *Post Mortem*. Well aware of the differences between the two versions, he often declared that he has no faith in his memory, and is completely uncertain as to exact facts, times, and places. In *Post Mortem*, since the narrative is focused on his relationship with his parents, and not first and foremost a historical testimony, issues of memory and forgetfulness regarding particular facts and dates are secondary—and indeed go unmentioned.

Chapter 10 of *Post Mortem* juxtaposes three scenes: Moshe Kaniuk punching his son, and the choice to forgo nativeness in favor of an affected immigrant identity; the lynching as a trauma witnessed by the young Kaniuk, with his mother failing to support him and Moshe responding with understanding—although more out of spite for Sarah than sympathy for Yoram; and the trauma of combat, framed as the loss of comrades—an event that, in 1948, follows the killing of the Palestinian boy, establishing a clear tie with the earlier-narrated prewar lynching scene. In the last case, in *Post Mortem*, as with the lynching, Sarah is self-absorbed, the exaggerated stereotype of a "Polish mother," complaining about losing sleep over her son being in danger, whereas Moshe responds sympathetically, again out of contempt for Sarah rather than empathy for Yoram. In such scenes Yoram emerges as the ultimate victim. Kaniuk's response, however, also mimics his mother's: just as she substitutes her own fears for his safety, even though he was not the target, for his horrific experience, he privileges his own fate over that of the murdered Palestinian victim.

Beyond valuing her son's physical return over what he has seen and felt, Sarah invokes what she witnessed as a child in Ukraine and a young woman in Palestine to effectively cancel Yoram's capacity for new painful experience. Her reference to the "row of bodies" is to the Odessa pogrom of 1905 and the 1921 Jaffa riots. The demand that he not "preach" to her implies that her suffering, before his birth, exceeded anything he could possibly experience today.

Yoram's mother's failure to support him intimates the binaries that pervade Israeli culture—self and enemy, Jew and Arab, assailant and victim. These national dynamics may seem barely perceivable in a narrative focused on parental betrayal and incompetence, and in the author's rage-filled recollection. All the same, the weight of the personal in the narrative has a particular collective political effect in Yoram's casting as the perpetual victim. In *Post Mortem* he writes:

During the 1905 pogrom Mintze [Kaniuk's maternal grandmother] remained with her family in the apartment and nursed baby Alexander [Sarah's brother]. The Russian maid had escaped and forgotten to shut the door behind her, and the rioters charging through the house ran past her, thinking that the residents had escaped. Simha [Kaniuk's maternal grandfather] climbed up on the roof to look for a family that had gotten

stuck, and shots were heard. Mintze-Miriam sat between sacks of pota-
toes and heard yells. Her hair turned white within a few hours. Simha
and his friends dragged the ladder to the roof and the Cossacks were too
drunk to climb. The family that had been on the roof were startled when
Simha climbed up to save them, and jumped down to the yard and were
massacred. The young Sarah walked out, and all she had to say many
years later was that there was a straight row of dead people there. (16)

In chapter 6 of *Post Mortem*, Sarah is described as being ashamed of her
son's occupation as a writer, as opposed to a bourgeois profession such as a
doctor. But when Yoram was a child, she supported his attempts at writing
unequivocally. Sarah was an excellent teacher, even according to her son's
testimony, and she wrote quite a number of textbooks for beginning readers.
Sarah's affair with a fellow teacher, referred to as B, occurred when the boy
was in fifth grade and illuminates her early stance on Yoram's writing.[57]
After the affair was over, Kaniuk writes, "B was just my teacher and no longer Sarah's lover" (109). Kaniuk and B got along quite well, but conflict arose
over Kaniuk's writing assignments: "I wrote straightforward compositions
and he would give me a C" (109). In the teachers' room Sarah once asked
B to read one of these compositions, and she erupted in defense of her son,
one of the few points in the book when she is portrayed as appreciating him:

Sarah ground her angry teeth and said, that bastard! What does he want?
Write him about pale sunsets! Give him a few highfalutin phrases!
    I wrote a lousy composition about how the sun flickers between the
clouds and I got an A. The teacher B read it in front of the class enthusi-
astically and I sat there ashamed. Sarah said, you should learn something
from all of this and I said I don't want to learn, and Moshe said, you are
teaching him the opposite of what you want from your education. You
want curiosity and daring, and you ask him to be like everyone else. You
want a revolution and you ask him to learn to compromise. She burst
out crying and told Moshe, look where your rigid uncompromising ways
have brought you! For a few days she was ashamed to look me in the eye
and it was nice. . . . I told [B] that yesterday on our balcony the sun farted

through the stormy waves of our anguished soul and I had to write five hundred times on the blackboard, the sun flickered! (109)

In one sense this anecdote is intended to criticize Sarah for teaching him to cater to the teacher's taste and compromise, but it also reveals mother and son's mutual ability to distinguish kitsch from clean prose and their common poetic values. These are values Sarah clearly does not share—as indicated in her instructions to Yoram—with B, who is still her lover. Her fury also betrays a sensitivity to B's underestimation of her son's abilities.

More often, Sarah's effect on her son does not encourage the narration and creation of a self. The most extreme instance of Sarah silencing her son comes in an often-repeated scene, like many of the formative scenes in Kaniuk's literature, introduced in his first Hebrew fiction book, *Ha-yored lemata*, in 1963. The scene occurs in the boy's fourth-grade classroom, where Yoram's mother was also his teacher. As told in *Post Mortem*, his mother announces that "we all come from different backgrounds and homes. . . . But what do we know about each other's families, about the homes they come from? So little. I suggest that you each tell the class about your home, and we will get to know you better" (105). The children enjoy speaking about themselves—no wonder, it is their chance to create an identity in class. But Yoram is not allowed to talk. Sarah ignores her son's raised hand until she can do so no longer, and he then ignores the tears welling in her eyes as she begs him to stop talking about the details of their broken household. The children snicker at Yoram until his mother slaps him and both mother and son break down crying. Kaniuk's narrative exposes her, and in denying her son the opportunity to talk, Sarah suppresses his ability to create an identity. As for Yoram, his recognition that narrating is essential to being and survival is clearly stated when he describes his childhood method for overcoming his fears: "I was then a compilation of fears. I taught myself to stand outside the painful experience and tell it to myself" (88). "Telling it" enables control, of which his teacher/mother deprives him. To penalize his mother further, Yoram offers silence.

Earlier in this discussion Yoram is described as identifying with the aggressor in the *ow/ay* game. But in chapter 11 of *Post Mortem* Kaniuk suggests it to be a legacy of his father. Like the lynching scene, this scene begins with the generic "one day," prompting a comparison between the two:

> One day my uncle Dov and my father went to visit a young woman that Dov was in love with, and saw her house on fire. Through the glowing fire they could see the young woman move as she tried to escape. The thugs, who held the bottles they drank from, poured gasoline on the fire and did not let her out. My father tried to fight them and got struck. Somewhere within him, I know this place from myself, he also admired those bastards' liberty to push him over. His pity was no greater than the feeling that he belonged to the burned as well as to those burning. (43)

In Yoram's telling, then, Moshe identifies with the aggressor. When Yoram writes "I know this place from myself," he recognizes his own potential and practiced position as an aggressor. Both father and son are observers who try and fail to change the course of an event. Readers must therefore ask if Yoram's implicit identification with the aggressor makes him an accomplice, even as his actions suggest the opposite.

Just as the scene in which Moshe watches the woman burn to death echoes Yoram's self-portrayal, the son invents other scenes that enhance the parallels between father and son. While in a hotel in Sweden a week after Sarah's death, writing about his parents, he has a dream in which he sees his father, Moshe, then long dead, wander the streets of Berlin, following a woman to whom he is attracted and who has no shadow. Moshe then runs into a man who is holding a baby but walks off, and Moshe suspects the man has eaten the baby. In a reverse blood libel, a bone is found on a church doorstep. Moshe calls for a policeman, who vomits on seeing the bone, and Moshe shouts, "Do something!"—just as Kaniuk cried to the policeman on Allenby Street when the Palestinian man was being lynched by Jews (53). In his dream Kaniuk unites his father's fantasized experiences of mid-1920s Germany and with own experiences in British Mandatory Palestine. His father, in the dream, eventually returns to a café and tries to tell his friends what he has seen, but no one believes him and he becomes angry. Thus Yoram's story is an attempt to invent his father's past through his own, and create parallel experiences and parallel reactions—in which his father responds as he has.[58]

In imparting his relationship with his parents in *Post Mortem*, Kaniuk figures them simultaneously as individuals and representatives in a collective national story. This universally representative role for the individual is common within national literature, wherein ethnic specificity is experienced as a current undermining nationality.[59] Indeed, Gershon Shaked's reading of *Post Mortem* shows that the specific ethnic identities of Kaniuk's parents are representative of Israeli nationality, and that Kaniuk is viewed as the ultimate Israeli, created by their union. His works, as noted already, are not read as critiquing Israeli nationality but as identifying with it. (Ethnic identities in Israeli autobiography will be discussed further in chapter 3, on Aharon Appelfeld and Shimon Ballas.)

Kaniuk, in this discussion, would seem to occupy the position of the *Ost-jude* (Eastern European Jew) who aspires to be accepted by German culture, despite the threat that this arrangement will annihilate his identity. When the young Kaniuk substitutes *ay* for *ow*, he accepts his father's conditions regarding identity; he asserts his preference for spinach over compote. In *The Last Berliner* Kaniuk writes: "The homeland of European Jewry is my real homeland. My family lived in Europe at least two thousand years."[60] For Kaniuk, adopting this European identity—being a Peter or a Robert—is also a bid for his father's love and recognition. This recognition is visible in instances such as their joint stand against his mother after the lynching, but it is never granted unconditionally. In identifying with Moshe and his adopted identity, and renouncing his native, inherited identity, Yoram also maintains his immigrant outsider status, which seemingly exonerates him from atrocities and other offenses committed in his native land's name. War will always be another pogrom. A native can be an aggressor, but an immigrant marginal Jew cannot be.

On the one hand, the juxtaposed experiences of the pogrom and the murders Sarah witnessed in Palestine, along with her eluding of the Shoah, might be seen to erase the legitimacy of her victimhood, considering that she herself survived these events. On the other hand, the adoption of these events as sources of trauma can preserve the native's "nonnative" position whereby he or she really cannot be an aggressor by virtue of still being a Jew.

At one point in *Post Mortem*, the family is "sitting shiva" in honor of Moshe's niece, whose braid was chopped off by an inconsiderate suitor. This potentially camp scene is framed as earnest. Moshe sits at his sister's house and sings hasidic songs: "In this rare moment Moshe evidently wanted to be a Jew among Jews without the Gymnasia Herzliya and the seminar's pagan Canaan [referring to the elite early Tel Aviv school and the biblical roots of Zionist 'new Hebrew' culture and songs, and alleged rejection of Jewish diasporic tradition]. . . . He had a good voice for lieder, but he had a better voice for these songs" (129). In singing the melodies of Europe, Moshe rejects the New Hebrew culture in Palestine.

Despite Moshe's support for aliya for pragmatic necessity, he and his peers reflexively detested Palestine and its Jewish settlement project. Exemplifying his continued affinity for the Continent, he takes Yoram, in chapter 30, to Haifa to visit the exiled German Jewish writer Arnold Zweig, who would return to Germany after the war. Moshe also arranged concerts at the Tel Aviv Museum, "magical moments" when the Yekkim would listen to chamber music "not only *for* the music itself but also *against* Tel Aviv, against the Russian and Oriental-like songs, against the sweat and the enthusiasm, against the exaggeration of it all, against the burning faith where the danger of a shattered dream lurks" (my emphasis, 139).

Yoram adopts his father's position despite harboring a festering anger toward him, an anger that does not dissipate even when Moshe is paralyzed by a stroke. On a visit to the rehabilitation center, he hears two women singing and compliments them. Pleased, the women promise to sing him "Ma yafim haleylot bekna'an," Isaac Katznelson's poem set to a popular Arab tune in 1911, which became an Israeli classic.[61] Kaniuk, who acknowledges elsewhere that this song represents everything Moshe hates about Israeli society, while serving as code for his revulsion for Sarah's Eastern European Jewish background, all the same invites the women to sing it for his defenseless father. Although the women lose their voices, and the performance never happens, the cruelty in the son's act is not lost on the reader (180).

Yoram, then, is not afraid to reveal his own behavior at its worst, leaving himself open to the reader's critical eye. Mindful of his father's descent toward death, Yoram races the wheelchair in the hospital yard in the hope of shaking him from his stupor, but Moshe only cries in helpless fear. He cries for his mother in Polish, "Mamushka," and recites verses from Goethe, and Kaniuk is infuriated that Moshe will not cry for his wife or his children, but only for his own mother and a poet (181).

POSTMEMORY, THE TERM introduced by Marianne Hirsch, characterizes the experience of those who have grown up in the shadow of narratives preceding their birth, and whose own stories are marginalized or repressed by the previous generation's stories, which were shaped by traumatic events that cannot be fully understood or reconstructed.[62] Postmemory, also known as retrospective memory, is often obsessive and unrelenting; it may be incomplete or absent, full or empty, and like memory itself, it is constructed.[63] Responding to a 1991 article by Kaniuk in *Die Zeit* about his confrontational meeting with the German author Günter Grass (discussed later), Hirsch writes that postmemory often maps and preserves cities that are long gone, as in Erich Kästner's and Grass's respective hometowns—although Kaniuk himself would never have paired the two authors—and in Kaniuk's Germany in *The Last Berliner*. In Germany Kaniuk can smell his father's fear; "the horror has been inherited" (127). But he cannot retrace his father's footsteps: "If I had only succeeded in being born here, into the horror . . . out of which the book stemmed, out of which grew my nightmare that I was supposed to be 'there' had my father stayed in Berlin and instead of being born free but guilt-ridden in Palestine, I would have been ashes in some German chimney" (128).

At the same time, postmemory in *The Last Berliner* serves a specific political end. The book is devoted to Kaniuk's attempts to unravel his identity as an Israeli in the face of the Shoah, and to extract it from the intertwined memory of his father. In *The Last Berliner*, as explained shortly, Kaniuk often depicts his position as an Israeli Jew in Germany as manipulative and self-righteous.

Whereas the opening chapters of a personal work are typically dedicated to gaining the reader's trust, in *The Last Berliner* the narrator engages in an extended exposition devoted to discrediting himself, and exposing his lack of reliability. Time and again he tells us how he sank into the "stupefying pleasure" of an "idiot of the first degree" (31). Be it a meeting with Katharine, his official guide, or the "righteous among the nations" couple who invite him for a beer, Kaniuk repeatedly stresses his adolescent insolence and inconsideration: "I now barter in other people's blood" (40, 46). Although *The Last Berliner* is closer to essay writing than all Kaniuk's other autobiographical works, rooted in emotion and plot, it is also the only work in which fiction seeps openly into documentary prose. This occurs when Kaniuk meets Adam Stein, the hero of his 1969 novel, *Adam Resurrected*, on the train in Germany (132).

THE MAIN NARRATIVE unit giving rhythm and momentum to *The Last Berliner* is the anecdote.[64] A string of polemical anecdotes carries the narrator forward, preventing him from settling at a defined destination. Kaniuk meets an endless stream of people whose company he seeks. He engages fellow travelers in conversation, sharing of life histories, and confession, using every method he can summon. Unlike *Post Mortem*, which focuses on the nuclear family and their life histories, *The Last Berliner* entails a sequence of meetings with figures who float in and out of Kaniuk's life, leaving their cumulative imprint on his German-Israeli experience. These anecdotes occur so close upon each other's heels that they become difficult to follow. The timbre of the sequence is emphatically emotional, with sentiments unable to be controlled or regimented, foreclosing rational debate. This tendency to defer to emotion explains why Kaniuk "lost" his public argument with Günter Grass about German involvement in the Gulf War (119–23). *The Last Berliner* is therefore a book about the inadequacy and vicissitudes of memory: "Everything I wrote in this book is about what memory is, and what can be done with it, and how one lives with it. What are steps without feet? What are feet without steps?" (216)

Obsessed as he is with the "cleansing of the horror" in Germany, Kaniuk is also preoccupied with cleansing Israeli horrors, and even more so with the points at which these two narrative obsessions intersect. The collision of these two stories, the collision of his memory with that of his parents, and the collision of the collective memory with the personal create problematic analogies. These analogies ultimately render a direct confrontation with Israeli national deeds impossible. Just as his trauma is erased by his mother's, the Palestinian Nakba (catastrophe) is overshadowed by the Shoah.

Kaniuk and Maimon

I have read the self Kaniuk created in *Post Mortem* as an outcome of the tension between imitation and alienation in his relationship with his father. But Kaniuk also had an adopted father—Solomon Maimon—and this imagined relationship deserves a look, given that it fortifies the attributes we have seen in his relationship with his biological father. The latest Hebrew edition of Maimon's *Lebensgeschichte* (originally published in German in 1792) appeared in 2009.[65] In his preface Kaniuk reveals his close affiliation to the Jewish-Lithuanian philosopher, who died 130 years before his birth:

> I read Maimon's *Lebensgeschichte* for the first time in Israel Haim Tavaiov's Hebrew translation, which was published by Tushia in Warsaw in 1898. The book found its way to a small Hebrew bookstore. . . . I remember I was twenty-two years old, I was living on Division Street on the corner of Canal in an old apartment without heating that cost me $18 per month in an area where languages besides Yiddish were hardly spoken. I went up to my miserable apartment from the store, wrapped myself in a blanket, and read the book twice in a row and felt that I had found a relative. Perhaps a new father. Someone I could have been if I had lived many years earlier.[66]

Kaniuk, then an aspiring painter and a wounded veteran of Israel's War of Independence suffering from shell-shock—or post-traumatic stress disorder (PTSD), as it is now known—living recklessly in New York, identifies Maimon (ca. 1752–1800) as a vision of either himself or a father. This is a significant attribute in any instance but especially so given the prominence of Moshe's emotional vacancy. Maimon—recognized as the first to narrate the Ostjude's journey from the Pale of Settlement shtetl to the West, and thus as creator of that geographic, cultural, and social journey paradigm—and the Tel Aviv–reared Kaniuk, a prolific if unruly Israeli novelist, do not seem obviously connected. Yet parallels can be identified in their position as Jews and life writers. Maimon, despite his misery, achieved what Kaniuk's own father could only aspire to by moving to and mixing within German culture, but he also filled the void left by Moshe in Kaniuk's writing and personal development.

In looking more closely for connections, one sees that Kaniuk's reading of the text while in the United States highlights his temporary poverty, and a dedication to reading despite uncomfortable living conditions. Both the poverty and the dedication echo Maimon's early experience in Germany. Beyond that, and more important still, Kaniuk's identification with Maimon stems from an existential identification of Israeli identity with that of the Ostjude. That is, the Israeli native is never simply that, a native, but always a newcomer, always marginalized, rejected, and a beggar at his own doorstep. The Israeli native is filthy, ill-mannered, unwanted by his own brethren, but in fact well-read, educated, and more original than those brethren.

Nor was Kaniuk the first to encounter revelation in a secondhand copy of Maimon's book. The protagonist Daniel Deronda, from George Eliot's 1876 novel of the same name, picked up a copy of "that wonderful bit of autobiography, the life of the Polish Jew, Solomon Maimon," at a London bookshop. The volume, on display alongside a "judicious mixture, from the immortal verse of Homer to the mortal prose of the railway novel," is seen to uphold this "judicious" selection.[67] By that time, however, Maimon was no longer remembered as a philosopher but rather as an emblematic Jew. When Deronda asks the price of the book, the shopkeeper takes it as a sign that he is "perhaps of our race?"

In Michah Yosef Berdichevsky's autobiographically based novella *Mahanayim* (The Two Cups, 1899), the protagonist, Michael, a philosophy student at the University of Breslau (now Wroclaw), reflects on Jewish intellectuals and authors whom he views as his role models. Over even Moses Mendelssohn, along with many other Haskalah eminences, he names Maimon as the figure to whom he is most attached.[68]

Nearly a half century later, Leah Goldberg likewise cited Maimon in her autobiographical novel *Ve-hu ha-or* (And This Is the Light, 1946) as a role model for young Lithuanian Jews seeking an education in Germany after World War I. Goldberg saw him as modeling ultraistic devotion to intellectual pursuits, whereby education stands above all other personal and material needs.

As he did for the earlier Hebrew writers, Maimon offers Kaniuk a tradition from which to build an autobiographical self. Maimon's narrative was crafted in the spirit of the German *Bildung*, a genre that encourages the individual to construct and reshape his identity and being.[69] Just as Maimon could learn German and become a recognized philosopher, Kaniuk can construct his own contradictory identity. By following Maimon, Kaniuk can observe his own father's identification with Germany, and can distance himself from his own native Palestinian-born identity in favor of his conflicted, fabricated, consciously fictive one.

CHAPTER TWO

"I Have a Pain in My Mother"

Natan Zach and Haim Be'er

It is not right to love only one human being so much,
even if it is your mother.—Romain Gary, *Promise at Dawn*

I could live without the Mother (as we all do, sooner or later);
but what life remained would be absolutely and entirely
unqualifiable (without quality).—Roland Barthes, *Camera Lucida*

I confess my mother, one always confesses the other.
—Jacques Derrida, *Circumfession*

THIS CHAPTER explores two autobiographical selves formed in relation to dying mothers, in the works of Natan Zach and Haim Be'er. Writing of their mothers, both authors create narratives that shape and delineate their relationships with their writerly identities and with Israeli nationalism. Notably, although Zach and Be'er—as well as Yoram Kaniuk—relate extensively to their fathers, with diverging resolution, details, and attitudes, each gives precedence to his relationship with his mother and her role in the formation of his self.

Kaniuk's *Post Mortem* delves into his parents' figures, their life stories, their deaths, and their influence on his being, but does not emphasize their contribution or lack thereof to his development as an author. Kaniuk's mother, Sarah, had lifelong women friends who remained at her hospital bedside when she was dying. These relationships are described as loving and symbiotic as well as competitive and petty. Kaniuk relates a standard exchange that occurred whenever the friends met, revolving around him: Sarah's friend Rivka would ask whether Yoram, who was perceived as a disappointment and a failure, was still writing. Try as she might to avert this line of questioning, Sarah would respond apologetically with her own rhetorical question: "What could he do at the age of fifty-eight? He can't go study medicine."[1] Likewise Natan Zach's parents failed to appreciate their son's vocation. They did not read his poems, nor did they realize that he had become the major poetic voice and great cultural authority of his generation. Yet even as both men describe their parents' disappointment with their chosen pursuit, they occupy notably different positions: whereas Kaniuk's reception within Israeli letters has been a matter of debate, Zach's memoir was written from a high perch in the Israeli literary establishment. That is, a clear discrepancy exists between Zach's public figure and his role within his family, a conflict that does not exist for Kaniuk.

In his 1997 memoir *Mot immi* (My Mother's Death), Zach writes of his mother:

> She never expressed any interest in my poems. I did not bother telling her and she offered no response to the rumors that reached her sometimes through friends and neighbors.
>
> She wholly accepted my father's verdict that poems were not something that would provide a person with a respectable income. Therefore they were worthless, simply a waste of time. She must have also remembered her father's music and his poverty.
>
> She herself did not read poetry, not even in her own tongue. The nuns, who had taught her when she was a child, had warned her to beware of wanton literature.[2]

For Zach, the need to care for his mother, who became ill after he was already an established poet, ended his decade-long stay in England, where he had completed his doctorate. He returned to Israel in 1979.

Unlike the respective mothers of Kaniuk and Zach, Haim Be'er's mother had a major role and deep involvement in her son's development as an author. *Havalim* (1998), identified in Hebrew as a "new book" without explicitly indicating autobiography or fiction, documents this progress, creating a link between the mother's advancing illness and her son's growth as an author.[3]

James Olney, whose 1980 collection was a watershed in the formation of autobiography criticism and theory as a field, proposed an explanation for autobiography's delayed entry into critical discourse.[4] He postulated that the genre, aside from not being considered "real" literature, makes critical self-reflexive reading redundant in many cases, because it seems to inherently contain this mode of reading. Translated as *The Pure Element of Time*, Be'er's book is a "self-contained" work of that sort. The delicate and constantly shifting relationship between the act of writing, memory, story, and self foregrounds Be'er's autobiographical discourse. Similarly, Zach's *My Mother's Death* is, at its core, a reflection on narrative and its relationship to art, poetry, and "experience." The two following sections focus, therefore, on very different narratives that share fundamental themes, debates, and core conflicts. Their distinctness highlights their affinities and common ground as personal life writings within the framework of national Israeli literature.

Zach's and Be'er's stories differ both in their social and cultural background and in their portrayal of the respective mothers' illness and subsequent death. They also entail diverging portraits of writers in an Israeli context. Zach, the defining generational voice, personifies Israeli identities in the 1950s and early 1960s.[5] His memoir, however, depicts him as existing at the margins of a financially secure Jewish-Israeli native-born society. Viewed during the last months of his mother's life, when she was suffering and losing her mind, the Zach family is depicted as a conglomerate of emotional vacancy, missed opportunities, and chilling alienation. Zach, for his part, had some reason to perceive himself as being marginalized, given his mother's Catholicism—along with the corresponding cultural alienation— and his family's lack of wealth.[6] Indeed, Zach's father was a vegetable seller, and Be'er's father was a grocer, with these similar professions existing far from the labor movement's agrarian ideal. And both fathers were rejected by their sons.

Each memoir also contributed to a change in the public cultural persona of its author. The work by Be'er, who was raised in an Orthodox Jewish family, signals his move from acknowledged margins to the center of the Israeli canon. Zach, from his loftier position, can reveal his marginality while reinforcing his already secure central status. While Zach's memoir remains marginal in his oeuvre, and was written decades after he established his influential position, Be'er's memoir is his most highly lauded work to date. Despite or because of its individual specificity, the book expanded Be'er's profile from "religious writer" to a place of wider recognition. Zach and Be'er, therefore, seem to have traveled different trajectories: Zach, a leader of his generation, reconstructs his potential marginality in a book that was well received but not considered his major or most influential achievement—those books were written forty years earlier. Be'er's autobiography writes its author from the margins into the center, representing a threat to a coherent, homogeneous cultural core and literary canon of clear-cut Israeli identities. At the same time, broader changes to this cultural core are what enabled his move from the margins to the center.

An additional intersection of formative Israeli narratives occurs in Be'er's *Havalim*: the narrative of immigration and settlement (his father's story) and that of the native-born Israeli (ostensibly his mother's story). But the lines of conflict between these narratives are dislodged from their normative tracks because his mother's family is ultra-Orthodox and does not necessarily identify with the newly founded Zionist nationalist establishments. Conversely, Be'er's paternal uncle, an immigrant, is depicted as the ideal of the Jewish native of Palestine—a hardworking, emotionally sturdy, successful farmer in Emek Yizrael (Jezreel Valley)—a center of Zionist agricultural settlement and the development of the Israeli labor movement. Thus both Be'er's and Zach's memoirs highlight conflicts between immigration and nativism, and between alienation and belonging in Israeli culture.

Where the Dwarfs Don't Live Anymore:
Fragments of Narrative and Self in Zach's *My Mother's Death*[7]

Natan Zach's fragmentary memoir, *My Mother's Death*, begins with the author's expression of hesitation about publishing it: "I have a need to apologize for bringing these private pages out in public. . . . Perhaps they will also interest those who have not been through such similar experiences. Our lives are, after all, similar to one another, no less than they are different."[8]

The apologetic tone of this passage, which nevertheless insists on the text's universality, places Zach's memoir within the Western autobiographical tradition—beginning with Saint Augustine, who wonders "why we confess to God, when he knows (everything about us)"; continuing to Rousseau, who, like Zach, insists on our attention because reading his story will teach us about the making of man; and on to the Hebrew tradition of "useful" instructive autobiography, in which the text purports to benefit readers, because the author has experienced conflicts and tribulations that readers themselves are destined to confront.[9] The useful bent in Hebrew autobiography merges with the voice of the autobiographer as a community representative, whether as a prophet or a prayer leader who evolves into a national leader.

Zach's opening also places him within the classic modern Hebrew convention whereby allegedly authentic papers are happened upon and brought to press untampered with. This form, a component of what Menachem Brinker has named in his reading of Yosef Haim Brenner "a rhetoric of honesty," and which Brenner incorporated into many of his greater works of narrative fiction, centers on an authentic unedited text, for example, left behind by a ship passenger or even "taken" from a traveler's satchel. It is thus a fabrication mimicking testimony or "genuine" life writing, published as a diary, confession, or memoir.[10] In this vein Zach creates a distance between himself and the text by noting that he does not recognize his own handwriting. The facade of a text composed of sketches that do not qualify as art and are far removed from poetry and from Zach's poet persona matters to Zach in this work, and he returns to this idea, as we shall see, at crucial moments.

In his introduction Zach relates having returned from Emile Habibi's May 1996 funeral in Haifa's Anglican cemetery. Characterizing Habibi as a close friend, Zach announces his affinity with the Palestinian communist, author, editor, and political leader. Willy-nilly the friend's funeral enables Zach to return to his mother's death. Looking through his drawers for some papers, he finds notes in his own handwriting—although, as he says, he does not believe in coincidences—which he had forgotten having written immediately after his mother's death, fifteen years earlier. Some sections in the memoir, however, were obviously written closer to the time of publication, a year after Habibi's death. In a fragment about Nelly, his mother's beloved dog, Zach writes: "Years later I wrote a poem about the two friends." The Nelly poems were published in his collection *Anti-mehikon* in 1984, three years after the memoir was allegedly written and forgotten. One fragment, devoted to sculptor Miriam Karoly's death in 1994, opens with the words "Many years later" (65). Another fragment opens with the statement "Fifteen years after my mother's death I dream the following dream," indicating that this section was written around the same time the old notes were found (111). In the analysis of a poem that Zach includes in his narrative — a poem originally published two years after his mother's death — he states that his mother did not appear in his dreams for a long time, and when she did finally appear, it was in his nightmares, one of which he records in this section. This further contradicts the claims in the introduction. Nevertheless, the statement serves to present the notes as a complete, untouched artifact found and published by Zach. This contributes, as we shall see, to the distinctions Zach tries to draw between poetry and life writing.

The memoir consists of a sequence of short paragraphs or page-long units. Each unit appears isolated on one or two pages, printed only on one side of the page, possibly to avoid a sense of continuity. Serving the same "countersequential" end, many of the units begin with "once" or "one day." The book's third section ties together three such singular instances with the markers "once" and "another time."[11] One section opens with "repeatedly." These events are formulated both as singular and as "examples" of similar events; either way the structure prevents the production of a narrative that develops or progresses because it positions whole, separate anecdotal units alongside each other, rather than as stemming from each other. We cannot know how long the mother's illness lasted or how much time elapsed between sections — which may go back and forth in time.

ZACH'S OPENING WORDS, as we saw, cast him in the contradictory position of individual and representative, unique and universal. This correlates with Zach's position in Israeli literature; however, this particular work highlights aspects of his persona that do not emerge through his poetry.

Whereas Zach's contemporaries Yehuda Amichai and Dahlia Ravikovitch might each have contended for the generation's leading poetic role, neither could claim responsibility for differentiating their generation in Israeli culture, as Zach did in his poetry, as well as in his influential essays and criticism and in his work as an editor. According to Hamutal Tsamir and others, Zach formed the voice of Israeli poetry and instituted the poetry of the new state.[12] Zach, as Tsamir points out, established the national Israeli poetic speaker in the national landscape, making his belonging a "given," taken for granted and obvious. Reading *My Mother's Death*, we are reminded what a directed and conscious effort this was. Zach, the ultimate Israeli and universal poet, returns in this text to his given name: Harry Zeitelbach, an unwanted child with all the hallmarks of an outcast within Jewish Israeli society. Harry Zeitelbach, born in Berlin in 1930, is the son of Italian-born Roman Catholic Tina (short for Clementina, the Hebrew word for tangerine) and Norbert Zeitelbach, a German Jew and World War I veteran who spent two years as a prisoner of war in Brighton, England. After escaping from Berlin to Paris, the family arrived in Mandatory Palestine in 1936. Having lost all his property with the rise of the Nazi regime, Norbert Zeitelbach arrived in Israel penniless. He became a construction worker and ended up as a partner in a greengrocer's shop in Tel Aviv, right across the street from Kassit, the café where his son would take his early steps in Israeli cultural bohemia in the 1950s. As for the son, he served as an officer in the Israeli army in 1948 and after the war studied at the Hebrew University of Jerusalem.

IN *MY MOTHER'S DEATH* Zach reveals glimpses of his erased family tree—one of his German non-Jewish relatives who served in the Luftwaffe (German air force), and on his mother's side, an uncle who was active in the Italian Fascist Party. Zach's parents, although living for years in Palestine and then Israel, never learned Hebrew.[13]

As Zach sketches out his mother's illness and deterioration, her loss of independence and bodily control, the blindness, the debilitating pain, and retreat into Italian, a language of which her medical staff is ignorant, he considers the possibility of euthanasia, for her and for himself.[14] This is a position that entails sympathy and care. But those qualities are what *My Mother's Death* so strikingly lacks.

Although Zach tells us little of his childhood, he provides insights by indirection. When, for example, he takes his mother out in the sun on the old-age-home balcony, she sees a boy walking home from school and says: "I could use one of those now. Back then, when I had one, I did not know how to appreciate it" (35). Even in her longing Tina cannot view the boy as a person in his own right, a person she might relate to. He is still "one of those," a generic boy. Zach confesses: "Actually, I never loved her. Maybe it was unrequited love. She welcomed everyone. She would even ask the postman or any stranger who happened to visit the house in for coffee. Perhaps she was wary of the strange country; perhaps such was her nature" (81).

The fragmented structure of Zach's memoir clearly correlates with the fragmented self that emerges from his book. Narrative, narrativity, the ability to tell a story all represent absences in Zach's volume: narrating creates a self, and *My Mother's Death* is, among other things, a reflection on the inability to create a self or a story of it.[15]

My Mother's Death concludes with a section entitled "A Short Fairy Tale, Purely the Fruit of the Imagination." Generically contradicting autobiography on several levels, a fairy tale is a narrative situated in no time and no place—such as "a long time ago in a distant land." Autobiography is necessarily of specific times and places. The fairy tale gains its universal value from its alleged lack of specificity; the autobiography may be universally representative precisely because of its specificity.[16] A fairy tale often promises a happy ending and closure. Autobiography cannot. A fairy tale is a complete and self-sufficient narrative, and yet Zach presents his chapter as a conclusion, a part of a larger autobiographical narrative. These differences may guide the reader's expectations in approaching Zach's conclusion labeled a fairy tale. This is the story that follows the title:

> Once upon a time there were three dwarfs. A big dwarf, a medium-sized dwarf, and a small one. The big dwarf had a big bed and a big room. The medium-sized dwarf had a medium-sized bed and a medium-sized room. And the small dwarf had a small bed and a small room.

They lived, the three dwarfs, in one house. But they hardly ever spoke to one another, apart from the acceptable words of politeness when they met in the morning, or when each turned to his or her room in the evening. Neither did they help each other. For the life of a dwarf is extremely difficult, and one must not demand of him more than what he possibly can give.

As the years went by, the dwarfs died one after the other. First the big dwarf died. Then the medium-sized dwarf died, and as for the little dwarf, if he has not died yet—he has left no trace.

And so, the three-room house was emptied, and three other people, not dwarfs, came to live in it. And if no harm has come to them yet, and I hope with all of my heart that it has not, they are still living in it until this very day. People satisfied with their lot, as if there had never been any dwarfs in the world. (115)

Several elements disrupt this "fairy tale." The "happily ever after" comes because the dwarfs have disappeared. No evil is punished, nor is good rewarded. An absence of parents is fundamental to fairy tales. Here the story of "The Three Bears" creates a positive frame of reference and expectations, but the family structure is upset: the relationship established among the three dwarfs is tolerant at best; the father-mother-child triangle lacks not only its nurturing bond but basic mutual sympathy. (The Hebrew discloses gender, which the English conceals—the medium-sized dwarf is female; the big and small ones are male.) In contrast to "The Three Bears," no external force violently disrupts the dwarfs' life, necessitating repair; rather hell is at home, and more so: hell is them, because once they leave the house, it becomes a fine place to live.

The dwarfs' story stands in contrast to the fragment Zach devotes to his uncle Heinrich Scher and his family. Uncle Heinrich married a woman who had an apparent intellectual disability and was heavily dependent on him. Their first daughter was similar to her mother, and the second had Down syndrome. When Heinz was wrongfully accused of embezzlement in the agricultural distribution collective he ran at his moshav, Ramot Ha-Shavim, he sedated and then murdered his wife and younger daughter, who were at home with him, and then committed suicide. Zach interprets the suicide as Scher's act of refusal to leave his beloved dependents alone, when he has been backed into a corner through the questioning of his honesty. Eventually Heinz's name was cleared of all suspicions, and the real embezzler was found.[17] This family's violent end and seemingly inseparable bond contrast sharply with the experience of the dwarfs, who simply drift apart and disintegrate for lack of empathy and ability to connect.[18] The dwarf family bespeaks a sterile, suffocating environment; as noted, no violent event occurs to disturb their daily routine.[19]

IF AUTOBIOGRAPHICAL NARRATIVES potentially work toward refiguring, reworking, understanding, exposing, or seeking revenge, salvation, or development, Zach's narrative reaches a dead end and, at best, disintegrates. It refuses to allow closure and corresponding meaning. The dwarfs have not left behind a trace, and that is for the better, but it utterly contradicts the essence of life writing. The disappearance of the big and medium-sized dwarfs is reiterated in the autobiographical sections. Zach is concerned with the process of death, with the ravaging of individuality caused by his mother's dementia and illness. Yet he is concerned with deterioration and death, not with separation or parting. When he receives the phone call from the Italian hospital—"We regret . . . "—he rushes to the morgue: "A cold shriveled body devoid of flesh, perhaps thirty kilograms, remained. The pointy chin she never had is the most distinct feature. The eyes are closed. I stroke the chilled face with shaking hands, kiss only to oblige. Is this my mother? No, no longer."[20]

In a "generically correct" fairy tale, the kiss would bring the mother back to life; her body would remain intact. Illness, suffering, and death would leave no mark on it. In Zach's dwarf "fairy tale," the two larger dwarfs die. What happens to the small dwarf is not of interest; all that matters is that he has disappeared. Notably this is commented upon by the first-person narrator, who intervenes with an abundance of empathy for anyone but the dwarfs. The refusal to provide closure as a narrative balm, apparent in the parting scene, is reiterated in a poem Zach appended to the book, part of a cycle named "PS" (נ.ב):

לֹא לֹא גְמַר
חֲתִימָה טוֹבָה
חֲתִימָה סְתָם
מַעֲשֵׂה יְדֵי אָדָם
בִּמְעַט כִּמְעַט כָּמוֹךָ

A paraphrase of this may be: "No, not to be written in the book of life, only an end, man-made, almost, nearly like you." The poem is based on the traditional greeting used on the eve of Yom Kippur, when Jews wish each other "a good signing," meaning that when the Day of Atonement is over they should be "written into the book of life." The Hebrew word for signing also denotes closure, so at the end of his book Zach notes that this is just an end, without grace or sublime value. That is where Zach leaves us: in mounting emotional strain and discomfort, with no tools to ease these states. Here poetry aligns with prose. But at the heart of this slim volume, Zach creates a sharp dichotomy between the two.

Immediately after the paragraph that describes his mother's death, Zach quotes from "Beintayim" (Meantime), a poem he wrote soon afterward, which is roughly translated here:

Meantime she returns to me in my dreams whenever I sleep
And I say welcome back; while you're here, have a seat,
And she props up the pillow, as is her custom,
For it is not natural for a mother not to prop a pillow for her son
And for the son to prop up his mother's pillow
And wipe her cold sweat and smooth her frazzled hair
And hold her cold hand and say fear not
The place you are going to, you will not return from
Empty-handed as you so often have
Because the place you are going does not store hopes
Nor loss, regret, or sorrow, not even a mother's pain
The place you are going to lacks nothing. It is whole.[21]

The poem begins with an allusion to the canonical Jewish hymn of praise to God, "Adon Olam": the Hebrew words for "whenever I sleep"—

be-et ishan—are a declaration of trust in God that one may recite in moments of liturgical joy, such as in the Friday night prayer that greets the Shabbat; the speaker entrusts his or her soul to the hands of God, when sleeping and when awake. The fear that arises near the end of the poem also ties in to "Adon Olam" ("the Lord is with me, I shall not fear," *adonai li ve'lo ira*). This allusion to Jewish liturgy frames the exchange between mother and son as a spiritual Jewish gesture of comforting that is at the same time ironic, given that it contradicts everything we have learned in this memoir about Zach and his mother, born a Roman Catholic and educated by nuns.[22]

Zach proceeds immediately to analyze the poem:

> This time, exceptionally, the poems are early to arrive. Having written them, they stir a disconcertedness in me that I cannot understand. I have never written about a "fresh" experience. The term *experience* always repelled me. . . . "Meantime she returns to me in my dreams whenever I sleep." But that is explicitly untrue. She only returned in the poem. Years went by until she began to return in my dreams.
> In my nightmares, to be exact.
>
> What are those fictional "markers" that find their way into every verbal experiment, in order to amplify its emotional content, and how can they be arrested without hurting the very capacity to write poetry. . . . But here, on these pages, are things only as they are. Not poetry.

> A rumbling: it is
> Truth itself
> walked among
> men,
> amidst the
> metaphor squall. (Paul Celan)[23]

Fully aware of his dance between *Dichtung und Wahrheit* (poetry and truth), Zach quotes Celan's poem as if to fortify his "truthful prose" premise, undermining the project as it unfolds.

If we recall now the family of dwarfs, we may discern that while the fairy tale lacks in mercy, empathy, and grace, elements present in the poem "Meantime," the poem and the fairy tale do share a common feature. Namely, the fairy tale is a universalizing genre; it attempts to generalize as it eliminates time and place, in opposition, as noted, to the specificity of life writing. In that sense, the fairy tale fits Zach's poetic public persona in Israeli culture, because this persona ostensibly surpasses the specifically local and present.

In trying to conceptualize his mother's life and marriage, and his place within them, Zach sees the fairy tale as providing a frame of reference. It helps him explain her inability, or unwillingness, to mother. Involved mothering therefore emerges as a component of fairy tales, not "real life." Had Tina had her own personal fairy tale fulfilled, she might have been able to mother, but because her own life broke the mold she couldn't complete it for her son:

> Actually she cannot be blamed. Her mother died when she was born. Her two elder sisters abused her, and turned her into a Cinderella, a kitchen drudge. A Cinderella without a magic shoe, without a ball, without a prince. Her father was too busy with his musical compositions. He was forty-two or forty-three when he died. What else had she left but to marry the first man who offered her refuge. She met him on a streetcar in Amsterdam. A couple that had not even a common language, other than the will to escape. He from his domineering mother. She from her sisters.
>
> She was seventeen when she married. What a *shidduch*. And what sort of love could she offer the son who turned up, uninvited, in the family portrait. (93)

Looking at his mother's pictures, Zach, like Roland Barthes before him in *Camera Lucida* (1980), does not recognize her. "Too young," he comments. Haim Be'er's *The Pure Element of Time* also ends with a lack of recognition. Be'er's dying mother asks, "How can we recognize anyone?" pointing to the multiple changing faces of every human being. Kaniuk's *Post Mortem* unites his parents' identities with their bodies—they can be dissected, as in an autopsy, and a palpable grain of unhappy truth can be found and exposed. Barthes recognizes, or discovers, his beloved mother in the "Winter Garden photograph" of her as a five-year-old: "In this veracious photograph, the being I love, whom I have loved, is not separated from itself: at last it coincides. And mysteriously, this coincidence is a kind of metamorphosis. All the photographs of my mother which I was looking through were a little like so many masks; at the last, suddenly the mask vanished."[24]

For Zach the masks cannot vanish. He observes a photograph of his parents from Berlin, dressed for a masquerade. They remain enigmatic: "Were they happy then? Did they love each other?" (95) The questions remain unanswered, and love remains unrequited. Stripped of what Zach terms "those fictional 'markers' that find their way into every verbal experiment, in order to amplify its emotional content," this "autothanatography" is not, following Derrida, writing against death but horrifyingly and starkly proceeding toward it, with his mother's death a preparation for his own:[25]

> Over and over, in the few clear moments, she asks: Do me a favor, bring me pills.
>
> And I know which pills she means. And I know she is right, that it is for the best.
>
> But shall the son rise upon his mother to kill her. I decide this way one day, and the other the next. And after all, a few days after her death I turned to my friend A. R., one of the founders of the illegal euthanasia society in Israel, and received instructions, what, who, and how. And I am resolved: I will not go through it. As soon as the first signs are apparent. . . .[26]

Nancy K. Miller, following Derrida, writes: "Autobiography—identity through alterity—is also writing against death twice: the other's and one's own. Every autobiography, we might say, is also an autothanatography."[27]

In his memoir, *From Year to Year* (2009), which has not been translated into English, Zach recalls returning to Israel after a decade in England. Having completed his PhD in English literature, he is offered a teaching position at Haifa University. His mother's situation has deteriorated; she can no longer live alone in her apartment, and his uncle is no longer willing to bear the brunt of being her caregiver alone.[28] An only son, he has, as noted before, no choice but to part with his life in England and return to Israel.

Describing a return visit to England, Zach contemplates the possibilities of his "road not taken"—pursuing life in England rather than returning to

Israel in 1978. He writes: "A door which has closed behind you will never open again, unless you wish to inflict pain on yourself for the sake of remembrance of things past, and I am not Proust."[29] This ironic declaration can be read in at least two directions. The first is that Zach declares himself opposed to the autobiographical impulse. Writing the past entails a contact with memory that he rejects because of the associated pain. Perhaps this is the same impulse that dictates his distance from *My Mother's Death*—found forgotten in a drawer, not searched for. As for the second direction, to "be Proust" means to permit a consciousness to develop and expose itself, a process that Zach is allegedly unwilling to take part in; however, his self-reflexive narrative does just that. By not "being Proust" Zach also differentiates himself from the major vein of the European modernist canon.

The self who emerges from Zach's memoir, like that of Yoram Kaniuk's *Post Mortem*, is a vacant self, almost, one might say, a "dead self." Zach writes of his dead parents, but his writing, and the self it erects, is experienced as "dead." A central image of Israeli culture during and after World War II and the 1948 war was that of "living-dead." Nathan Alterman's poetry formulated this image to perfection, with dead soldiers returning from battle and dead lovers haunting their living wives.[30] Zach and Kaniuk, both born in 1930, belonged to the generation envisioned in Israeli literature as the living-dead, and they rewrote their selves as the dead-living: those who go through life as if dead (as opposed to the speaking-dead, whom death cannot silence). The dead-living replaced the living-dead in Israeli prose of the late 1950s and 1960s, and fifty years later they are still dominant in life writings. In Zach's writings, as in Kaniuk's, this state is epitomized by the absence of a parent, mother or father, or the parents' inability or refusal to see their son or empathize with him, leaving him "dead" in life. As we shall later see, for Shimon Ballas, exactly the same age as Zach and Kaniuk, and for Aharon Appelfeld, two years younger than the other three, the image of the living-dead, despite its prominent role in Israeli culture, does not serve as a frame of reference. Both these authors, unlike Kaniuk, and Be'er, immigrated to Israel, and their relationship with Israeli identities, as I will explore further in chapter 3, separates the paternal from the national.

The Boy Who Brought Light: Haim Be'er

Haim Be'er often makes cameo appearances in his fictional works, entering the revolving door between autobiography and fiction. In his recently published novel *Halomoteyhem ha-hadashim* (2014; Their New Dreams), Be'er's fictional heroine, a novelist, reflects on the ethics of writing, and her mentor tells her "a story about his friend Haim Be'er." After the publication of his book *Havalim*, in which he had written about the world of his father and mother, quite a few readers wrote to him to share their feelings. Several of the letters were moving, but the one that shook him most came from a friend of his deceased mother, who wrote: "When I saw you had written a book about my best friend, Mrs. Brakha Rakhlevski, peace be upon her, I rushed to buy your book in hope of finding fresh water from the well. How disappointed and wounded I was when all I could find was nothing but the family's dirty laundry, which you had hung out openly in the sun on the 'line.'"[31]

In this later work Be'er reflects on *Havalim* to confront the accusation that self-exposure is, in fact, filth and slander. Without being willing to reveal intimacies, the writing mentor tells his student in *Their New Dreams*, following from the anecdote about Be'er, that "true" fiction cannot be produced. Be'er's autobiographical book, *Havalim*, is therefore a fitting search for the origins of his authorial persona.

Haim Be'er was born in "Southern Syria," as he wrote in an early poem, which is what Ottoman Palestine was called before national divisions were introduced.[32] His mother's family had been living in Palestine for several generations. His father, Avraham, was a Russian Jewish immigrant. Be'er was educated in Orthodox schools in Jerusalem, where he grew up. His *Havalim* (literally "bonds," translated as *The Pure Element of Time*, as part one is titled in the Hebrew) recounts his Jerusalem childhood and his initiation as a writer. The book, structured like a *Künstlerroman*, traces Be'er's path to becoming an author through several contradicting narratives, which Be'er interweaves but does not reconcile: a narrative of genealogy and inheritance, a narrative of careful, gradual grooming and apprenticeship in a craft, a romantic narrative of the author as an individual genius, a psychological narrative of trauma and survival, a national narrative of native and immigrant identities, and a narrative of supernatural or metaphysical decree.

Be'er recounts his storytelling apprenticeship with his maternal grand-mother—who "ordains" him to preserve the family history, reflecting her broader philosophy—and with his mother, who poses different demands. Be'er's father, for his part, holds that "Geshtorbn, bagrobn, arop fun mark," the past is dead and buried, and "children should grow up facing the future," an outlook countering the autobiographical impulse (76).[33] His narrative is thus generally silenced in the book. Alongside the fact that Haim's mother dominates his childhood and his narratives, and marginalizes his father in the family's story as in daily life, no room remains for Avraham Rakhlev-sky's story in his son's autobiography because the father rejects narrating the past.

Generally, whereas the mother struggles with her own mother over own-ership of the family narrative, and over what sections of the past are worth preserving and how, the father is for eradicating it all, or protecting his son from it. The mother, for example, critically acknowledges her mother as the source of Haim's storytelling ability and tendency toward anecdotal narra-tion.[34] Reflecting the open hostility between Brakha and Avraham on this issue, Haim's mother one evening revives an old grievance over a toy pistol a neighbor borrowed and returned broken. She curses the neighbor, the neighbor's husband, and her good-for-nothing son, when suddenly:

Father, who sat mute all evening, burst out, without any warning, in a medley of furious, unclear words, in Hebrew and Yiddish, studded with Russian curses, and when he finished he banged the kettle on the floor. In the silence that prevailed after the sound of metal striking the floor tiles died out, Father stared at the puddle of water with the slivers of brown enamel scattered in it, and said that what was was and what advantage would come from her ugly custom of constantly explaining the past all her life, especially when children should grow up facing the future. And then, passing his hand over his mouth with an obliterating gesture, he said, 'Geshtorbn, bagrobn, arop fun mark.' Mother, who froze on the spot at first, pulled me into the kitchen and closed herself up with me there, waiting until father went to bed, and her lips muttering over and over, "At least I've got you." (75–76)

Elsewhere, the son reflects:

When I look straight at him, now, from the sober distance, lacking the recoil of the present, and try to straighten out the life that was wrinkled between the walls of that house . . . my heart is torn with pity—the pity felt by someone who is himself now a father of grown children for that forsaken man, my father, sitting idly long evenings . . . or busy by himself in the kitchen. . . . And more than pity, maybe it's sadness that will never find redemption, for the father who sees his only son, born in his old age, becoming alien and even hostile to him, a son who formed an alliance with his inconsolable mother, a secret alliance against the whole world, but also against him, and he doesn't have a hint of how he sinned and why he was condemned to have the two go far away from him. Sometimes, Father would reconsider [in Hebrew: תשעתמ], and taking advantage of Mother's absence, he'd succeed for a little while in finding the way to me, but then she'd appear and cleverly restore the situation in a wink" (75).

Aside from his distance from his wife and son, the father's notable appearances in the story reveal instances of what the son terms "violent altruism," such as during Haim's bar mitzvah dinner, described as reminiscent of a Hieronymus Bosch painting because Avraham insists on inviting beggars, "handicaps," the mentally ill, or simply deprived souls, few of whom the family personally knew.[35] A different humiliating image, evoking pity, emerges when Avraham escorts Haim on an overnight school field trip and, partially exposed in his old-fashioned pajamas, tries to silence the boys' midnight riot with an anachronistic limerick, which is viciously mocked by Haim's classmates from then on (182).[36]

As for the opening story, emerging from the grandmother, it involves a broken-down truck loaded with chickens, and workers quickly transporting the chicken cages to a functioning vehicle. Fixing on the image, the grandmother explains to the boy that when one truck fails, a "transfer" must be made to another truck. Thus she transfers the stories of her family's heritage to Haim to carry, preserve, and retell. Haim the child thus memorizes his family tree stretching back generations (29).[37] The grandmother's stories are anchored in place and time; they have a physical presence in the world—they can be corroborated by artifacts. A wooden pole on a street in Vienna, for example, which she read about in an 1880 guidebook, is still there when years later Haim and his wife find their way to it.

According to the Hebrew autobiographical tradition, parodied as early as the mid-nineteenth century, the canonical Hebrew autobiographer comes from a line of great scholars. (Even Kaniuk abides by this norm when he describes his father, visiting Mea Shearim, as better versed in the Talmud than the local scholars he meets there.) Through his grandmother's stories, Be'er incorporates a few magical artifacts, lost and preserved, that materially contain the family's past—a cracked washbasin that saved his great-grandmother Hannah from the 1837 earthquake in Safed when she was a baby; the Napoleonic coat for which a forebear traded his own tattered coat in a Russian forest.[38]

Whereas the grandmother's story is entrusted to Be'er to be memorized, preserved, and faithfully transmitted, his mother's legacy provides no such narrative. It holds secrets to be revealed and a groping after memory, the attempt to pinpoint moments of revelation, when facts were first known and uncovered. His mother's story is about how to tell a story, how a story unfolds, how it is twisted and unraveled. It is about remembering: events, pictures, objects, expressions, and texts. She offers him her life so that one day he may "do something" with it; that is, she offers her pain as raw material he may process (64).[39]

WRITTEN STORIED LIVES, autobiographies, tend to lean on one another for support. They develop their individual paths in relation to and in the footsteps of others. *The Pure Element of Time* is a very personal and specific story, imbued with detail, but it leans on at least two other autobiographical narratives: Romain Gary's *Promise at Dawn* (1960) and Vladimir Nabokov's *Speak, Memory* (1951), from which Be'er's English title is pulled. When Be'er demonstratively incorporates these two narratives into his own text, he brings to the fore, and exposes, the act of narrating memory. When readers are continuously made conscious of the craft of narration, the text does not permit them to languidly suspend their disbelief and uncritically follow a linear, advancing and direct, story with a coherent message. When we are constantly made aware of the making of the story, it cannot be consumed as unmediated or "naturally flowing." By relating to former autobiographical texts, Be'er directs our awareness to the act of construction in which he is engaged. He exposes his narrative workshop, and impedes our ability to ignore it. This referential narrative influences the concepts of self and of memory that the book constructs.

Promise at Dawn, like *The Pure Element of Time*, is the story of a mother who, for better or worse, devotes her life to raising her son as a "great author." For Be'er the reference to Gary promises that the mother-son relationship and the mother's vision of her son encapsulate "a magical world, born out of a mother's murmur into a child's ear, a promise whispered at dawn of future triumphs and greatness, of justice and love."[40] The mother-son relationship in Be'er's work thus plays out in light of Gary's precedent. In the last stages of her illness, Be'er's mother

> waved Romain Gary's book like a fan and declared that the books that were dearest to her heart were those where the characters were described honestly, but lovingly. The desirable balance between those two contradictory demands is very complex, even though it looks quite simple. . . . "If you read Romain Gary without yielding to his charming French sentimentality, you'll understand how paralyzing and castrating love is, and how here, in this pleasant and sticky novel, the mother and son, maybe even reluctantly, become tools in each other's hands." (68–69)[41]

This sort of self-reflexive writing debilitates Be'er in his attempts to draw a critical portrait of his mother. She has imposed her literary values on him before he can even begin writing, and her open acknowledgment of their familial enmeshment paralyzes him.

Speak, Memory, for its part, surfaces at a key moment in the narrative, when Be'er stops to reflect on the project of writing his life. In this consideration he reflects on a great devastation that predated his birth: the death of his mother's two daughters—the first because of a botched blood transfusion, the second, three years later, to diphtheria. The daughters were from Brakha's disastrous previous marriage. Be'er offers several versions of his discovery of his sisters' existence. According to one, this occurs when their dresses—one saved for each daughter by Haim's mother—are torn from the closet by officials sent on behalf of the Ministry of Rationing and Supply, which enforced the country's 1950s austerity policy, in search of black market activity. The ransacked closets also reveal a small cylindrical amulet, which, as we later learn, is meant to prophesy the birth of the girls' brother, Haim.

This version of the discovery is framed within a national context. Haim and his mother return home from a social visit and encounter their neighbor, who informs them of what has happened:

> [She] announced with obvious joy that a gang of rioters of the military governor Bernard Joseph had invaded our house and made a pogrom.
>
> At home, we found Father sitting and gazing among the mountains of clothes and wide-open closets. Mother froze on the spot, and then she wrung her hands and asked in a whisper how this was different from the sights of destruction in Hebron, that were described in the newspapers after the riots of 1929. (89)[42]

Later that evening his father collapses with chest pains: "Mother led him to bed and said he should thank God that the apparatchiks of *di yiddishe medineh* didn't take him along to prison in the Russian compound" (91).

Like Kaniuk, Be'er was born in Mandatory Palestine, although in its very waning years. But whereas Kaniuk's parents both identified with the prestate Jewish institutions, the Be'er family felt alienation toward them and the eventual apparatus of the nation-state. The Jewish nation-state, specifically, they perceived as part of the continuum of ruthless institutions that had threatened and endangered Jews, whether in Eastern Europe or in Palestine. This view is evident in Be'er's terminology, which groups Israel's institutions with others previously responsible for fatal assaults on Jews. The minister Dov Yosef is marked with his English name, Bernard Joseph, as a "military governor," as if he were an official of the British Mandate; the inspectors are thugs, a gang of rioters carrying out an Eastern European pogrom; and the raided apartment is compared to Palestinian-targeted property belonging to Hebron's historic Orthodox community. The father's chest pains and collapse are likewise tied to officials so blindly devoted to a doctrine that they unscrupulously commit abuses in its name, as Soviet Communist officials might, and Be'er refers to the new state in Yiddish: *di yiddishe medineh*. Taken together, such language distances Be'er's family from the Jewish nation-state. Be'er's mother's six-generation legacy in Palestine exists distinct from the Zionists and their institutions, whose agents are cast as perpetrating violence on other Jews, as if they still lacked the protection of a nation-state. This hostile and aggressive state also represents and enacts an invasion of the private family sphere. Avraham's narrative, although silenced here, is different. Even as he, too, is portrayed as a victim of the state, he nonetheless collects national memorabilia and cherishes its tokens.

As indicated in the multiple narratives of his lost sisters, the search for the moment of primary knowledge reveals Be'er's concepts of remembrance and autobiography: He writes of the ransacking:

> This scene was the first thread I pulled out of that tangled skein of the past, intending to attach other threads to it, every single one separated, in order to weave them into the fabric of life constantly flowing dark and changing. But I had already used it many years ago in my first book of prose, where I embedded it, distorted and adapted to the needs of the plot. Now, when the person in me rebels against the story teller, as Nabokov confessed, and I came to redeem it from captivity and restore it to its original place, I realized, like the author of *Speak, Memory* after he borrowed the portrait of his nanny for the lad in one of his stories, that the scene had been swallowed up in the artificial world where I had placed it without much hesitation, and there it was assimilated into its new place, an assimilation more complete than in the previous reality, where it had once seemed to be protected from the interference of the artist. (91)[43]

The conflict between fiction storyteller and autobiographer is mediated here by the presentation of autobiography as a conscious literary genre and tradition. If Be'er can view his conflict through Nabokov's, then the conflict emerges as part of a form—autobiography—that is as crafted as fiction and governed by its own clear rules. This conflict reappears when Be'er cannot describe his mother's illness and death because he has already characterized them fictionally in *Notsot* (1980; *Feathers*, 2004), a novel he was writing at the time of her death (280).[44]

As he puts it in *The Pure Element of Time*:

> Mother's final torments and her death that I impetuously granted to the character of the mother in the book I went back to writing after she passed away, I now wanted to take them out of there and copy them here now, where they belong, but her shining face, which accompanied me during the two years since I began to realize what she had announced in Ruhama Weber's ears—that one day I would make something of her life—suddenly grew dark. What echoed in my ears was, "We interpret 'Thou shalt not steal' different from usual," the moral lesson she preached to me when she noticed that I had embedded in one of my literary texts some sections that had already appeared in my earlier books, in another context. "We interpret 'Thou shalt not steal' as thou shalt not steal from yourself." (280)[45]

In *Feathers* the discovery of the lost sisters is complicated by the exchange of the two dresses for a sailor suit with gold buttons. This shifts the scene's anxiety from the mother's alleged infidelity to her son—rooted in his accusation that she has loved a child other than himself, that he is not the entire focus of her life—to the boy's own fear of annihilation. By changing the gender of the dead sibling, Be'er brings death nearer to the protagonist in *Feathers* than to his childhood self in *The Pure Element of Time*. The boy whose sailor suit is unearthed by Dov Yosef's supervisors is dead and unknown, not spoken of, buried at the back of the closet. The same could happen to the protagonist; he too could disappear. What is more, in the novel, when his mother mentions the Hebron massacre, she names Eliezer Dan Slonim and his family as specific victims who have been murdered. The protagonist recalls having seen a picture of the one-year-old Shlomo Slonim, the family's sole survivor, whose expression reminds him of his own father's after the officials left their apartment, an expression of bereft solitariness. The dead brother is thus replaced with a survivor, but the horror and guilt of having survived and of remaining behind endure, as does the imminent danger of losing one's beloved protectors, or the threat of one's own death. Thus the source of the protagonist's fear differs from the source of young Haim's fear in the autobiography.[46]

In *The Pure Element of Time*, Be'er emphasizes his distance from the revelation of his dead sisters by invoking the memory and words of another— Nabokov—whose autobiographical self introduces the concept of "chronophobia." Literally a fear of time, in Nabokov's case it involves the fear regarding significant events that happened to his parents before he was a part of them, marking that life could have proceeded without him and his writing self. Indeed this is a fear Be'er also experiences in *The Pure Element of Time*.

An issue more directly articulated by Be'er through Nabokov involves material previously used in fiction and how an author's *inability* to directly reincorporate this material in autobiography facilitates the surfacing of additional memories. Having lost the "obvious" choice of memories, Be'er can access an alternative and earlier path of memory.[47] Here it involves the father's story, a narrative dissociated from repetitive historic developments, as they emerge in the mother's imagery, and instead rooted in an eternal, mythological, theological concept of time. On the eve of Passover, at synagogue, young Haim has gone with his father early in the morning "to the feast of the firstborn" who owe "thanks to the Lord of Hosts for distinguishing between us and the Egyptians" (92). The synagogue sexton, Rivkesh, distributes cookies to break the fast:

> When he came to me, Rivkesh pinched my cheeks with his skinny, rheumatic fingers that emanated a sweetish, disgusting fragrance of vanilla intensified by the smell of medicinal cognac and the juice of chopped fish, and said that, according to the law, he didn't have to give me any cake. "Thou are not a firstling," he explained in biblical language, and when he realized that I didn't understand, he said in simple words, "You aren't your mother's firstborn. They didn't tell you that she had children who died before you were born?" Father chased him away with a furious gesture. . . . [H]e was counting on me to forget the stupid incident in the

synagogue, and mainly not to ask Mother anything, for she was busy enough with the store and the holiday and her mind wasn't free to give me answers to such questions. (92–93)

Indeed this memory does not surface until the writing of *The Pure Element of Time*, when Be'er realizes that the pogrom scene, because already appropriated into *Feathers*, cannot serve as the moment of discovery: "And then, when I thought I had succeeded in the work of extrication, which was accompanied by an oppressive sense of shame for my frivolity and extravagance during the writing of *Feathers*, one of those blessed moments came to me when spacious plains of life are suddenly opened before you and you see with bold clarity sights that speak in the direct present tense, even though they were meant for other times" (91).

Be'er then probes his initial impulse to suppress reckoning with the sexton's comments:

I don't have a satisfactory answer to the question of why I didn't protest then, when father quickly and firmly moved me away from the pit gaping at my feet . . . or simply, why I repressed my curiosity and didn't persist in clarifying what the deranged sexton meant. Was the abyss he exposed so menacing and tempting that I yielded . . . so the void wouldn't draw me into it? Or was the answer enfolded in another question, a harder and more complicated one, emanating from the previous one, like a box from a box, the question of how the repression of that incident, as Father called that scene, was so successful that only now does that distant memory return and come to stand before me so vividly? (93)

Thereafter both narrative options yield to yet another thread, a scene of self-discovery that brings the lost sisters into the open. In this scene Be'er, home alone during the summer between sixth and seventh grades, describes rummaging through his mother's belongings and finding the girls' pictures. Here, too, a connection is forged with the opening words of *Speak, Memory*, in which Nabokov describes "a young chronophobiac" who experiences a sense of panic when viewing a family film taken a few weeks before he was born, including a baby carriage, anticipating him but perceived as a coffin.

Be'er sees his mother with little children who are not he. Existing before his birth, this domestic world of child rearing does not recognize his existence: "I don't know how long I was absorbed in the photos, but in every one of my reflections which suddenly looked at me when I raised my eyes—the closet was wide open and I was standing between the two doors with mirrors on their inside panels—I was at the same time both observer and observed in the billows of this discovery that froze on my face. Feelings . . . madly accelerate into a one and only moment, and if I want to talk about it today, all I can do is spread it out, static and lifeless, like a hide stripped from an animal carcass" (104).[48]

In the book, time past is depicted as a corpse in several crucial instances, which I will now look at in greater detail. Be'er read the first novel he was writing in installments to his mother. In contrast to his imagery of death, she saw telling and writing as an opportunity for correction and revival.

For example, he reads her the scene of father and son rising at night to climb Mount Zion to see the sunrise, where it had risen "on the fourth day of creation,"

> [s]he shut her one eye and said quietly that her heart tormented her sud-
> denly for being so hard-hearted to the two of us back then, and by mobi-
> lizing all possible arguments—the early hour, the cold, and the danger of
> the border—she prevented him from taking me with him on his walk to
> Mount Zion, as he had been preparing to do for several days.
>
> "At least now you can repair that sin," her chin trembled, where bris-
> tles of hair were turning gray at the bottom. "Too bad I never tried to
> write. Someone who writes can live his life over, but for me it's late, too
> late." (278)[49]

Paul John Eakin has described the layered role of remembering in auto-biography this way: "It is memory itself, memory as an act, 'remembering remembering' rather than any of its possible contents, that is central to the recovery of self-experience."[50] As Be'er puts it, he is "at the same time both observer and observed." The development of a comprehensive linear narra-tive in Be'er's book is conflict-ridden and made impossible by the corpses of memory he stumbles on. He likens his grasp of memory to the chalk mark that forensic investigators use to trace a dead body.

In this light Be'er describes a scene he arguably mistook for years to be his first memory. And this memory introduces a possible source in Be'er himself for his identity as a writer, suggesting this identity does not, in fact, originate in his grandmother's plans or his mother's ambitions.

Be'er was three years old when war broke out with the Arab states in 1948.[51] During one particular bombardment, he is sheltered under his bed, on the floor together with his parents, some shoppers who happened to be at the grocery store when the shelling began, and some neighbors. The apartment above theirs is hit, and when the shelling ceases, the little boy crawls out from under the bed:

> [I] looked in amazement at the strips of whitewash and plaster that kept dropping from the ceiling one after another, illuminated by the thin tubes of light coming through the cracks between the bags covering our floor of arabesques with a thin, whitish layer. "*Vayse murashkes.*" "White ants," I shouted with foolish joy, the happiness of a child rescued from death. "*Vayse murashkes,*" laughed the momentary guests, surprised at the image, and Mrs. Vine . . . kissed Mother's cheeks that were flushed with fear and said that her son would be a writer.
>
> But it's precisely the crystallization of the memory, its ostensible perfection, and mainly the fact that it's sealed with the stamp of destiny that have made me suspicious over the years. And Mother, with her repeated attempts to express it in words so I'd preserve it in my heart and never forget it not only doomed to destruction the amazing, primal nature of the scene and its thin impression as envisioned by the child, with his fresh sight, but she also confiscated it from me. What could have been the quivering, forming shadow of a surrealistic fluttering of flakes became the white line homicide detectives draw in chalk around the body of a murdered man stretched out on the ground before it is cleared away.[52]

Far away from there in the heart of the quicksand territories of oblivion, another memory still sprouts, maybe even before the first one, and unlike it, we didn't dare ever remember it again, and we let its illuminating streams go on, search for their path in the silent and shapeless depths of our being as long as they don't rise to the visible layers of real life and flood them. (135–36)[53]

The second early scene that Be'er recalls, and which competes for the title of "first memory," is not an imaginative revelation, as is the "white ants" scene, or a collective expression of adult admiration for the child, but a violent argument between his parents over finances—an argument that ends with his father cracking a table with his fist and demanding that the boy be either on Father's or Mother's side, because they are not one. His mother stalks off with young Haim in her arms to wander the streets. The material evidence of the cracked table opposes the memory of the white ants by his mother, whose insistent affirmation of the memory confuses her son as to whether he remembers the event itself or her narration of it.

In these alternative memories, a maternal narrative is juxtaposed with a paternal one, with the latter rejected throughout the memoir. Be'er's father does not reveal the facts; he tries to protect his young son from them, so that in erasing his memory of the synagogue scene Be'er also loses his father as a protective, caring, and supportive figure. It is of no small consequence that Avraham Rakhlevsky takes his son to synagogue on the eve of Passover: this action serves as a bridge between father and son. The rejection of the knowledge that Haim is not a "firstling" preserves the similarity between the two—with Avraham also being an only child—so unattainable throughout the book. As Be'er reflects:

The preference for the one memory and its persistent cultivation by careful repetition, which evoked words about it and led to a crystallization of it, and especially to an artistic shaping, might be what blocked the earlier, vivid but shapeless memory and prevented it from floating up. And who would guarantee me that that memory itself, an act that surfaced at long last, even before the flesh of the words was closed beneath it, won't ward off what it now wants to destroy from those internal places that never know peace. And the hand wants to hold onto those abstract things, that no longer have shape but essence, as they were back then in fact vibrations, an eternal and direct present—that hand will return empty. (94)[54]

Narrative form and shape allow for clear vision—what is shapeless cannot be remembered. But artistic form also obstructs memory; once created, the form cancels alternative visions, it gains independence and confiscates the memory from the rememberer. If we are to follow Be'er's perception, the narratives we construct are our identity, and identity does not precede that narrative; rather the opposite is true.[55]

The stories in Be'er's narrative conflict and collide, often ruling each other out. Hannan Hever has pointed to the book's anecdotal structure, as noted earlier, comprising complete, autonomous, and self-contained units that do not require the sequential connection that would build a linear, developing narrative, from beginning to end, inherently creating its own goal and meaning.[56] The anecdotal structure, as Hever has claimed, frustrates the formation of a subject as developing until a point of coherent completion. This structure also blurs clean lines of Israeli identities drawn between religious and secular, the "old" and the "new" Jewish settlement, urban living versus the workers' agricultural settlement, center and periphery. What is more, the developing and "explanatory" narratives in the book contradict each other. At the painful heart of the book stands Haim's mother's confession to him, when he is twelve years old, about her own death wish after the death of her two daughters. The mother's monologue, however, is interrupted so that the narrator can return to his outrage, a child's fury, at her failure to shield and protect him from the horror, as well as his present attempts to reconstruct how he felt "towering over the unconscious body of that distant afternoon hour" (86). Be'er's narrative repeatedly questions his mother's choices—of mercilessly exposing the young child to the hard facts of her life, of irreparably alienating him from his father. Meanwhile the loose structure of the book maintains its multiperspectival fractured quality. Every fact can be turned around to reflect a different view.

The difference in narrative views between Be'er and his mother is apparent when the son tries to reconstruct his mother's narration to him of her suicide attempt, before she married his father. Her body and life are saved—but her telling him about the act constitutes a dead body that he cannot revive.

After the death of her daughters, Brakha's brother Isaac opens a fish shop to get her out of the house, asking for her help. This keeps her busy and functioning during the day and asleep with exhaustion at night. Still, during the noon break she would stay alone in the store:

> "Sometimes, when I couldn't bear my life anymore, I'd sneak up to the roof."
>
> . . . Once again Mother fiddled with the clasp of her purse, and asked if I knew that every young woman gets a period once a month and menstruation is the indication that the body is preparing for pregnancy. Not only didn't I understand the strange turn in her talk, as if she were planning to begin a lesson in sex education—like a school nurse—but a blush also rose onto my cheeks. . . .
>
> "I knew all the roofs here, from three stories and up," Mother returned from the slight deviation from the track of her story, a deviation whose meaning became clear only later, and looking up, carefully combing the skyline of large buildings facing us and next to us, she said, "You understand, I wanted to take my life. . . . I practiced so that at the crucial moment, I'd have the strength to take the last little step to liberating destruction, and after it there'd be no more grief or longing." (85)

The story is then interrupted by the narrator's reflection on it. But this time Be'er writes not with rage toward his mother but compassion, even as he observes that her confiding in him amounted to abuse, since he was far too young to understand the information she imparted.

The last time Brakha Rakhlevsky climbs a rooftop, at the moment of jumping, she feels her period: "[A]nd all of the sudden, like a bolt out of the blue, I knew I wasn't lost, that I was still young enough for a new life to sprout in me, that if only I wanted to, I could be a mother to a living child again" (88). This physical moment of revelation, which ties the corporeal to the sublime while excluding divinity, is the "rational," "secular" explanation supplied for Be'er's place in his mother's life. Brakha is repeatedly described as a rational woman, realistic and practical, even cold. But alongside this rational explanation centering on the mother's wishes, body, and desire, Be'er offers a contradictory, but equally valid, metaphysical explanation.

As a young girl Be'er's mother chanced upon an old Jerusalem mystic, a palm reader, who gave her the protective amulet mentioned before, and prophesied that she would never leave the country and would mother a son: "A precious and special son you will have and with his birth he will fill the house with light" (117). The prophecy is forgotten when two girls are born, and revived only with Haim's eventual birth. Buried deep in the closet, the amulet resurfaces together with the small dresses, when the rationing office trashes the family's apartment. The prophecy of a hero's birth embodies Brakha's expectations of her son, and his tacit acceptance of them. The white ants—that is, his own individual gift, appreciated by those around him; his bookishness; his mother's coaching; his grandmother's expectations; literary talents possibly inherited from his father: of all these, it is the mystic prophecy that leaves him most uncomfortable:[57] "By dint of foggy words of prophecy, I was forced to live my life as an echo, and maybe it would even be more correct to say that I was imprisoned in a fictional image of myself that was preordained for me from the day I was born, and in fact long before, to be the realization of a document I didn't choose and that I wasn't free to accept or reject, bearing on my shoulders a cursed cloak whose exterior is grandiose and whose depressed lining corrodes" (118).

It would be easy, too easy perhaps, to accept Be'er's mother as the epitome of a secular worldview. But her whole life, like her son's, is effectively dictated by the Jerusalem mystic rabbi who reads her palm when she is a girl and gives her an amulet to insure a prophecy.[58]

Be'er's struggle to probe his mother's character simultaneously smudges his own portrait. Yet this ambiguity allows for a freer deliberation of multiple layers and identities in the text.

THE PURE ELEMENT OF TIME ends with mother and son sitting peacefully together at home when a bird flies into the room, a reference to the ending of Gary's *Promise at Dawn*, which similarly tells of an enmeshed, symbiotic mother-son relationship and an author's development. In the book's final paragraphs Gary ironically, but also quite seriously, counts his contributions to the world:

Once . . . I found, one morning, a humming-bird in my living room; it had come there trustingly, knowing that it was my house, but a gust of wind had slammed the door and it had been held prisoner all night between four walls. It was perched on a cushion, miniscule and incapable of understanding, all courage gone, no longer trying to fly, weeping in one of the saddest voices I have ever heard, for one never hears one's own voice. I opened the window, it flew out and I have seldom felt happier, and I knew that I had not lived in vain.[59]

By comparison, in Be'er's closing chapter, the author writes himself, rewrites Gary. The bird acts as a migrating spirit of autobiographies, flitting from one book to the other: "A small, silly sparrow, who had slipped away in his flight and passed between the waving cloth sheets, suddenly found himself trapped in the room, and by the time I threw the pair of windows wide open, he had banged himself time and again on the lintel, and then he dropped helplessly onto the sofa beneath him" (281).

Even beyond the anecdotal structure, the relational subjectivity Be'er offers here creates an analogy. In Gary's story the rescued bird adds to the sentimental affirmation and value of his identity. In *The Pure Element of Time* the bird unites Be'er and his mother in bewilderment; together they wonder whether the bird is the same one that flew through the room before. All that is certain is that they can look together without necessarily seeing the same thing. Be'er's confession that he cannot ultimately pin his mother down, or settle on one finite story, frees him to tell his contradictory stories. His very attempt to remember and tell becomes a vital sign that overcomes the chalk marks around dead moments of memory strewn throughout his book.

CHAPTER THREE

Languages of Immigration

Shimon Ballas and Aharon Appelfeld

I mistrust childhood stories, just as I mistrust stories of dreams.
In particular I mistrust novelists' childhood stories: those whose
strength is in fiction are the least reliable in conveying things
as they are, not to speak of their own childhood.
—Shimon Ballas, *Ba-ir ha-tahtit*

Childhood is an atemporal zone belonging more to imagination
than to reality. It is an experiential wholeness which one cannot
disassemble into parts or encapsulate in words.—*Ba-ir ha-tahtit*

The city where I was born exists only in my imagination.
—Aharon Appelfeld, *A Table for One*, 109

S HIMON BALLAS (b. 1930) and Aharon Appelfeld (b. 1932) both immigrated to Israel, and they both relinquished their mother tongue in
favor of Hebrew. But these similarities only highlight the distant poles
Ballas and Appelfeld occupy on the Israeli spectrum of literature and ethnicity. Appelfeld was born in Czernowitz, in what was then Romania; Ballas
grew up in Baghdad. Until he was seven years old, Appelfeld belonged to a financially well-off family. Ballas, from a young age, was aware of his mother's
struggles to make ends meet. Appelfeld survived the Shoah. He arrived in
Israel alone at age fourteen. Ballas was twenty-one when he immigrated to
Israel and was accompanied by his reluctant two siblings and by his mother,
who could not stand the idea of him enduring immigration alone. Ballas
transitioned to Hebrew in a painful process after experiencing success in
Arabic journalism and fiction. After abstaining from Arabic while gaining

proficiency in Hebrew, he maintained a bilingual position as a professor of Arabic literature and a translator from Arabic into Hebrew. Appelfeld's official education was interrupted in first grade, only resuming in 1946, when he arrived as a survivor refugee in Israel, five years before Ballas. By then he had learned German, Romanian, Ukrainian, and Yiddish. He eventually studied Yiddish at the Hebrew University of Jerusalem and later became a professor at Ben-Gurion University in the Negev.

Both authors have been deeply critical of the Zionist movement. Yet Appelfeld has been embraced by the Israeli cultural establishment and received every prize it has to offer; he has gained international acclaim and is mentioned as a Nobel Prize contender. In contrast, Ballas holds a marginal position in the Israeli literary landscape. In line with his high profile, Appelfeld has been accused of ingratitude toward the literary establishment, whereas Ballas has not.[1] The establishment's recognition of Appelfeld and rejection of Ballas suggest it is willing to tolerate Appelfeld's distance from established Zionism but not that of Ballas.

Despite clear divergences in their biographies, Appelfeld and Ballas respond, in their life writings, to similar demands and accusations leveled by Israeli culture at immigrant writers, and at immigrants in general. Israeli immigration and immigrant identities are thus illuminated by a close analysis and comparison of these two writers' works.

Shimon Ballas: The Nightingale Who Declined a Position in Court

Biography is a conflict zone for authors, readers, publishers, and critics. Immigrant authors are typically expected to write if not about their own immigrant experience then at least about their country, culture, and community of origin, and about their new surroundings from an outsider's perspective. Given this context, both Appelfeld and Ballas confront critics and readers in their autobiographical writings, demanding to be released from what Ballas has appropriately called the "ethnic parentheses."[2]

Appelfeld, for his part, declares: "Despite all the external and internal pressures, on the whole I kept my faith with my core and I wrote only what I had experienced. I didn't stray into other pastures, though there were times when I was tempted to write historical short stories. I thought that the historical angle might deepen my writing. After the Six Day War, I tried and failed again. It was then clear to me once and for all that it was simply not in my power to write something outside my personal experience."[3]

Ballas, like Appelfeld, has always been read biographically, but when he has written about events he did not experience, such as in *Tel Aviv Mizrah* (East Tel Aviv; finally published in 1998), publishers have rejected his work, recommending instead that he write about Baghdad.[4] Ballas writes about the present, and is asked to write about the past, presumably reflecting an expectation that he maintain his outsider and immigrant status in Israeli society—one who cannot participate in its current debates but may show pictures of the past that justify Israel's existence in the present. Ballas's writing does not comply with this call. Am Oved publishers, which published his first novel, *Ha-ma'abara* (1964; The Transit Camp), rejected the sequel on the grounds that it was not "up to required standards": "Yeruham Luria [the editor], in his gentle demeanor, told me: 'You wrote an important novel, a first and brave novel about the transit camps, what have you got to do with Ha-Tikva neighborhood? Write something about Baghdad. You must have plenty to tell.'"[5]

When Ballas writes about his reception in Israeli literature, and referring here to his 1972 novel *Hitbaharut* (Clarification), he notes that it was rather well received, but that none of the readers commented on his symbolic representation of Israel's position and role in the Middle East, depicted through the character's triptych painting of biblical-mythological giants:[6] "In this case the disregard was caused not by a lack of awareness on the part of the critics of the significance of the symbol, but by the segregated, not to say racist, concepts held by teachers and scholars of literature that separate me from the authors of my generation, native born and originally from Eastern Europe, and place me within ethnic parentheses, as a 'Sephardic' writer."[7]

Ballas, an overtly political author, has likewise noted his resentment at being introduced as a member of the "Babylonian" community, a term that goes back to ancient and early medieval times, and to the Iraqi Jewish community's glory years; as he points out, the term erases his Arab identity. His characters are concerned with and conscious of ideologies and politics. The first page in his autobiography, *Be-guf rishon* (2009; First Person Singular), encapsulates the complex position of Iraqi immigrants in Israel—sprayed with disinfectant, driven on trucks to transit camps on the Israeli periphery, and meeting the Palestinian victims of 1948. On the final count, such figures include the last Palestinian left in Ashkelon, formerly the Palestinian town of al-Majdal, a nonvocal guard at the local cinema.[8]

The title of Shimon Ballas's autobiography signifies a shift in his work. After publishing more than fifteen volumes of fiction, translation, and scholarly research, mostly in Hebrew, but also in Arabic as well as French, Ballas promises to shine the light directly on himself. In this slim work Ballas commits to the "autobiographical pact" and to an identity between the name appearing on the cover, his own, and the first-person narrator and hero of the story.[9] Ballas is well aware of the genre's laws. His novel *Ve-hu aher* (1991), published in 2007 in English as *Outcast*, is written as the fictional autobiography of a historical figure, Ahmad Nissim Soussa, a notorious Iraqi Jewish convert to Islam in the 1930s, cast as Ahmad Haroun Saussan.[10] Whereas in fiction Ballas proved a rather obedient autobiographer, he challenges bounds of the genre in his self-portrayal, slipping from essay to memoir and straightforward autobiography. In trying to reconstruct the sequence of Ballas's life, and his personal trajectory, one stumbles into cavities and cracks rather than following a comfortable, self-explanatory linear narrative. Ballas here introduces himself as an impulsive adolescent who, like most youths, does not seek adult advice. He was fed up with the political persecution of communists in Iraq; he wanted to be free to enact his political agenda. But in his eagerness to leave Iraq, he imposes an immigration journey on his whole family. He ends up registering to immigrate to Israel before the Iraqi Jewish legislator Ezra Menachem Daniel, who employs Ballas as an assistant, can present him with a generous offer to fund his studies in France. Writes Ballas in *Be-guf rishon*: "I wanted to leave alone, to start a new life, but my mother sensed something unusual in my behavior and started asking questions, and when she could not find my ID card in the closet she forced me to confess" (7).

The confession brought Ballas, along with his mother, brother, and sister, to Israel in 1951. It also suggests to us that if we succeed in entering Ballas's closet, we may elicit a confession. Indeed the closet trope here intimates the scene in Haim Be'er's *The Pure Element of Time* (discussed in chapter 2) in which contents from Be'er's mother's closet reveal his deceased sisters and the amulet foretelling his own birth. Ballas's closet, however, remains inaccessible, and thus he manages, even in this personal book, to keep his identity concealed and encoded. He sketches possible contours of his identity but leaves it to us to connect them, and often refrains from clarification or tying up loose ends. Generically this book places the author in the public rather than the private sphere, and positions his meeting with history within wide circles of belonging rather than intimate circles, emotional or spiritual. As such, the book introduces underground Communist Party members in Iraq, as well as 1950s and 1960s activists in Israel. It heralds a line of dominant, inspiring, and complex figures, each of whom could sustain a novel and some of whom already serving as models for Ballas's fictional characters. In Ballas's 1984 novel *Horef aharon* (Last Winter), Maxime Rodinson (1915–2004), the Jewish Marxist historian and scholar of Islam, and the Egyptian Jewish communist and revolutionary Henri Curiel (b. 1914), who was murdered in 1978, both served as such models. These figures expand their presence in *Be-guf rishon* until, near its closure, he almost permits them to take over. In withdrawing from his "first person" narrative, Ballas calls to mind Natan Zach, who brought family photos and distant relatives and friends into his narrative; or Appelfeld leaning on parallel images and depictions of other children who survived and of children who did not; or, at the end of Appelfeld's *Sipur Haim* (1998)—*The Story of a Life* (2004), in English translation—the description of seeking financial and emotional support in an immigrant club, a description that slips into the first person plural, thereby dimming the book's revelatory intimacy. These techniques, in which the autobiographical narrative opens itself to other figures or adopts the plural first person, may have the effect described by Virginia Woolf in "The Lives of the Obscure"; that is, by rubbing shoulders with the famous, the relatively lesser-known life writer gains visibility.[11] In Ballas's and Appelfeld's respective works, however, the plural first person also becomes clearly representative, as it has in Hebrew life writing since the mid-nineteenth century. The plural asserts and validates the voice of the autobiographer as representative of a community, even as the narrator simultaneously insists that he refuses to represent anyone but himself.

Relational writing is fundamental to autobiography.[12] This is the case even though traditional critics of autobiography, in a perhaps surprising collaboration with early feminist critics, maintained the myth of the auto-biographical canon as fundamentally comprising narratives of autonomous, singular, differentiated individuals, while relegating relational narratives to women and other outsiders. This conceptualization narrowed and limited the form's complexity, or, as Paul John Eakin succinctly puts it, "so-called traditional autobiography became the province of the Marlboro man."[13] However, later readings such as those of Nancy K. Miller and Eakin himself clearly demonstrate that autobiography extends to multiple voices and rela-tionships. As Erich Kästner puts it: "When one sets out to tell about himself he generally begins by telling about other people altogether. People he has never seen and never could have seen. People he has never met and never will meet. People who are dead long ago and whom he knows next to noth-ing about. When someone sets out to tell about himself, he generally begins with his ancestors. And that is understandable, because without ancestors one would be quite alone on the ocean of time, like a castaway on a tiny uninhabited island. Quite alone."[14]

Thus the meaningful relationships that fill Ballas's narrative constitute the coordinates mapping his self and his world. In particular, the writer's childhood was marred by the absence of his father, an unsuccessful busi-nessman who at one point went to jail for unpaid debts. Ballas relates going with his nanny to jail bring his father home-cooked food. As a result Ballas's mother almost single-handedly raised him and his two siblings. Their father came "for short visits on holidays, mostly to stock up on the goods he was trading in" (14). Ballas does not, however, dwell on the financial hardship that plagued the family, the humiliation and anger it stirred in him as a child. His mother's helplessness and loneliness, as well as the family's sepa-ration from the father when immigrating to Israel, are condensed into two pages. At the small house where he and his siblings and nanny lived, the father's visits would "disturb the daily routine of the household, especially in the evenings when he would sit by the dinner table with a glass of arak in front of him" (14). Reading this description, one is struck by the strength demanded of the young Ballas, whose mother never had enough money to buy him a book or notebook to help forge the man he became. The family's financial situation improved when he and his older brother chipped in: "During my first year of junior high I began giving private lessons to children of the younger grades in elementary school." Unlike his father, who declined immigration to Israel, saying, "I am not at the age for a new beginning," Ballas emerges from this text as a person whose entire life consists of brave beginnings (15).

Ballas was in the third grade when he made his first attempts at writing, and his composition was hung for display with other outstanding students' work. But the school environment was also a stage for humiliating blows such as the one he suffered when he was publicly ridiculed by his teacher and peers for singing off-key in the school choir. Later a composition Ballas wrote was cruelly parodied by his junior high school teacher. These responses, writes Ballas, enhanced his "tendency toward seclusion and the fear of exposing myself. I would cling to Gibran's famous saying: 'You have your Lebanon and I have mine,' and paraphrase it in my notes: 'You have your world and I have mine'" (18). But beyond a personal tendency toward introversion, *Be-guf rishon* presents a conscious literary choice in approaching life writing.

As suggested before, Ballas has not, until very recently, received much favorable critical attention. Among his boosters have been Hannan Hever and Yitzhak Gormezano-Goren, who have helped bring Ballas to a new readership and enable his recognition as an Israeli fiction writer. Taking advantage of a particular opportunity provided by life writing, Ballas in *Be-guf rishon* assesses his own works, and how he would prefer them to be read.[15] Ballas is not apologetic, nor does he flatter his readers, but unlike Amos Oz, he is reserved and not purposely confrontational. He opens his writer's studio before us and offers a reading, while attempting to transport his texts from "the ethnic parentheses" in which they have been set. Rather than position himself as a member of a broader group of Iraqi-born authors who switched from Arabic to Hebrew (such as Sami Michael), Ballas places himself in the context of Israeli authors such as A. B. Yehoshua, Oz, and Appelfeld, who began publishing in the late 1950s and 1960s. Like them he inhaled Agnon and founded his stories on mythical and allegorical infrastructures rooted in a national context—as demonstrated in his reading of his novel *Hitbaharut.*

Autobiographers in the "great Western tradition," as well as within the Jewish autobiographical tradition, beginning with Augustine's command to "tolle lege," are what they read. That is why their disclosures often include their reading lists, and an autobiographer's perspective is commonly shaped by his or her meetings with books and the company in which they were read.

Be-guf rishon is similarly strewn with books that formed Ballas's identity. As a young man he read nineteenth-century French realists and Arab modernists, with the latter including the Egyptian Taha Hussein. Books paved his way to communism: "My attraction to communism was of a romantic sort, meaning it did not stem from experience in social activism, or the influence of a friend who exposed me to Marxist ideology, but simply from reading books, especially romantic books. I admired heroes who fought to defend the weak, who preached social justice and confronted the supporters of aristocracy" (16). A specific book Ballas identifies as leading him to the Communist Party is Jack London's *The Iron Heel* (1908), which he read in French translation.

In one scene Ballas describes participating in a communism study group at a café and being asked by the discussion leader to explain the difference between materialism and idealism: "Without hesitation I explained that materialism characterizes the person who pursues materiality and wealth, whereas idealism marks the faith in sublime values that the intellectual aspires to. 'True,' the secretary gave me a thin smile, 'that would be the literary meaning. But we need the philosophical meaning.' And here the Shoemaker intervened with quotes from Lenin and Marx, directing his words at me, ridiculing my bookishness" (25). This reading group is a revelation and Ballas's communist initiation to intellectual humility.

Books posed risks to Ballas's safety in Iraq: on one occasion he is summoned to the censor's office to check a package of books he had ordered from France (33).

BALLAS'S ARRIVAL in Israel, like Appelfeld's, was not the result of Zionist belief. Immigration to Israel was Ballas's way of escaping the spiritual and ideological suffocation he was subject to in Iraq, as well as the immediate danger then faced by Iraqi communists. The prospect of arrest, imprisonment, and even execution was imminent. Ironically, once in Israel Ballas did eventually go to jail for being a communist.

In the late 1950s Ballas reported on Arab issues for the Hebrew communist daily *Kol ha-am* (Voice of the People). As such, he applied for a visitors' permit in Umm al-Fahm, a city then still under Israeli military rule. The permit application was enough to warrant summoning a plainclothes policeman to the Ballas family shack, still in the transit camp in Beit Dagan, near Rishon LeZion. A search revealed nothing more than forms Ballas had brought home from his army service confirming he had not lost army equipment, in the unlikely event he might be held responsible for such items later on, and outdated maps that his brother, Abud, then still in the service, had saved as souvenirs. But Ballas's overcaution carried a heavy toll—both he and his brother were imprisoned. Abud was court-martialed and sentenced to a month in prison. Other soldiers had taken these discarded maps home as well, but "Abud was the only one punished because he was also the only one who had a communist brother who had felt like visiting Umm al-Fahm" (59). Ballas himself, after several appeals, was sentenced to three months in prison under espionage charges. It was during this period, in summer 1959, that he first bonded significantly with Hebrew and considered adopting the language as his own. His jail term gave him ample time to catch up on reading the classics and, more important, to read his first novel in Hebrew—Avraham Shlonsky's translation of Mikhail Sholokhov's *And Quiet Flows the Don.*

For Ballas the first thrill of immigration was not a meeting with the Land of Israel, or Jews from around the world, nor the humiliation of being sprayed with DDT upon landing, but his first encounter with a copy of *Kol ha-am*: the communist daily was openly on sale, along with other papers, at an Ashkelon shop. A few days later Ballas found his ideological peers selling the party's weekly journal in Arabic on the street, and made his way to the party. The Israeli Communist Party became a home to him: "On my fourth day in Israel I was among friends with whom I would share a worldview and deeds" (7). From this description, written sixty years after the fact, communism truly seems, despite the internal feuds and power struggles, to have been a unifier: Arabs and Jews, post-independence and post-Nakba, shared a common language and goals.

BALLAS'S PROSE often tries not to call attention to itself; his tone is understated and refrains from emphatic statements. One exception is the densely alliterative opening passage of *Be-guf rishon*, in which Ballas describes landing in Israel after a crowded, stifling flight, his fellow travelers having vomited on him. The scene ends with a young man boarding the plane and spraying its passengers with a strong-smelling substance. Ballas strays from understatement in two other instances, both involving texts he wrote under different circumstances and inserted into his autobiography. (Life writings are often receptive to such external excerpts.) The first is a quotation from an autobiographical text written almost thirty years earlier; the second is a newspaper column. As we will see, the contrast between the tone of these passages and the bulk of *Be-guf rishon* emphasizes the choices Ballas made in constructing his autobiographical voice. Ballas notably specifies that the first piece was written in response to a specific request, and the other as part of his journalistic duties—neither was initiated by him:

> In an epilogue I included in the short story collection *Ba-ir ha-tahtit* [The Lower City], entitled "The Childhood of the Imagination," which was originally an answer to a survey the *Ha'aretz* newspaper initiated among writers about their place of birth, I described at some length the experiences that have remained with me from the world of my childhood.[16] Below I quote sections of it.
>
> "I grew up in the Christian neighborhood in Baghdad. . . . On our right lived a wealthy Jewish family, and their house was the only large and lavish house in the alley. It had a cone-shaped lantern hanging on its facade, made of slabs of colored glass, and topped with a jagged tin crown. At nightfall, when I heard the heavy steps of the sentry, I would rush to the

window to see his shadow in the dark lean a wooden ladder on the wall, and climb it to light the lamp. The flame would dance on his scorched gaunt face and send a fearful flash in his black eyes. After that I would watch him climb down, carry the ladder on his shoulder, and disappear down the alley. Alert, I would wait for the continuation of the ceremony, and when the new long whistle would rattle the stillness of the night, I would feel a chill down my back." (34)

These "foreign" paragraphs inserted in *Be-guf rishon* are filled with sensual detail. The text just quoted is followed by descriptions of his Armenian neighbor's singing and the tolling of the church bell. A compelling indicator of the difference between these passages and Ballas's usual prose comes in his brief, restrained description of his father's visits to the family's home in the contemporary text, versus the "Childhood of the Imagination" description of the same visits. In *Be-guf rishon* Ballas writes: "My father never had property of his own, or even a bank account. He was a small fabric merchant who spent most of his days in Shatra, the small southern town where he was born and where he had a small fabric store. . . . [On his visits home] he would sometimes take my brother and me with him to a café, where we would be treated to a soft drink. On holidays he would sometimes grant us a few coins" (14).

In the imported description from "The Childhood of the Imagination," the tone is different:

My favorite holiday was Passover. I liked sitting 'round the set table, reading the Haggadah, and drinking the sweet wine that my mother made herself. But as the holiday drew near, I was filled with anxiety that my father would not be with us and we would not have a Seder dinner. . . . When he came, he would fill the house with bustle; upon entering he would call my mother and our maid and shout at the man carrying his goods lest he ruin anything. . . . But just as the celebration grew when he came, so the agony lay heavy in his absence. He used to announce his visits in his letters, but there were times he would leave us in doubt until the eve of the holiday. My mother and the maid would work all day in preparation for the festive meal, and I could not budge from the window until late afternoon. A miracle did not happen on such days, and a hard feeling of spite swelled in me toward him. (38)

Ballas is describing the same situation in these two paragraphs, but the descriptions are distinctly different: the pathos-filled, sentimental earlier account against the reserved later one. For the Hebrew reader the former passage evokes the classic story by Yosef Haim Brenner, "Ba-horef" (Winter), a paradigm of autobiographical short fiction. In a memorable scene the protagonist, Yirmiya Fierman, recalls his mother, Golda, waiting for his father to return for the festive meal. The mother is crushed when her husband does not bother to appear. The child is left at home with his bereft mother, harboring anger and pain. When Ballas alludes to this scene, he places his memoir within the major Hebrew tradition, while at the same time distancing himself from it by not pursuing the Oedipal narrative or bringing it to a climax. Ballas, like Brenner before him, moves away from his father, but unlike in the model his mother and siblings join him. A comparison of Ballas's two passages thus stresses his later decision to avoid the earlier, more florid approach.

"That is what the childhood stories we read are like," Ballas summarizes, still quoting his earlier self, "they are stories." In *Be-guf rishon*, following the excerpt from "The Childhood of the Imagination," he turns abruptly to describe the campaign for the second Israeli Knesset, at its peak when Ballas arrived in Israel (38). The contrast between the narrow streets of the imagined childhood and Israeli propaganda is sharp. One explanation for this sudden shift might be that, for the period being described, Ballas did not yet speak Hebrew: "My entire vocabulary consisted of sentences such as: 'Communism very good, Ben-Gurion not good'" (39). The choice to make this shift becomes clearer through the second inserted text, his last column for the right-wing daily *Ha-yom* (Today) just before its closure. *Ha-yom* was published by Gahal (an acronym for *Gush Herut-Liberalim*, or the Herut-Liberals Bloc), and Ballas's column was included as part of the paper's policy of publishing diverse opinions. The piece ran November 14, 1969, not long after the Soviet invasion of Czechoslovakia:[17]

Last Friday two festive assemblies were to be held in Tel Aviv–Yafo to mark fifty-two years since the October Revolution, the first on behalf of Maki [the Israeli Communist Party] and the second on behalf of Rakah [the New Communist Party]. . . . That Friday night, November 7, it rained in Tel Aviv and I faced soggy and dismayed posters from both parties, wedged between scores of colorful announcements, longing to be observed by sympathetic eyes. I stopped by them and read the names of the speakers on the program, and as I did, I recollected the boisterous assemblies in the old 'People's House' [*Beit ha-am*], when Maki was at the summit of its success. The great auditorium would be decorated with red banners, and loudspeakers were placed on the roof and blared Russian songs down quiet Ben-Yehuda Street. The leadership would be sitting on the stage, in proper observance of Soviet tradition, with two giant-sized portraits of Lenin and Stalin hung behind them. I remembered the fiery speeches, the roar of applause, the rhythmic chant of the celebrating crowd: "Sta-lin! Sta-lin!" and the revolutionary songs sung by the party youth choirs. Maki had three superb choirs at the time (one of which was an Arab choir from Nazareth); on the eve of the celebrations of the revolution they would assemble on the stage together, and the wooden walls and the plaster ceiling of the auditorium would quake with their clear voices. . . . Songs, songs, emotional meetings, embraces, a clenched fist. (108)

In the article Ballas uses nostalgia to express the pain of the present, and juxtaposes this nostalgic gaze with his disillusionment following the invasion of Czechoslovakia. He expresses his disillusionment by describing a radio broadcast he listens to after returning home from the wet streets; the broadcast, marking the day of the revolution, is a reading of Aleksandr Solzhenitsyn's *One Day in the Life of Ivan Denisovich*, the first open, though fictional, account of Stalin's atrocities in Soviet Russia. Because Ballas's article is brought into *Be-guf rishon* as an excerpt, a foreign text, the distance from nostalgia is double. Ballas does not declare his choices in his life writing; he presents us with the options, and his preferences emerge from them. Ballas ultimately rejects nostalgia.[18]

IN 1970 BALLAS WROTE a children's book dedicated to his daughter: *Ash'ab me-Baghdad* (Ashab from Baghdad). The story follows Ashab, "chief of the idlers of Baghdad," who has been in exile, like many characters with whom Ballas identifies.[19] Being a children's book, this story has a happy ending: Ashab returns to his hometown, is received with open arms, and settles there for good.

The former exile Ashab's "idling" consists of being a poet, a troubadour, a drifter. Upon his return to Baghdad he improvises a poem (translated literally here) before the governor:

> Rejoice my heart and heed: My time has found its frame!
> The brook has returned to its bed
> and every mineral to its mine
> the wanderer returned from his roam
> and every exile to his home.
> And sin is seen on the sinner, and the hunter fell in his own trap!
> And the king is back to his kingdom
> and every sovereign to his rule
> God's will is my delight: My time has found its frame! . . .

When Ashab finishes his song, the governor is smitten with pleasure, his face aflame with drunkenness. Slapping his hand on the table, he says: "My decision! I now pronounce you the nightingale of the court!"

> "Is this a prize or a punishment?" asked Ashab.
> "Whyever a punishment?"
> "If thou shall not be angry with me, please permit me to refuse!"
> "But why? Here you would be a free man!"
> "I wish to go back and be an idler. Only in this idleness do I find my true freedom!"[20]

Ashab is Ballas's author figure—the idler is the artist who refuses to be court nightingale. In the children's story this refusal is accepted in laughter. In the adult world it causes discomfort—but the conscious choice to be the onlooker, bystander, observer who will not hire out his or her oud or pen reflects Ashab's choice.

Everything Is Jerusalem: Aharon Appelfeld[21]

Aharon Appelfeld's fiction has been read autobiographically since he first began to publish in the mid-1950s. Critics have responded to his work within the context of his Shoah survival and postwar immigration to Mandatory Palestine. His autobiographical works, the works that commit to the "autobiographical pact," address this frame of reading and respond by raising a debate regarding fiction and autobiography within a national context. Like Kaniuk, Be'er, and Ballas, Appelfeld is preoccupied with the relationship between his fictional and autobiographical writing. *The Story of a Life* signals this preoccupation in several instances. In chapter 22, for example, Appelfeld describes his theft of a watch, and in doing so demonstrates his awareness of joining a tradition of autobiography.[22] Ever since Augustine confessed to having stolen inedible pears with his friends, for the sheer pleasure of taking what did not belong to him and could not do him any good, autobiographers have made a trademark of confessing to thefts of objects they did not need or want. In modern autobiography this type of theft is emblematized by Rousseau's stealing of a ribbon. Rousseau's theft introduced a new theme adopted by subsequent autobiographers: not only is the stolen object useless to the thief, but the theft has a ruinous impact on an innocent other. In Rousseau's case the maid Marion is accused of the theft to which Rousseau does not confess, and her life is destroyed—she is fired and has little chance of finding other equal employment given the circumstances of her dismissal. As for the particular theft in *The Story of a Life*, Appelfeld recalls picking up a lost watch in an Italian transit camp. The watch turns out to be the last remnant another survivor has of his family, but rather than return it, the young Appelfeld buries it in the sand.

The confession of a theft not only signals Appelfeld's belonging to the great tradition of autobiography but also grants him reliability, as such autobiographical confessions always do. By sharing a low point with his readers and exposing his moral weakness, the autobiographer earns the readers' trust. We assume that a person willing to reveal such a shameful event is not hiding other facts.

Appelfeld's *The Story of a Life* highlights the implications of "story" throughout.[23] Chapter 6 is dedicated to the memory of Gustav Gotesman, the principal of a school for blind children in Appelfeld's hometown. Gotesman's story is framed within a familiar narrative that dictates how the story should be read: "Every town, it would seem, had its own Janusz Korczak," referring to the renowned Polish-Jewish educator.[24] In this chapter Appelfeld reconstructs the journey of the principal and schoolchildren to the train station to be deported. The children make stops along the way, singing a musical piece at each. About two of the stops Appelfeld remarks: "No one was there apart from them, and their song sounded like a prayer. . . . On the second stop, in Labor Square, there was also no one waiting for them" (45). Here Appelfeld's autobiographical narrator turns into an omniscient fictional narrator. (If no witness survived, how could he otherwise testify to the events?) Again, as in the story of the theft, Appelfeld signals his conscious production of narration, and deferral of his commitment to testimony. When Appelfeld steps into the role of fictional narrator, he allows a sentimental tone to permeate his narrative. This tone does not filter into the professed autobiographical sections.

Like Ballas, Appelfeld mainly refuses entry to nostalgia. Appelfeld does so by attempting to transform the experience of past and present: "I'm no historian. . . . My form of accuracy is different from that of the person who writes history. I'm interested in other details. I'm trying to make the past—present; perhaps the future too."[25]

In 2001 Aharon Appelfeld published an elaborately designed coffee table book, *Od ha-yom gadol*, translated by Aloma Halter as *A Table for One*. The added appeal of a collaboration between Appelfeld and his son, the painter Meir Appelfeld, and the subject matter, Jerusalem cafés, cannot prepare us for the earnestness and intricacy of the project. The Jerusalem here is of the 1950s, '60s, and early '70s. The cafés mentioned are long closed, but during this period they provided Appelfeld with a home. For Ilana, the *owner* of Café Peter, he brought in the women he was seeing to accept or reject, as one might do with one's parents. His studies were supported financially by fellow customers in the same cafés, who gave Appelfeld what little money they had. During his university years, and many years later, except when he was teaching, he spent his waking hours in cafés.

In Appelfeld's story of immigration, cafés (and their regulars) play a role similar to that of the Communist Party in Ballas's work. Both represent familiar territory in strange new surroundings. On this count *A Table* offers more than a glimpse of midcentury Jerusalem café culture but rather an expansive exploration of the foundations of Appelfeld's writing, and of his concepts of literature, of past and present, Israeliness, ideology, art, and individuality within a national context. Here Appelfeld asserts his Israeli identity as that of the immigrant survivor, and his immigrant identity as constituting Israeliness.

Israel is an immigrant society, and Appelfeld's fiction stands out in Israeli literature in its deliberate universalization of survivor immigrant figures. Appelfeld elevates them from "human dust" to individuals representing suffering, complexity, and sensitivity. Appelfeld notes that, in this respect, he was "the *halutz* before the troops."[26] Appelfeld uses a Hebrew idiom here from a specific ideological context: the *halutz* translates literally as "pioneer" or "scout" and refers to the early twentieth-century Zionist immigrant initiating Jewish settlement in Palestine—a figure whose move is motivated by devout Zionism. Appelfeld adopts the term and applies it to his own worldview, which is far from Zionist settler ideology. In Zionist terminology *halutz* is the polar opposite of "immigrant." In Israeli culture the *halutz*'s pure Zionism differentiates him or her from an "immigrant," whose move was triggered by necessity, such as anti-Jewish violence or expulsion. Although Zionism is founded on the idea of creating a Jewish refuge, those actually seeking refuge have not always been valued in Israeli culture—that is, arriving in Israel by choice is generally viewed more favorably, and those who find refuge in Israel are rarely received as Zionists, or as fulfilling a Zionist goal. The ideal *halutz* is a man who rejects his diasporic Jewish past in favor of a New Hebrew identity. The immigrant stereotype is a figure branded by a Jewish ethnic past of victimhood that cannot be shaken off. Appelfeld's writing upsets this cultural hierarchy. In his work immigrant, rather than *halutzi*, stories are related as a true realization of Zionist values.[27]

When *The Story of a Life* was published, Gershon Shaked, the major scholar and critic of Appelfeld's generation of Hebrew narrative fiction, offered a lengthy, mixed review of the book. His critique included the insinuation that Appelfeld was telling half-truths—by not mentioning, for example, his father's survival and their meeting in Israel after the war, as he does in *A Table for One*—and showing ingratitude to the Israeli establishment, which had reviewed his works so supportively and granted him the most prestigious prizes.[28] Shaked's review is very personal in its tone—he begins by pointing out the parallels between his own life and Appelfeld's. They shared German as their mother tongue, but Shaked was not a Holocaust survivor. As his autobiographical essay writing reveals, he was exposed to violence and antisemitic brutality in Austria, which he left after the Anschluss for Palestine. There he found a home away from home in the local boarding schools.[29] Shaked's writing and teaching indicate that he justifiably saw himself as a cornerstone of the Israeli literary establishment's backing of Appelfeld. In the early 1970s Shaked hailed Appelfeld along with Amos Oz, A. B. Yehoshua, and Amalia Kahana-Carmon as major forces in Israeli literature. He identified the four young fiction writers as the new Israeli canon, an uncontested position that they still hold alongside others who have now joined them.

Shaked's later writings indicate that he viewed himself as a mentor of the three men in the group. With respect to *The Story*, perhaps he was offended by not being mentioned. Otherwise it is difficult to explain why he lists all the cultural institutions that Appelfeld wrongly failed to include in the text, such as publishing houses and universities where he taught. He insists further that Appelfeld characterizes his relationships with his teachers, the generation's leading Jewish studies scholars at the Hebrew University— Martin Buber, Gershom Scholem, Dov Sadan, Hugo Bergmann—as closer than they actually were. Aside from being merely personal, the tone of Shaked's review thus includes injury and offense. Shaked reads the dominant role given to specific figures in Appelfeld's story—as opposed to others, such as possibly himself—as a political statement. Injury is transformed to accusation when Shaked reads Appelfeld's *Story* as "wanting to get rid of Israeli identity."[30] Overall Shaked's critical discourse blurs the borders between personal injury and political difference, and frames Appelfeld as an Israeli author who has effectively shirked his duties as a spokesman and representative of the imagined community.

On one level *A Table* may be read as Appelfeld's response to criticism Shaked leveled toward him after the publication of *The Story*. More significant, however, *A Table* stems from the closing chapter of *The Story*, which is devoted to the "New Life" Shoah survivors club in Jerusalem: "Sometimes it seems to me that all my writing derives not from my home and not from the war, but from the years of coffee and cigarettes at the club. . . . Every member carried within him a double and sometimes triple life. I borrowed a little from each of their lives. . . . The steam from the coffee and the haze of the cigarette smoke enveloped us for years and brought us to where we are today."[31] The closing note of *The Story* illuminates the author's self as constructed upon the selves of the club members, and his own first-person plural voice, in the tradition of Hebrew writing, as a representative of theirs.

In *A Table* Appelfeld affirms his own centrality to Israeli culture, while positioning immigrant marginality as the inherent, or even "true," Israeliness. He thus describes Israel as his home, while clarifying that "my homeland is not, after all, the land of the Hebrew revolution but the land of émigrés."[32] Correspondingly, in a chapter devoted to his winning of the 1972 Brenner Prize, he outlines his own oeuvre's commonalities with Yosef Haim Brenner's, positioning himself as a genuine heir to Brenner's literary estate: "Upon arriving in Israel, most Hebrew writers changed their subject matter and even their style; but Brenner stayed Brenner. . . . Brenner did not believe that changing one's place meant changing one's destiny and I too, like him, do not believe it. In this sense, he was and has remained close to my heart."[33]

Therefore, when Appelfeld rejects Israeliness modeled on the New Hebrew ideal he gains this license from one of his culture's most cherished and venerated authorities. The affiliation between Appelfeld and Brenner is enhanced when Appelfeld relates how Rachel Yanait Ben-Zvi (1886–1979) invited him for a congratulatory visit after he received the prize. Yanait, who immigrated to Ottoman Palestine from Ukraine in 1908, was a leader and founding figure of the prestate labor movement and early Israeli political institutions. She had founded the agricultural school Appelfeld was sent to as a child immigrant survivor in 1946, and she possibly provided the model for the "unmarried woman," or "spinster," in *Mikhvat ha-or* (1980). This was the case even though she married Yitzhak Ben-Zvi, who would serve as Israel's second president, and had two sons. Yanait had of course known Brenner, but she disapproved of him. For a time they had both worked for the same journal, *Ha-achdut*, for which he was on the editorial board and she contributed articles: "He never saw any light on the horizon," she decreed. "He was discouraging." She also recalled Appelfeld's faults as a teenager, as Appelfeld himself recounts: "I had been a rather withdrawn child . . . I was uncooperative and rarely mingled with others, and . . . I would sit reading books in German. . . . She had read two of my books. To judge from her expression she was far from pleased, but she complimented me on my Hebrew."[34] Yanait represents a rather blunt articulation of a common response to Appelfeld's work, and therefore is an easy target for retaliation.

Brenner and Appelfeld are therefore equalized by Yanait's criticism. But Yanait's response to the much younger author's work can be seen as common and almost crude, based on the New Hebrew ideal. This suggests how retaliation against Yanait could be easily waged. Moreover, given her gender, she could be cast as unable to truly fulfill the ideal but instead merely mimic it, enabling Appelfeld in his later narrative of the exchange to frame the cultural demands she represents as superficial, artificial, and reductive. Thus his immigrant position may be accepted as the "truer" and more "authentic" one, thereby revealing Yanait as disingenuously pompous and rigid.

In the closing paragraphs of *A Table*, Appelfeld writes:

Again and again I'm asked when I'm going to write about Israel. This question, which I was asked forty-five years ago, never goes away. It looks like it's going to haunt me until the end of my life. Once I couldn't restrain myself and I said, "I only write about Jerusalem. The Carpathian Mountains are also the Judean Hills. All the streets and all the cafés, even the trees and the flowers, everything that appears in my books—is Jerusalem. It's hard to persuade people that a city is, among other things, a private matter. It molds everyone differently. Sometimes it is actually the man in the street who instinctively picks up what journalists and professors don't see. The taxi drivers in Tel Aviv can immediately spot the Jerusalemite in me. Many years ago, in New York, I hailed a cab. The driver turned around to me and said in Hebrew: "You're from Jerusalem?" "What makes you think that?" "Your bag and the way you are holding it. I was a taxi driver in Jerusalem for ten years. I know who's from Jerusalem." (106)

In *The Story* memory is enacted by the body: "The palms of one's hands, the soles of one's feet, one's back, and one's knees remember more than memory" (vii). Later he writes: "I was only seven at the outbreak of World War II. The war was etched inside my body, but not my memory. In my writing I wasn't imagining but drawing out, from the very depths of my being [in Hebrew: body], the feelings and impressions I had absorbed because of my lack of awareness [in Hebrew: my blindness]" (186).

Likewise the book's preface problematizes its title. Appelfeld opens by noting the proximity of memory and imagination: "Memory and imagination sometimes dwell together" (v). He promises "segments of contemplation and memory" rather than a linear retrospective story, and confesses lacking memory of events during the war: "During the war I was not myself, but like a small creature that has a burrow, or, more precisely, a few burrows. Thoughts and feelings were greatly constricted. In truth, sometimes there swelled up within me a painful sense of astonishment at why I had been left alone. But these reflections would fade with the mists of the forest, and the animal within me would return and wrap me in its fur" (vii).

The body both constitutes and contradicts identity ("I was not myself"). Although the body cannot produce a story, it does, contradictorily, have a memory and a story to tell. In addressing this difficulty, theory of autobiography has dwelt extensively on the Cartesian dichotomy between body and mind and its applications to narrated memory and autobiographical selves (see chapter 4 for a discussion of these issues within a gendered context). Along these lines Paul John Eakin has recently introduced neuroscientist Antonio Damasio's terminology to the theory of autobiography. Following Damasio, Eakin suggests that the term *embodied self* constitutes a tautology, since the self is inherently corporeal. Eakin quotes Damasio: "There must be a nonverbal self and a nonverbal knowing for which the words 'I' or 'me' or the phrase 'I know' are the appropriate translations, in any language. . . . The idea that self and consciousness would emerge *after* language, and would be a direct construction of language, is not likely to be correct."[35]

Following Eakin's reading of Damasio, we can conclude that Appelfeld's "body" is not mute and blank but an agent enabling a sensation of being and a recognizable identity. The body is also crucial later in establishing Appelfeld's Israeli identity, when he undergoes the physical tests of the New Hebrew—of manual and agricultural labor—and the military placement committee, which pronounces him unfit for combat. The body is here ruled a failure.

The body is one layer of memory; literature is another. Appelfeld writes in *The Story* that it was from Agnon that he "learned how you can carry the town of your birth with you anywhere and live a full life in it. Your birthplace is not a matter of fixed geography. And you can extend its borders outward or raise them to the skies. . . . And he taught me that a person's past—even a difficult one—is not to be regarded as a defect or a disgrace, but as a legitimate source to be mined" (152).

In *A Table* it is through others that Appelfeld reaches himself, and in Jerusalem that he discovers his lost relations, through observing immigrants who shared the cultural and ethnic background of his childhood. Jerusalem has always held metaphysical ties with the past, but here these ties allow for the reconstruction of lost families, and transport the lost European past into the Middle Eastern present:

> When the war broke out I was seven. . . . My childhood crumbled as if it had not existed. For years I neither saw my grandparents nor experienced the wonderful summers in which I had reveled in their presence. But one day, as if by chance, they were revealed to me as I was going up Agrippas Street on my way to Mahaneh Yehuda market, and I knew then that the gates of light had been opened to me, and I saw what I had not seen all those years: hills and Jews are connected to one another and above, there's the sky's clear dome. And I knew then I was now permitted

to enter those gates and write what the heart remembered and what the eyes had seen. (83)

The ability to see his past and his loved ones in the present supplies a license to narrate (to write) unmediated by narrative—to produce unprocessed emotion and visual sensation. This holding of the past in the present—seeing Jews and hills tied together, whether the Judean Hills or the Carpathian Mountains—is directly linked to the autobiographical impulse. Appelfeld describes frequent visits to the ultra-Orthodox Jerusalem neighborhood of Mea Shearim, where the inhabitants not only bring to life but *become* his grandparents and create, rather than revive, memories of his Carpathian vacations.[36]

As he muses on Mea Shearim, Appelfeld wonders why thousands flock to the living history museum in Sturbridge, Massachusetts, while Israelis can't appreciate their own such museum, smack-dab in the middle of Jerusalem, with no admission charge and no need of period actors. He is not here invoking the quaintness of Mea Shearim, where one might imagine picking up a shtetl souvenir, but expressing the value of a present space in which the past dwells. His defense of Jewish ultra-Orthodoxy in Israel does not ignore its harmful sociopolitical impact and power dynamics, but he nonetheless insists on its merits, which might somehow be extended to Appelfeld himself, or to his writing. In other words, Appelfeld perceives himself writing the Shoah, or his role in it, as akin to an ultra-Orthodox Jew preserving his or her tradition. In neither case can the relationship be questioned or altered. The past in Mea Shearim, like literature for Appelfeld, is a burning present. As he recounts in *The Story*: "I don't feel that I write about the past. Pure and unadulterated, the past is no more than raw material for literature. Literature is an enduring present—not in a journalistic sense, but as an attempt to bring time into an ongoing present" (125).

The literal Hebrew here says not "enduring present" but "burning present" (ספרות היא הווה בוער), a change that prevents English readers from perceiving a crucial element of Appelfeld's concept of writing and of self. He strictly refrains from use of emphatic language, reserving it for critical moments such as this.

Appelfeld finds his lost grandparents in Mea Shearim, and his parents and their social circle in Jerusalem cafés. We return to Café Peter in *A Table*: "I don't remember who first brought me to Café Peter, but I do remember that no sooner was I through the doorway, than I knew that these people were my lost uncles and cousins, they had brought their language here with them—their attire, their little shops in the pastoral villages and their splendid department stores from the towns from which they had been uprooted. I had been in Israel for some seven years, yet only now I returned home" (6).

The cafés and the Shoah survivors club constitute a mix of public and private that enables Appelfeld to experience impersonal relationships, some not involving a single word exchanged, as intimate ties. The deep past is recovered as sites in Jerusalem become fragments of the Austro-Hungarian Empire, where the gestures of fellow patrons embody those of murdered family members and "at Café Rehavia and Café Hermon you could get a cup of coffee and a piece of strudel that tasted just like the ones served in [Dresden, Leipzig, or Berlin]" (16). A clear example of this recovery occurs for Appelfeld at his regular seat at Café Atara: "There was a corner by the window where my imagination conjured up the sights I needed" (60) (הפינה ליד החלון הביאה אל דמיוני מראות מדוייקים). The translation here omits the Hebrew adjective: "*precise* sights." Also important to note is that Appelfeld sits near the window but does not look out. His view is from the outside in—that is, the window reflects his internal experience.

For Appelfeld the café demystifies authorship and the act of writing. He finds the privacy, tranquility, and domesticity of his own room suffocating, and noisy cafés and cheap coffee inspiring. In *The Story* Appelfeld describes his passion for staring, and eavesdropping, his capacity as a young child to sit silent for hours, watch, learn, and internalize the ways of others. He recalls being slapped and scolded for such tendencies by an old man in the ghetto. Cafés, however, permit such behavior and can allow the observer to view his or her object without being intrusive. The regulars at Café Peter are Appelfeld's "literary salon" and his "writing school." The café teaches him diction, modeling his poetics through patrons with accents and modes of narration—or omitted narration—echoing his childhood and its terrain.

In the Hebrew version of *A Table*, the centrality of human relations to

Appelfeld's Jerusalem is highlighted by a particular contrast in his son's paintings—namely the absence of people, even though their presence is implied in the houses and streets depicted. Like the text, the son's art avoids the mythological, historical, and heavily symbolic Jerusalem.

A TABLE holds thirty-four chapters. At the center of the book, in chapter 17, is a poetic manifesto Appelfeld stages as a dialogue with a friend. He concludes the section with this:

> Since the publication of my first story, I've been treated as if I were the chronicler of the Holocaust. I'm not someone writing a chronicle, nor am I a historian. I try to be a novelist. What is important for the historian does not concern me. The historian makes a distinction between one place and another, between past and present. I do not distinguish between them. In this respect, and not only in this respect, the artist continues to be a child. For him, what was "then" and what is "now" are intertwined. There was a right-wing critic who claimed that I refuse to relinquish the trauma of childhood and insist on bringing it here. Another critic, this time a left-winger, claimed that my writing on the Holocaust inflames nationalistic sentiments. Such allegations will only flourish in a country constantly in the throes of ideological obsessions.
>
> There were years when I suffered from this. But as I grow older, it becomes increasingly clear to me: you simply have to be yourself. Just that.
> (54)

Amia Lieblich has described *A Table* as the more psychologically reconciled, or forgiving, of the two autobiographical texts.[37] This is indeed the case, but beside or beyond that, the coffee table book asserts the immigrant's position as no less "Israeli," and perhaps even more Israeli, than that of the empowered New Hebrew. In other words, rather than accept his position as eternal immigrant (as Lieblich sees it) from his seat at the café, Appelfeld upsets the balance of center and margins by painting Israeli society as a society of immigrants, and marginalizing the New Hebrew culture and its values.[38]

Ostensibly this is what Yoram Kaniuk did as well, only Kaniuk needed to revise his identity as a native in order to adopt an immigrant identity that would serve a political end. Appelfeld's position entails a refusal to adhere to the demands of "integration" and "blending." His refusal to adopt the image of a New Hebrew opens the possibility for different definitions of being Israeli. However, Appelfeld's choice, like Kaniuk's, excludes others.

AS FAR AS APPELFELD'S worldview is concerned, Israeli immigrants come from Europe. When Appelfeld and other Ashkenazi writers universalize the experience of immigration, they thereby run the risk of generalizing Israeli immigration and ethnicity. This view can erase the specific identities of immigrants who arrived from countries outside Central and Western Europe and elsewhere in the West.

Reading Appelfeld and Shimon Ballas side by side thus highlights the differences between their life writings and their lives; surprisingly it also illuminates striking resemblances and affinities. A divide, for example, separates the authors' recorded reactions to the Six Day War. Appelfeld is a metaphysician, Ballas a former communist. Yet both authors' responses to the outcome of the war differentiate them from the collective Israeli enthusiasm.[39] For Ballas the war's end is at once an exciting time of bonding and meeting with Palestinians from across the border, and gaining exposure to bookstores and intellectuals previously inaccessible to him, as well as a time of alienation from the messianic spirit sweeping the Jews in Israel:

> I heard veteran party members justifying support of the war: "The Christians have Rome, the Moslems have Mecca, why shouldn't we have Jerusalem?" This came from old-time communists who had never held a prayer book their whole lives.[40]

Ballas feels that his lack of enthusiasm distances him from friends.

In *A Table*, meanwhile, Appelfeld describes the anxiety and old fears of destruction that resurface at the threat of war, the feelings of danger and nervousness and the hoarding of food: "The prophets of doom have been declaring that our coming to Israel has been useless: it's our fate to be wiped out" (68). He continues:

> Just as the danger and threat had brought to the surface words from the Holocaust, victory brought with it terms from Jewish mysticism. On the

radio and in the press people talked of miracles, of Redemption and of the coming of the Messiah. These terms were beyond me. I love the mysticism of daily life . . . particular spots in Jerusalem toward evening, the light that glints out from the ancient walls and the rocks, the plants that rise out of the parched earth. And even more than them, I love the people who embrace children and the people who pray. This mysticism is close to my heart, but for me the cosmic or historical mysticism remains a complete abstraction. (68)

Appelfeld therefore does not tie mysticism to nationality—or history, in his words. However, the occupation and military rule over the Palestinians do not appear in Appelfeld's text. Neither does East Jerusalem figure in his map of the city, which is limited to the western part both before and after the war. Like Ballas, Appelfeld is not carried away with the public celebration, but for different reasons. Palestinians remain invisible in this landscape. As in other major Israeli literary works of Appelfeld's generation, Palestinians figure as ominous Others, but they do not have specific faces or characters. After a month of reserve duty in 1963 on Mount Scopus, then a Jewish enclave within Jordanian-ruled Palestinian East Jerusalem, Appelfeld, writing in *A Table*, returns from "a small island in a sea of enmity. While I was on guard duty at Mount Scopus, I wasn't afraid, but since my return I've been dreaming that a horde of Arabs are at the outpost, overrunning it, and our guns have jammed" (54). Appelfeld's genuine experience aligns with the Zionist cliché of experiencing Israel—and not only Mount Scopus—as a fragile "small island in a sea of enmity." That is, as far as Israeli ideology concerns Israel's relationship with Palestinians, Appelfeld's position is not marginal but mainstream and conventional. Ballas's position on these matters is anything but cliché.

After the 1967 war Ballas enlisted himself as a mediator between Jewish Israelis and Palestinians. He translated Palestinian literature and introduced it to Israeli readers of Hebrew. Literature, he presumed, would enable Jewish Israelis to see the Other. *Be-guf rishon* portrays a cultural bridge as part and parcel of Ballas's concept of writing since his youth, when he was selecting news items from underground communist papers in Baghdad in service of the party. Ballas has engaged in writing historical novels. He finds himself in historical figures. Appelfeld, in contrast, professes in *A Table* that his attempts at historical novels would result in "everything—except literature" (71). He rejects roles of representation, which Ballas takes on.

APPELFELD'S CONNECTION TO the past, his corporeal memory and the obstacles on his path to articulating it in straight narrative, should be read in the context of trauma. Nevertheless, his autobiographical works do articulate related ideas in a clear ideological frame, and from a confrontational standpoint. In *The Story* Appelfeld's description of his first years in Israel would fit Ballas's position as well:

> And above everything hovered the familiar slogan: "Forget the Diaspora and root yourself in the present!" But what could I do? Within me there was a deep refusal to efface my past and build a new life on its ruins. The idea that a person has to destroy his past in order to build a new life seemed to me totally misguided even then, but I didn't dare voice this thought, not even to myself." (114)

CHAPTER FOUR

Gendered Margins

Narrative Strategies, Embodied Selves, and
Subversion in Women's Autobiography

IKE MODERN Hebrew literature and culture in general, Hebrew autobiography has been dominated by men's voices. Nationalism has enhanced this dominance in Hebrew letters and contributed significantly to the marginalization of women's writing. However, as early as the
1920s in prestate Palestine, women began to produce life writings, memoirs,
and testimonies of their experiences as Jewish immigrants and settlers in
Ottoman and Mandatory Palestine. A large number of these writings revise
national narratives of Jewish settlement in prestate Palestine, not only expanding the stories to include women but also shifting and changing their
very structures, their perspectives, and the events they relate. Life writing
has therefore allowed women writing in Hebrew to write a nation that is
inclusive of women and that recognizes their failures and their feats within
a national context. Although many parallels and affinities exist between
men's and women's autobiographical writings, perhaps seeming to eliminate
the need for separate readings, the construction of gender and gendered
identities within nationalism demands a particular effort or investment by
women nationals that clearly differentiates their autobiographical writing
from men's. This chapter considers this special effort or investment in a
variety of writings by women of different generations and positions in Israeli
culture; however, the five women considered here are unarguably a part of
Israeli hegemony—they are not immigrants, they are all Ashkenazi, they
are not Shoah survivors. Thus the marginality of gender surfaces as part of

these writers' hegemonic cultural position, and reconfigures their cultural dominance as conflict-ridden and diverging from the main channels of Israeli culture.

It has often been proposed that autobiography offers a means of "talking back."[1] Autobiography is a platform on which the silenced, the marginalized, and the ostracized can speak, and their speech, it has been implied, might disturb the power hierarchies that have relegated them to the cultural periphery. As Sidonie Smith has pointed out, autobiography is where women can write themselves out of culturally imposed embodied subjectivity and ruffle the clean hierarchical dichotomy between the universal self and the embodied self that is characteristic of the Western autobiographical tradition.[2] As the second wave of feminism showed, Western culture positions body and mind at opposite ends of a hierarchical binary that is gender marked.[3] This dichotomy has influenced concepts of self. The Cartesian subject, conceived as male, is described as "unique, unitary, unencumbered . . . by all forms of embodiment," eternally rational, and, at the same time, universal.[4] In contrast to this human/male Enlightenment self, women's selfhood is constituted as essential, embodied, and nonuniversal.[5] Woman has been conceived as natural, speechless, inarticulate, and unreflective. A bind thus emerges whereby "the woman who would reason like a universal man becomes unwomanly, a kind of monster."[6] However, by writing herself and, more so, giving the body a story and writing it, woman may write her way out of this dichotomy. Writing may not be easily accessible to the woman, given that, until very recently, "women," as Carolyn Heilbrun memorably writes in *Writing a Woman's Life*, "have been deprived of narratives, or of texts, plots or examples, by which they might assume power over—take control of—their own lives."[7] Shoshana Felman has questioned whether the problem's core was indeed the lack of models and women's hesitation to take power, given that this would be an aberration from their womanhood, or whether the problem instead stemmed from a linguistic unavailability of "*structures of address*": "we cannot simply *substitute ourselves as center* without regard to the *decentering* effects of language and of the unconscious, without acute awareness of the fact that our own relation to a linguistic frame of reference is never self-transparent" (emphasis in original).[8]

In contemporary Israeli autobiography, the body—male or female, vulnerable, unsheltered and failing, ill, badly injured, dead or foul-smelling—appears to unsettle power structures. The embodied autobiographical Israeli self offers a point of departure for critical meetings of individual identities with the national collective. These meetings probe Israeli axioms and cultural strongholds despite the authors' otherness, or perhaps because of it.

The fractured embodied autobiographical self makes its appearance in both women's and men's works. This chapter is concerned with the gendered specificity with which the self is represented in women's autobiographical writing.[9] It offers readings of Esther Raab's memoirs, which receive the most attention, along with Netiva Ben-Yehuda's *1948—Bein ha-sefirot: roman al hathalat ha-milhama* (1981), Yehudit Kafri's *Kol ha-kayitz halachnu yehefim* (1995), Nurith Gertz and Deborah Gertz's *El ma she-namog* (1997), and Nurit Zarchi's *Mishakey bdidut* (1999).

Notably all but the first of these texts are related to kibbutzim. Kafri was born and raised on Ein Ha-Horesh, in central Israel, and Gertz's parents left Ein Ha-Horesh after she was born but maintained close ties with the community. Indeed Gertz quotes Kafri in her autobiographical volume.[10] As for Zarchi, she moved with her mother to Kibbutz Geva, in the Jezreel Valley, at age five, after her father died. Despite their common kibbutz background, these three authors present very different perspectives on childhood in a kibbutz specifically, and on life writing in general.

As elsewhere, works on the Shoah are omitted from this chapter, but many have yet to receive the close attention they deserve.[11]

ONE MIGHT QUESTION what exactly frames the authors discussed here as "marginal." As noted, in many aspects all are integral to Israeli cultural hegemony. They were born in prestate Palestine to Ashkenazi families. The books of Ben-Yehuda, Gertz, and Zarchi were published by leading publishing houses, and Kafri's book, although now out of print, was originally published as an issue of the kibbutz movement journal *Shdemot* dedicated to her work.[12] That is, her perspective was adopted as representative. The work of Esther Raab (1894–1981), although self-published by her nephew, who runs her estate, is widely recognized. Raab's father was among the founders of Petah Tikva, the early Jewish prestate agricultural settlement founded in 1878, and is recognized as having plowed "the first furrow" there. Netiva Ben-Yehuda (1928–2011) hosted a program on Israeli national radio.[13] Her father, Baruch Ben-Yehuda, was principal of the prestigious Gymnasia Herzliya, director of the Ministry of Education, and an Israel Prize laureate (1979). Yehudit Kafri (b. 1935) has won the prime minister's award for authors, her poems are included in the Israeli high school curriculum, and her parents were among the founders and leading figures of their kibbutz. Nurith Gertz (1940) is a prominent literary scholar and critic. Her parents were among the founders of their kibbutz, and after they left it in the early 1930s, her father served in a high government position. The childhood of Nurit Zarchi (b. 1941) was marked by the death of her father, the author Israel Zarchi, who, although not a central figure in the Hebrew canon, has been acknowledged.[14] Zarchi wrote *Mishakey bdidut* after years of international acclaim as a children's writer, and a stable career as a poet and fiction writer for adults. She teaches and lectures in Israeli universities. She does not seem to fit the description of a culturally marginal figure.

In their writings these authors, like Yoram Kaniuk, Aharon Appelfeld, and Haim Be'er, establish relationships with Israeli culture that are based on belonging, suspicion, conflict, and intimacy. They all crumble the Israeli subject and frustrate any attempt to grasp it as a single, stabilized, united whole. Ben-Yehuda, Kafri, Gertz, and Zarchi all write from a marginal position that is centered on their lived experience as women. They are women in a patriarchal national society; thus their view is necessarily from the margins.[15] Furthermore, their choice to distance themselves from the dominant strata of Israeli society to which they ostensibly belong is enhanced by the prism of gender and the alternative critical view it offers. Their autobiographical writing delineates gendered marginality, and articulates and chisels a critical tool out of it. It is through gender that they make audible a voice both confrontational and representative.[16]

Esther Raab's position differs distinctly from the positions of her four followers. Rather than view herself as marginal, as we shall see, Raab narrates herself as a definer of the national Israeli native self. Her depiction of this self is strongly influenced by her concepts of gender, and creates a national image that digresses from the conventional power arrangement of gender roles within Zionist literature and culture. Like her poetry, her autobiographical voice creates a subversive and different constellation of gender, nationality, and narrative.

A Stroll through the Zionist Orchard: Esther Raab

Esther Raab is considered to be the first native-born Hebrew poet. Readers of Raab's poetry in recent decades have problematized the place of nativism in her poetry and its reception, and the complexities of gender in the construction and understanding of that nativism. These issues, which have dominated the discourse on Raab's poetry since it was first published in 1922, illustrate the various historical uses her work and public persona have served for different generations of readers.[17] In past readings Raab's memoirs have served as a backdrop for or corroboration of these discussions. But rather than consider these memoirs as background or scaffolding, this section puts them in the foreground, and also examines them in relation to the memoir of Esther's father, Yehuda Raab.

The following section relies on autobiographical writings that span Raab's lifetime, encompassing the periods recollected as well as the times of writing, in order to study the author's construction of her native identity in relation to the images she creates of her father and mother, and her different relationships with her parents.

Raab's memoirs were written in bits and pieces, each a page or two long, mostly relating to her early childhood in Petah Tikva. She published fragments during her lifetime, but the majority were collected and published posthumously by her nephew Ehud Ben-Ezer, first in the collection *Gan she-harav* (A Garden in Ruins) and later in *Kol ha-proza* (Collected Prose).[18] The collections do not differentiate among memoir, diary, and fiction. However, Ben-Ezer's notes are helpful in determining which sections were originally introduced as fiction and which were meant to adhere to the autobiographical pact.

Raab's roots in Palestine were deep. Her great-grandfather had immigrated to the Ottoman territory sometime after the Hungarian revolution of 1848, the name Raab having come from the family's Hungarian town of origin. Raab's grandfather, however, remained in Hungary, and this is where her father, Yehuda (1858–1948), was born. Yehuda Raab immigrated to Palestine in 1876 and took part in the founding of Petah Tikva two years later. Yehuda narrated his memoir, which covers the years 1862–1930, to his son Benjamin Ben-Ezer.

In Hungary the Raab family leased a farm from local gentry. They raised sheep and made wine, and were appreciated and respected by their non-Jewish neighbors. Yehuda Raab does not remember his father as singular or different from other Jews.[19]

Yehuda Raab describes his family as sturdy, self-confident country people unintimidated by anything or anyone. Their Jewish identities are exact opposites to those found in autobiographies such as Solomon Maimon's or those of his followers, Mordechai Aharon Guenzberg and Moshe Leib Lilienblum. In fact, Raab constructs his family in Europe as "natives" before their immigration to Ottoman Palestine. Therefore, the family's physical and mental power is part of their identity, without the need for Jewish-Palestinian nativist discourse. That is, Yehuda Raab's memoirs do not coincide with the Zionist norm of the land changing the people, since the strength his family brings to Ottoman Palestine is what enables their settlement there in the first place. Rather than depict his family members—after Theodor Herzl's model, to name but one example—as feeble, diasporic, feminized figures in need of rescue by a change of place and independence, the memoir depicts them as leaving a safe homeland in favor of a dangerous unknown terrain that demands all the strength they have brought.[20] Their story also diverges from the mainstream narrative of the Zionist settlement project in Eretz Yisrael because it does not tie national, religious, or ethnic violence and threat to the cause of immigration. The Raabs came to Ottoman Palestine long before the horrendous pogroms of 1881, which are recorded as the trigger for the first wave of Zionist immigration. Their Zionism is inseparably linked to their religious belief and practices, and thus has little to do with the prevalent narrative of disillusionment with hopes hinged on emancipation. One of Yehuda Raab's anecdotes summing up these differences tells about the killing of the family cat:

> As my memory has preserved it, my father was not the only Jew to live in this way at that period. There were many Jews who lived in villages and worked in agriculture. . . . These Jews were honest in their interactions with the locals and held their heads high, they were proud Jews, not like the Jews of the other countries of the diaspora. This is what once happened to Father: One day two men from the rural gentry drove by our house in a carriage drawn by four horses. One of them, in high spirits, shot our beloved house cat, which was wandering in the yard, and killed it, and immediately the rogues continued on their way. As soon as my father discovered what had happened, he grabbed one of the horses in the stable, without a saddle or reigns, and galloped after the noble carriage. He overtook them at the gates of the town of Veszprém. They were ashamed to enter the town with a Jew close on their heels. They turned from the road to a remote village. There they stopped at an acquaintance's home, and Father—at their heels. A fight broke out immediately, and the landlord to whose home they had escaped, who was a friend of Father's, made peace between them. The guilty noblemen had to ask for Father's forgiveness and pay him compensation of 52 Gulden. Father gave the sum to the village elder-man to be handed out to the poor. This event was so well known in the area that many years later, when those two noblemen would walk into a club or a pub, their friends would tease them, calling "meow" in remembrance of the story of the cat and the brave Jew. (20–21)

This is clearly a far cry from the stampedes described by Solomon Maimon, during which he was once dropped and lost as a child, that took place whenever a member of the Polish gentry approached the neglected rickety bridge on the family's hired estate.

Esther Raab's relationship with her father carries incestuous connotations, as suggested by her writing. Her relationship with her mother, Leah, was strained. As she writes in a segment from the 1960s, published in her

Kol ha-proza, "I never earned a caress from my mother. The reason for that is unclear to me until this very day" (63). Mother and daughter, however, were united in their adoration and admiration of Esther's father, Yehuda:

> Not tall, but sturdy and well built, he would boast in front of Mother and me—on Fridays, when she would hand him his clean shirt, he would take off the worn one, and show off with his broad chest, powerfully pound his chest with a fist, and the two of us, Mother and I, would shriek and stop him from doing it, and he teased us, his two "weak women." . . . They both seemed very young and wonderful to me. I once saw Father take Mother in his arms and kiss her—I never forgot that movement of his, it had a wonderful tenderness and superior manliness, I've never seen anything like it since. They did not notice me, and I have saved that picture within me until this very day. (32)

Esther Raab's erotic admiration of her father's physique appears in writings throughout her life. In a section written in approximately 1970, Raab tells of an event that most likely took place in 1887, almost a decade before she was born. Raab recalls the narration itself, when her father told the family this story. It is a cozy family scene—the family is gathered around a warm stove in midwinter, with a lively fire of scented eucalyptus, drinking coffee with "Mother's cakes." The description of this scene appears twice in her memoirs; both descriptions convey the warmth of intimacy, the scent of the eucalyptus wood in the fire, and her mother's cakes, and in both Raab describes the child's observation of her mother viewing her father with fresh eyes—although the cause of the mother's altered gaze is relayed only in one case. As Yehuda tells it, when the Baron Rothschild first visited Ottoman Palestine, he was asked to drive the baron and baroness from Petah Tikva to Zikhron Yaakov. The carriage broke down midway and they proceeded on foot. The baroness was wearing delicate high-heeled shoes, so Raab took off his shirt and tore it into strips, which he used to wrap her feet. As Esther recollects the narrated scene, her father knelt before the baroness and gently "wrapped her tiny feet with wide bandages; he was nude to the waist and handsome beyond description in the dusk, in the rocky landscape." Eventually the bandages fell off and Yehuda carried the baroness the remainder of the way, while the baron and their escort trudged behind. When they reached their destination, the baroness parted from Raab with "a long kiss on his tanned cheek." Her father's physical strength and power are accentuated by the baroness's diminutive feet and helplessness. This story is related by the father in a familial setting. He is a powerful object of attraction, while the baroness herself is not described other than in her incompetence, dependence, and gratitude to Yehuda. Thus mother and daughter can join her vacant perspective of adoration. The daughter here observes her mother viewing her father "with new eyes," and Esther describes herself as "dissolving" with affection toward him.[21]

Raab's desire directed toward her father is often mediated through descriptions of other women's desire. Her written observations of her parents' relationship as a child sometimes holds traces of gloating at her mother's insecurity. In one fragment Raab describes her father's visits from Manya Shohat, the former Russian revolutionary who was dominant in prestate Zionist military and labor movement circles. Again Raab, who wrote this fragment in about 1975, and just past eighty, dwells on her father's physicality: "My father was about forty years old at the time, in the prime of his virility and vitality, and his green eyes shone in his tanned healthy face. He was broad-shouldered, and his shirt collar opened to reveal a broad manly chest, a dandy no less than a hippy of our days." On these visits Shohat and Yehuda would have lengthy heated arguments in German in the dimly lit sitting room, while Esther's openly envious mother would serve coffee, and they would fall into silence when she walked in. Raab's mother ostensibly regained her self-esteem by turning the visitor masculine: "'Nu,' she would ask in a mix of Yiddish and Hebrew after the visitor had gone, 'What did the half-male tell you?' Father would smile into his beard and tug jokingly at the tip of Mother's white apron, and then all would be set right" (165). The father's childlike gesture, with the tug like that of a boy at his mother's apron, rearranges the power structure—the mother is now seemingly the adult in charge. Masculine and feminine are set in order, and Manya Shohat's threatening performance of gender is laughed aside. But the fragment closes with the child observing her mother trying on her father's hat in front of the mirror to see if she too can cross-dress like Shohat. Caught in the act, the mother laughs her attempt away, but the event itself has taken place, even if it is overtly negated.

Raab's father is a more sensual figure in her writing than her mother. The scent of his body is mentioned particularly often: "healthy sweat and the scent of vegetation and also something that had the odor of the cowshed and milk" (62) emanate from his shirt. His bed exudes the "smell of tobacco mixed with healthy sweat" (9), and when Esther is bitten by a scorpion she is comforted in his arms, "and that is how the day turned into a holiday— a sad and painful holiday, but still—to smell Father's arms, which always emanated the odor of a pure suntan, to be nestled in his arms as in a cocoon woven out of an iron web, to be protected and happy" (14). Her father's body is experienced as warm, nurturing, and protective. It smells of milk— albeit cow's milk.

Raab's relationship with her mother does include instances of affection, as she describes it in a letter: "I must have been two years old then—and Mother—she used to play a game with me, and those were perhaps the only moments in which I felt the warmth of her heart—because we were always on polar ends. I would slap myself on the cheek—and then Mother would shout—'Why are you hitting my daughter?' and I would feel a strange and very warm split: I am Mother's girl, and I am hitting Mother's girl, it is difficult to explain where the pleasure was derived from" (46).

This scene provides a subtle counterpoint to the father beating his chest as the mother and daughter admiringly watch him dress. At age two the daughter mimics the father, and she too elicits shouts of protest from the mother. Mimicry through a form of aggression creates belonging—being her mother's possession enables her to allegedly injure her mother by injuring herself. It is the father, rather than the mother—who teaches Raab how to knit, a task the daughter finds exceptionally dull—who is repeatedly represented as the primary educator: "I always tried to be like my brothers— not to show weakness or excessive femininity—and Father understood me and agreed to teach me like my brothers: to shoot, swim, and ride a horse. I followed his instructions, and my ability matched my brothers' in these three skills—Father instilled a kind of fearlessness in me—until my daring sometimes surpassed that of my brothers, and that angered them. It was rare in those days, when girls followed their mothers, knitted, sewed, played with dolls—in all three of those skills my ability was nil" (64). Later passages continue to portray Esther as distant from and unfamiliar with stereotypical feminine roles.

In a section written in the late 1950s, Raab describes herself as a young girl with a friend in an abandoned orange grove, picking orange blossoms. The friend imagines herself as a bride covered in the blossoms, later a mother to daughters who will in their turn grow up to marry and bear children, and so on until the end of time. But Esther says:

> "Until the end? No, I want to do different things."
>
> "You can't. Everyone, everyone, always does it this way."
>
> "I want to be like Deborah, the prophet in the Bible; I want us to have a king again like Saul, a king like David, and I want to fight the Arabs." (118)

Following Zionist culture of this period, Esther the child links the present national struggle to the biblical past. The Philistines are the Palestinians, she is a biblical prophetess, and she can connect to male kings of a later period as long as she can join these powerful figures in national war. This childhood fantasy is famously reprised in Raab's poem "Holy Grandmother's in Jerusalem."[22] Hannan Hever points to the intersection of the new native and tradition in the poem, which connects Raab's early childhood in Petah Tikva with her visits to her maternal grandmother in Jerusalem, and the fantasy of meeting Deborah and having an affair with her lover King David.[23]

Despite Raab's representation of her father as enabling her to cross set gendered borders, he in fact interrupted her education at age fifteen (the age given in family records, rather than sixteen), in 1910, when mixed classes were introduced in Petah Tikva. This strict or cautious approach seems incongruous with other aspects of Yehuda's parenting style and general attitudes concerning gender.[24]

One of Raab's most striking passages is a description of the family's relationship with their neighbors, known as the "English family"—*ha-Englander*, a mix of Hebrew prefix and Yiddish adjective), attesting to the hybrid language environment in which Raab grew up. In this fragment, titled "Two

Suitors," which Raab did not intend for publication, she describes a habitual scene from age three. The Englander neighbors had two older boys:

> Frank's looks repelled me, but he played the violin outstandingly, and I loved the sound, and he noticed it immediately. He would give me a look and then shift his eyes to the violin case, and smile into his moustache. After that came the tea ceremony, English tea to the letter, with silverware and crystal clinking—and it captured my attention—and I would keep visiting.
>
> After Frank drew my heart with his melodies, he would pull me on his knees, and with one hand fatten me with sugared almonds and huge slabs of "cake"[25] that melted in the mouth, and with a second hand he would stroll under my short starched dress—I did not find it pleasant at all—but out of respect for his charming music I stayed still until the tea ceremony was over, and everyone rose and moved to the balcony. (11)

This sexual assault takes place in public, during tea, and passes unnoticed, or uncommented on by adults. No one attempts to stop the pedophile neighbor, stop his invasion of the three-year-old body, with all the inevitable damage, or even comment on his behavior. Oddly this same girl, whose body is forsaken so young in her neighbor's hands, will be forced to drop out of school to avoid simply attending mixed-gender classes.

The scene is difficult because the invasion of Raab's body takes place amidst the most proper social ceremony, with all decorum observed just so. British tea, as Raab describes it, will cloak abominable behavior as long as the china and cake are right. Elsewhere in her writing, sexual violence is overlooked in relation to adults. When a Palestinian housemaid is raped by a Palestinian coachman, the event is silenced in the Raab household and the victim "disappears" (37).

Strikingly the neighboring Englander home is the scene of yet another formative moment, and of Raab's first memory: her mother giving birth to her younger brother. It is notable that Raab frames this memory as her first, despite the alienation she describes in her relationship with her mother.

Raab's fragment "First Memory: Birth," written circa 1969, relates to the late 1890s and was first published in 1976 in the literary journal *Keshet*, and again in the collection *Gan she-harav*.[26] It opens with a view of the land-scape, its shades, contours, and scents. Anemones arouse the senses, and as Esther sits in her carriage her father's hands are described as pouring red anemones at her feet; he is from this very initial point depicted as molder of the landscape. The landscape description here evokes one of Raab's early poems, "Al ma'arumaikh hogeg yom lavan" (A White Day Celebrates upon Your Nudity). Here, too, a haze rises from the desiccated earth, forming a curtain. In the poem the land is constructed as an erotic female partner/mother figure. In the memoir fragment the father is linked with the sensual creation of space, confining the mother to the mysterious indoor bed. The possible lesbian eroticism that emerges from the poem is traded here for a relationship between the father and the landscape; both dote on the child and, in the opening paragraph, the mother becomes redundant.

Raab's narrating gaze gradually redirects from the wide expanse outdoors to the house, then the bedroom—to her parents' beds, her father's of simple iron and her mother's canopy-covered bed. Outside, in her own protected canopy of the carriage, she is with her father and the maternal earth. In-doors it is her mother who becomes the focus, but she is inaccessible to the baby who has by now grown into a little girl:

Mother in the canopy-covered bed lay in another world. The white trans-parent curtains swayed in the wind, and the bed was laden with mystery. In that bed my brother Elazar was born one night, with Mother writh-ing and letting out strange choked sounds, and me weeping and wailing from fear, I was shaking all over and in the middle of the night my father wrapped me in a blanket and took me to the Samuels, or the "Englander," as they were called, where the head of the family began singing Sabbath songs even though it was an ordinary weekday, just so that I would not hear Mother's yells—I was shaking with chill and fright. The older son began rolling on the rug, performing antics to distract me; logs burned in the English-style fireplace arranged neatly one on top of the other, and a shiny tool set leaned on the wall: huge silver-coated tongs that reflected the flame, and a poker, made of silver as well. Their gleam hurt my eyes;

I sank on the carpet in front of the fireplace—I sank in it, and felt as if I was sinking in a bath of warm water, and salty tears ran down my lips and I fell asleep.

I awoke to the sound of the swish of the bead curtain in the door across the hall that I liked to play with. Sunbeams crept over me—someone had picked me up and carried me home.

I stood before Mother's bed—she lay pale, the smell of carbolic acid (phenol) filled the room and made me nauseous—and, listless, she extended a thin arm toward me, as if in her sleep laid it on my head—next to her lay a pink creature and I was filled with rage toward him—was this worth hurting Mother so? (9–10)

The bodily symbiosis between daughter and mother here does not match Raab's descriptions of her mother's distance and lack of intimacy. The young girl is frightened by her mother's pain. The men are enlisted to distract her, preventing her from witnessing the birth. She does not clearly state that she knew her mother was giving birth until they reunite and she is introduced to the baby; however, the language points to her identification with the process. Describing herself as wrapped in a blanket and then sunk in the rug as if it were warm water, before the fire, Raab summons images connoting a preborn child in the womb. Raab too is born—into her first memory. The narration of the first memory and the entrance into narrative memory accept or define the division of roles between father and mother: he creates protective and sensual space and vision; she is mysterious and apart. Raab's identification and compassion bring her close to her mother, and enable her to direct her anger at the baby brother, rather than feel betrayed by the mother for having had him. The intimacy between mother and daughter is reinforced by the opposing settings—the fireplace tools with their blinding glint at the neighbors' house, versus the warm, caressing sun once she returns home.

I read this scene in light of another by a different author: Rachel Yanait Ben-Zvi's 1959 autobiographical narrative of immigration, *Anu olim* (We Immigrate, or Our Immigration).[27] Clear similarities exist between Raab's description of her mother giving birth and a description of a birth scene in the memoir by Yanait, a Ukrainian-born agronomist, educator, Zionist labor movement activist, and leading member of prestate military organizations in Palestine (also discussed in chapter 3). Unlike Raab, whose memoirs emerge from her life as a poet, Yanait is a public figure, and her memoir is part of her actions as such. Yanait's book documents her first years in Ottoman Palestine, to which she arrived in 1908, until the end of World War I, her meeting with the land through touring it, and her initiation into the local political institutions: Hashomer, the prestate military organization, and Poalei Zion, the Zionist socialist party. Her memoir does not follow her life into old age as Raab's does.

Like Raab, Yanait devoted attention to the Palestinian landscape, but despite being an agronomist and founding an agricultural boarding school, her narrative hardly touches on the Palestinian flora and fauna. She focuses on buildings, ancient and new, and the people she encounters. Yanait often writes in grandiose, pseudobiblical language and often uses the first person plural. Despite the clear differences in their poetics, a resemblance holds between Raab's first memory and Yanait's description of her younger sister's birth in Ukraine. A comparative reading of these birth scenes highlights the role of locality and nativism in Raab's writing and identity building.[28]

Describing a return visit to her hometown of Malyn in Ukraine, after she had already immigrated to Ottoman Palestine, Yanait mourns the decline of the hasidic court of Rabbi Gedalya of the Chernobyl line and recalls the following:

> The night the Rabbi "saved" my mother. A frightful night it was in our household. My mother was in labor and my sister and I—both still young—stood with our father and Aunt Gittl by the door of her room anticipating salvation. It was a difficult birth. Mother had been suffering in labor for two days . . . and it was already midnight. Father urgently called for the Polish doctor who lived on the outskirts of the town, and the doctor left Mother's room, and waving his hand in a gesture of despair, he said: "Only God can help."
>
> At the sound of the doctor's words my aunt Gittl sprang to her feet and cried: "Girls, hurry, hurry to the Rabbi to annul the decree! To Mother's

rescue!" And we run with our aunt in nightgowns twisting between our legs, we run crying to the court of the Rabbi. . . . Here he is, he raises his eyes to us, and we boldly clasp the rim of his robe with our shaking hands, sobbing in tears. Silently the Rabbi turns to our aunt and places his red kerchief in her outstretched hands. Amazed, we look at the handkerchief with the sense that the Rabbi is providing our mother with a proven remedy. And our aunt races back and we run with her as fast as our feet can carry us, and here we are at Mother's side, and our aunt wraps her face and head with the kerchief. Mother's face is wrought with pain, a cry of pain erupts from her mouth, and we weep too. At this moment we hear the sound of a baby's crying. . . . Our mother was in deadly danger, and she is still very weak, we do not move from her bedside. (255)

Here, too, the physical and emotional experience of the mother is shared by her daughters, even if they are too young to contain it. In both accounts the daughters cry with the mother, in both they are removed from the mother at a moment of crisis, but Yanait runs to bring her mother a mystic remedy, ultimately taking part in the birth, whereas Raab is removed for her apparent protection. Raab was younger than Yanait at the time, which may explain some of the differences, but it does not explain all of them. If in Raab's memory the Sabbath songs need a rational explanation—as noise to drown out the mother's screams, just as the neighbor's son's extravagant antics are meant to distract the daughter from her mother's pain and dangerous situation—in Yanait's narrative the seeking of the religious authority, and faith in the rabbi's power, has an immediate and direct effect, saving her mother's life.

Although Yanait sets this metarational experience in her hometown of Malyn, her meeting with Ottoman Palestine is also imbued with religion. Similarly the Jewish life cycle helps organize consciousness in Raab's early memories of Petah Tikva—but, contrastingly, the divine does not enter Raab's birth scene. In Yanait's worldview, that of the immigrant socialist settler, ostensibly secular, the divine occupies a place as central as the secular. On the other hand, Raab's family, who never clearly broke away from the

Orthodox circles from which they originated, produces a seemingly secular narrative, exhibiting how autobiographical discourse can often shuffle our fixed expectations.

In a passage written and also first published in 1952, "Paris or Jerusalem?," Raab recalls being summoned into the house by her mother, a scene that points to the broader strain in the mother-daughter relationship:

> I had just bathed Mitzi, my Angora cat, in soapy water, and her long hair clung to her skin, making her seem miniature, her small thin body shaking and chilled. I wrapped her in an old towel and placed her in the sun and sat down next to her.
>
> Gradually she began to purr and blink, and it seemed that she would fall asleep, when suddenly came the order: "Come!" When my mother gave an order, it was impossible to disobey her. Her hands were small and roughened by work, and when her palm was wedged between my shoulder blades, she could lead me in whichever direction she willed. And so she directed me, as she straightened the red ribbon in my hair, and cleaned the sand that clung to my bare feet, she pushed and led me straight into the "salon," where a mix of Yiddish, German, and Russian bubbled. Tourists, Zionist party activists from abroad, were regular visitors at our home (*Kol ha-proza*, 119).[29]

A stark difference exists between Esther's gentle and nurturing treatment of the delicate cat and her mother's harshness. The cat and the girl are analogous, only the former gets to laze in the sun and the latter must perform before guests; the former gets wrapped in a towel and the latter tugged and manipulated. Esther is ushered into a room filled with unfamiliar adult guests. She shakes the guests' hands mechanically as if she were buttoning her boots:

> But my heart was elsewhere. Now I knew just what I had to do. I had to do a "number"—I must entertain the guests, recite a poem or sing. . . . This time I chose to sing Psalm 121, "I will lift up mine eyes unto the mountains," which my Russian teacher had set to a rather difficult national Ukrainian tune; there were a lot of ascents and descents and one

had to really "perform" them. I had a smooth soprano voice, and I applied myself right to it, to faithfully fulfill my duty: I opened my mouth wide and innocently, as many girls do when they sing, and pronounced the words of the ancient text simply and with ease, but where other little girls would tire and run out of breath and end off with a hoarse pianissimo, I ascended to the high notes of the finale easily and ended with a clear loud tone.

A thunder of applause descended on me. I held my place like a duck in the rain stubbornly staring at my mother. I was waiting for the sign that I could be excused. But it was not given.

And Mitzi must have already left the towel to roll in the hot sand and collect straw and thistles in her long silky hair. . . . Suddenly two strange cold eyes appeared before me, and a hard voice addressed me:

"Tell me, my girl, where would you like to live, Paris or Jerusalem?"

Paris or Jerusalem?—I must answer immediately, I must do my duty —Paris? I'd never heard such a name. Different names raced through my mind: Rosh Pina, Zikhron, Rehovot, Gedera . . . Maybe it was an Arab village after Gedera?

I answered promptly: "Jerusalem!"

Immediately I saw in my mind's eye the small window in Grandmother's home in Jerusalem . . . and the mountains around—"I will lift up mine eyes unto the mountains . . . ," the words echoed in my ears— and suddenly I felt in the atmosphere around me that I had "hit the mark" and fulfilled my duty by all accounts, and without waiting for a sign I took one leap and another, and flew outside.

Years later, during one of the Zionist congresses, I was staying in the same hotel as the cold-eyed "iron man" [the Zionist leader Menachem Ussishkin, 1863–1941]. I sat in the lobby before a heap of envelopes and postcards, absorbed in writing home—suddenly those cold eyes appeared above me: "Writing home, eh?—I will lift up mine eyes unto the mountains . . . ?" (120)

As it turns out, Raab was rooted in her homeland, but she also traveled. In 1922 she moved to Cairo, following her husband's business endeavors.

Separately Yehuda Raab also mentions the Ussishkin episode in his memoir, *Ha-telem ha-rishon*, but his description differs somewhat from his daughter's, warranting a comparative reading. Yehuda died in 1948, and his memoir, as told to his son, was published nearly a decade later, four years after Esther's version of the event was written. We may, however, safely assume that she knew his version, and chose to omit the linguistic negotiation he emphasizes. As Adriana X. Tatum has shown, Esther's meeting with the "iron man" Ussishkin maps the horizons of the native child, who has never heard of Paris and whose world is defined by her front doorstep and her visits to her maternal grandmother in Jerusalem.[30] The native imagination is governed by these self-imposed limits—it does not travel beyond Gedera, and fails to imagine towns or settlements outside the Jewish or Palestinian context. The words of the sophisticated ancient psalm flow easily and naturally from her lips, even when they are matched with a tune supposedly foreign to them (chosen by the Russian teacher). The native child embodies sensuality and tenderness in caring for her cat, whose eyes, which she describes as "two green pearls," are juxtaposed with Ussishkin's judgmental eyes. Esther intuitively gives the right answer to the "Paris or Jerusalem" question because she is inherently a native, and so earns the license to flee the living room. Her "authenticity" is so striking that a prominent audience member recalls it years afterward, when, abroad, even at a Zionist congress, she still has not changed and is busy writing home. She is at once proud of her intuitive nativism and annoyed by the obligation to parade it before the foreign guests, but it is precisely their gaze that tests and frames her as a native. Nativism needs to be performed. Also noteworthy, although Raab's father was present in this scene, he is not mentioned in his daughter's version—the performance of nativism is orchestrated by her mother, who, in summoning her to appear, disengages Esther from her "native" activity—sitting in the sun with her cat. Whereas Esther positions her emotional map as a definer of her nativism, Yehuda places linguistic codes of the developing Palestinian Hebrew at the center of his depiction of Esther's confrontation with Ussishkin—who remains nameless in Esther's narrative. Ussishkin speaks Hebrew to the child Esther. His Hebrew is marked by his foreignness, and identifies him as being of the diaspora:

He turned in Hebrew to my daughter, Esther, who was then a child, "Where would you like to sit?" (that is—live). "In the eighth grade." "No, not that, where would you like to live? In the capital?" "You mean Jerusalem?" she asked. "No, here in Petah Tikva." Ussishkin was not satisfied with this and pursued: "I do not mean Jerusalem, but Paris. Would you like to travel to Paris?" "No, I want to be in the land of my fathers!" answered the child angrily. With all due respect to Ussishkin, I have not forgotten the test he put her to until today. Ussishkin, who was not very tactful, did not refrain from saying: "Those words were put in her mouth."[31]

The father's version, highlighting the politics of linguistic code, omits the daughter's thoughts on where Paris may be; instead the young girl knows and answers accordingly, with strong conviction. In the daughter's version ignorance "proves" nativism, which is characterized in the father's version as unshakable conscious devotion. Moreover, in the father's version, language's role in the construction of a grounded nationalism is clear. As Orly Lubin puts it in a different context, in her work on Ziona Rabau: "The Hebrew language became not only the declared public unifying glue but also the central national façade. . . . The otherness of the languages that threaten Hebrew exposes the true common denominator—the coming together of Jews/Judaism to form one (imagined) community which glosses other distinctions within it, through unifying around the Hebrew language."[32] Thus a recurrent memory invoked by Raab in her writing is her Petah Tikva kindergarten, and the teacher, about whom she says: "It was unknown if she had ever studied Hebrew—her Hebrew was dreadful: she used to sing a few Hebrew songs with us, and when she realized that I have a pretty voice, she said: "You songs so prettily!" [At mashira kol kakh yaffe]" (40). Raab's security within language and her familiarity with it thus mark her nativism.

Zionist locality here declares itself as authentic and true as opposed to Zionist leadership abroad. Ussishkin's dated, foreign Hebrew also marks the borders of his worldview. He uses the word sit instead of live or reside, he uses the term capital in reference to Paris rather than Jerusalem, and he dismisses the child's answer by casting her as a trained parrot. The response by Ussishkin to Esther in Yehuda Raab's version inversely highlights the creation of her devout and solid nativism, when set against Ussishkin's confident view that the child's words were rehearsed and therefore inauthentic.

In 1962 Shlomo Grodzensky (1904–1972) published a short essay in the journal *Amot*, which he edited, about relations between the State of Israel and Jews living outside it.[33] Israel, he postulated, had discarded something Jews in the world had: a sense of continuity. The Israeli-born generation did not see the importance of being Jewish, so Jews of the world might not see the importance of being Israeli, if continuity could not be preserved and maintained, as it always had been. Israel, claimed Grodzensky, had much to contribute to Jews outside it, but not if it ceased to nurture the cultural and communal links that had tied Jews to one another in previous generations.

Raab responded to the article in a letter published in *Amot*'s next issue. Grodzensky, she claimed, was writing as an "outsider," viewing the issues "objectively." She wanted to speak "from within and subjectively." The biographical fact that she is native-born permits Raab to disqualify Grodzensky's immigrant position—the *Amot* editor was born in Lithuania, immigrated to the United States as a child, and came to Mandatory Palestine in 1924—and legitimize her own. However, she does not state her position to be absolutely true and correct, given that Grodzensky's is described as "objective" whereas hers is a "subjective," overtly biased, and personal opinion. All the same she claims her exclusive validity as a native:

> I want to speak from within and subjectively. There is not a nation in the world that compares to the Israeli nation in terms of the mystery and the sense of deep, inscrutable layers that characterize its spirit, its fate, and its wondrous existence. We, Israelis who witnessed the first and second aliyot firsthand, we have a different perception; our views are from within, and more so, they are the essence of our being.
>
> Zionism is a belief imprinted in our ancient blood; Zionist religiosity —a commonsense concept to me and many others—was not a "necessity" for the Zionist generation as the emancipation was a necessity for the generation of the emancipation. Its origin was singular and different: the Zionist generation of the two first aliyot was a wave sent here by the deepest heart of the nation, moved by its own ancient mysteriousness.

The State of Israel is undoubtedly the essential, privileged, and exclusive product of the nation; it is the result of a prolonged process of thousands of years, and like the lava that accumulates deep in the earth, and breaks out in due time, such was the establishment of this state.

Different social circles are temporarily pecking at the nation. Furthermore, we do not ask permission for daring to be the heart of the nation; we are the heart of the nation, and if there are others who do not feel the organic quality of the foundation of the state, and say we are too daring, it seems to me that these are remote and stifled layers within the nation.[34]

According to Hamutal Tsamir, like many of Raab's supportive readers, Raab depicts the native as the polar opposite of a figure embodying conscious idealistic nationality.[35] But Raab does not speak exclusively of the native-born. Rather she constructs Israeli identity as a lived experience. She refers to the generation of the Zionists as those who were present at a certain time and witnessed certain events. Those who witnessed the first and second aliyot, who were part of formative events, are those who will accept Israel as inevitable. They are the heart of the nation. As Hannan Hever has claimed, nativism, or the positioning of the native as organic, natural, constant, and immobile—in binary opposition to a political and ideological system of nationalism—can allow the culture to overcome the lack of a natural, organic Jewish colonial presence in prestate Palestine and cast it as such.[36] In aspiring to portray Zionism as natural, organic, obvious, and eternal, Raab can conceal the newness, frailty, and instability of the settlement project. Her nativism can make Zionism a given.

Hever describes the native as inherently paradoxical and contradictory: on the one hand, the native claims ownership of the land through the eternal continuity of his or her existence, while on the other the native claims this ownership as a brand-new being who will invigorate and fertilize the land.[37] Hever views this very duality as a political mechanism to establish the Jewish settlement project as simultaneously new and eternal. This is why Raab objects to Grodzensky's privileging of world Jewry as having a voice equally valid to the Israeli voice. But Raab, it must be restated, clearly refers in her response to settlers—those physically present at the onset of Jewish settlement in prestate Palestine—whether native-born or not.

Raab's position clearly differs from that of Yoram Kaniuk, who ceaselessly tries to overwrite his born nativism with an immigrant identity and who views the native position as that of a victim of one's (his) parents, the immigrants, who do not permit him to inhabit their immigrant likeness.

Establishment of the State of Israel is imagined in Raab's writing as a natural, inevitable act. Grodzensky's essay counters that many or most Jews did not perceive Israel's establishment this way, and that "natives," or what he calls the "Zionist generation," did not acknowledge this different perception.

In her use of "pecking" Raab rather unsubtly critiques those outside the settler generation. Focusing on this critique allows one to probe the nation's "mysteriousness," "Zionist religiosity," and "deep, inscrutable layers," as imagined by Raab, and then to question the organic naturalness of the Israeli native, along with the native's construction and construal. Such a reading may frustrate the paradoxical polarity between mysteriousness, depth, organic being, and the nation's heart, on the one hand, and doubts, reservations, shadows, scrutiny, and distance, on the other.

Raab's nephew and estate executor, Ehud Ben-Ezer, quotes her comments on his own experience: "You are like all the young people. Your ties to the country are loose, even your Hebrew is not rich, it is seasoned with a lot of pepper, and some nervousness and the desire to shock, like all young people—I don't have all those characteristics, and I don't wish under any circumstances to be included in *such* a frame" (448).

Are nativism and being Israeli therefore generational markers? What is the difference between identifying as a native and as a child of immigrants? Why was Amos Oz, the dominant representative voice in Israeli literature since the 1960s, motivated to reinvent himself as a native by leaving Jerusalem for a kibbutz at age fifteen, despite having been born in Mandatory Palestine, whereas Kaniuk reinvented himself as German-born? Why is Nahalal, where Haim Be'er visits his uncle's farm on vacations, the "true" Israel, as opposed to the narrow streets of the Orthodox neighborhoods of West Jerusalem? What attributes enabled or compelled Raab to present herself as native that diminished after one generation?[38]

The role of Hebrew in the construction of nativism may further explain Raab's response to Grodzensky's essay. Grodzensky questioned whether the preference for Hebrew over Yiddish—with other outlier languages such as

Ladino or Arabic unconsidered—was not the act of a "Jewish movement for assimilation in a national form," even if it was "a valorized assimilation," and whether negation of the diaspora did not constitute upsetting the very ground on which the State of Israel stood. For Raab the essential adoption of Israeli Hebrew enables the dual position of nativism and national revival.

As commentators on Raab have noted, one cannot understand her nativism without considering gender. A representative intersection of these meanings appears in Raab's often-quoted prose piece about her initiation as a poet, "The *Hedim* Days"—with *Hedim* referring to a major journal publishing Hebrew modernist poetry in prestate Palestine. The journal ran between 1922 and 1930 and was edited by Asher Barash (1889–1952) and Ya'akov Rabinovitch (1875–1948), who had both immigrated to Ottoman Palestine as part of the Second Aliya, before World War I began. By the time Raab met these men, they had both established their dominant positions in Hebrew letters. The short piece connects the early days of emerging urban Tel Aviv in the early 1920s to the literary assemblage of modernists that Barash and Rabinovitch had assembled around the journal. Raab initially describes herself as an observer of this troupe. This is a significant and formative section, and I will therefore quote it at length:

> Lamdan—tall, thin, and mysterious; Shlonsky—flashing sparks and winds blow in his thick hair—anguished winds—and a rich, translated Russian spirit. And Shünberg: tall, thin, his head the size of a child's; smiling with his eyes half open, and the space between his two front teeth reminds one of traces of mother's milk which have not been wiped off his innocent lips—he comes from the [Jezreel] Valley, the overgrown child, dressed in work clothes. In summer his sleeves are rolled up above the elbow, and his beautiful long muscles play under the tanned skin. Of course he is the focal point that most attracts the eyes. The two old men, Barash and Rabinovitch, watch him admiringly: it seems the young man embodies all their forsaken desires—they dance around him and he laughs. The one feels his muscles; the second touches his faded shirt: a scent of physical labor, of health and new homeland terrains—they observe him, breathe him, swallow him bit by bit, and he stands and

squints and laughs. But he also writes poetry, understated, crystallized poems, which are a sketch of something to come, something that does indeed come later.

[. . .]

One spring day I took Rabinovitch and Barash for a stroll through blooming almond orchards—they were both cheerful, they prattled; something of the magic around clung to them until the boundaries were blurred and they seemed like friends despite their age. Jokingly I pulled a poem out of my pocket and gave it to Barash. He stopped, read it, and became very serious; his heavy black eyes rested on me, and in his confident shapely voice he decreed: "You must write."

From then on I, too, was included in the "gang." (317)[39]

The scene is laden with homoeroticism, of which Raab partakes; she joins Barash and Rabinovitch's admiration of Yitzhak Shünberg's physique. Shünberg is scrutinized but does not return the gaze; his eyes are half closed, and his mouth half open. He is a product of the fertile center of the Jewish settlement project—the Jezreel Valley. Shlonsky's physical description blends with his poetics—the despair and the Russian influence. He is a body of mood and cultural spirits, just as Yitzhak Lamdan's mystique blends his writing with his body. But Shünberg's description clarifies that he has yet to become a writer—mother's milk has not dried on his lips. He is still an object observed by the editors and by Raab herself. Shünberg's exposed body—his sleeves are rolled up, his muscles dancing—and the uninhibited way in which the older men surround and touch him turn him into their text ("but he also writes poems"); his body enlivens theirs, as they cannibalistically consume him. In his old shirt and scent of new frontiers, the mix of infantile and masculine physicality, dependence and eroticism, he encapsulates the paradoxical nature of "nativeness."

Barash and Rabinovitch's admiration and erotic attraction enable Raab to follow in Shünberg's footsteps. She turns herself into an object of seduction as well. Whereas Shünberg brings his physical enmeshment with the land to the poetic salon in Tel Aviv, infantilizing the older cultural authorities, Raab takes them out into the landscape itself. She thus avoids needing to represent the land with her own body, as the female body would conventionally do within Zionist culture. Just as Shünberg "also writes poems," Raab pulls a poem from her pocket. In the apocryphal Book of Susanna, two old men try to seduce the young married Susanna, and when she refuses them, they falsely accuse her of having an affair with a young man in her husband's orchard. At the last minute the prophet Daniel saves her from execution. The setting of Raab's poetic initiation provides a counternarrative echo to the Susanna story. Raab leads the two adoring men into a liminal area that is also a quintessential Zionist zone: an almond grove. The grove is significantly not of oranges, which came to symbolize the Zionist settlement project, but of the native almond, associated with and belonging to the land. It is in these surroundings—where Raab is at home and Barash and Rabinovitch are her guests, where cultural hierarchy is unsettled and the editors are not clearly her superiors—that she can be recognized as a poet.

Because Raab's memoirs were written in bits and pieces throughout her lifetime, formative events are often repeated at different points and from different perspectives. Like her father's memoirs, Raab's writings do not proceed beyond the 1930s. In the later 1970s, when Raab was in her eighties, she kept a diary entitled "The Hell Notebook," the entries of which were devoted to her hallucinatory present, slashed by clear visions of the past. The present-day sections describe delusions of reference and paranoia. Raab feared that gas, poison, and electric currents were being injected into her home and her body, and that she had contracted an incurable disease that the doctors refused to treat. The medical and nursing staff were named "the wardens," and cars passing in the street were perceived as part of a plot directed against her.

The threatening outdoors, once united with her body and her language, now belong to immigrants she fears; Shoah survivors, she is certain, are part of the conspiracy to gas and poison her. Raab's paranoia and psychotic thoughts need not be brushed aside as such. Their content is significant. Isolated, she faces her fears: "I never imagined such cruelty in people—after all, most of them suffered torture in the camps, perhaps it is revenge, an opportunity to unleash on someone else the poison that has accumulated in them—And the native-born? Simply fools I think—" (409). Within this painful narrative appears a struggle for clearness of mind and sanity, in a section titled "Present Time":

> I embrace my head and feel its bone structure; a lovely skull, shapely, graceful bones. My dear head! You who bestowed me with so many thoughts, who attached wings to my spirit—how beautiful and precious to me you are—I enclose you in both my palms and I am proud of you—you have produced something in me along the stretch of road named life.
>
> If I was asked if I wanted to be born again, I would answer yes, but just as I have been so far—I love myself, am at peace with myself, have done everything according to the data set and etched in my blood, in my soul, and in my body. I have not betrayed the mold that God created me in—and it was not as perfect, perhaps, as others'—it was mine, and I have completed the intent preserved in it by my creator—for better or worse.
>
> I look at my beautiful body: the long straight legs, the chest, the waist, the back—Thou created me beautiful, my Lord—have I not kept my soul within it abiding by your rules? I have tried to live elevated—but I have not always succeeded—a great deal of the fault rests on people around me, who pulled me downward. Now I must part with this body I love. Where will the soul go? This complete cluster of beauty? The love, the pity, the maternity, the pure tears, the spread of wings that I sometimes knew—can my soul spread its wings without a body?
>
> Will I see my dear ones? (408)

Raab's description of the perfect, complete mold in which God created her possibly echoes the famous opening to Rousseau's *Confessions*. Raab's corporeal perfection, alongside her being in language, may offer a key to her nativism. The beauty of the landscape, described in her complete works, is now harbored in her body. In "The Hell Notebook" the landscape outside her body has been lost to her. It is a hostile, dangerous space she dreads and fears. The body has so far enabled her to soar.[40] Without it, she may no longer be able to do so. The threat of imminent death reinforces the split between body and soul, a split powerfully challenged and rattled in Raab's poetry, along with all its ideological baggage.

Raab's expressed love and adoration for her body go back to her memory of her mother in labor and the anecdote in which she "punishes" her mother by striking herself. The mother's and the nation's beds are alike described as a mystery. "It is difficult to explain where the pleasure was derived from," she muses; it is difficult to explain belonging and not belonging to the mother's body (46).

Raab's descriptions of her childhood often relate to the scars inflicted on her brothers' and her own body by the many diseases they survived. Her father used to mock her sickly looks, nicknaming her *greener cloister* ("green nun," in Yiddish), and she views her adult beauty as a sort of "revenge." Her autoeroticism again reflects the father's physical self-admiration. Thus, while Raab's recognition of her own beauty counters her father's earlier deprecation, it also mimics his self-admiration before a female audience, an arrangement she possibly alters in her waning days by acting as the *subject* admiring her own self as *object*.

Netiva Ben-Yehuda: A Dead Woman Speaks for the Dead

At the heart of Ben-Yehuda's *1948—Bein ha-sefirot*, as Dan Miron has shown, is a detailed and revealing description of suffering from post-traumatic stress disorder.[41] As Yael Feldman has shown, the author's gender was central to her traumatic injury.[42] On February 22, 1948, Ben-Yehuda, then a nineteen-year-old officer in the Palmach camp at Ramot Naftali, led a group of just-drafted trainees, some new immigrants who did not understand Hebrew, to a field exercise. Not enough guns were available to go around, and most of the group had never held a firearm before. Although she disapproved of the site chosen for the exercise, fearing it was too isolated and remote, she had been bullied into using it by a male superior, and did not want to be pegged a female coward. Cornered in a ravine, the outnumbered group was attacked by a Palestinian force. The attack was in part a personal revenge act against Ben-Yehuda herself, who had recently been dominant in a deadly onslaught on a Palestinian bus, killing civilians and military personnel. Her gender and blonde hair made her easy to identify. She was nicknamed Shagra ("Yellow Demon") by Galilee Palestinians, who set a price on her head.

One of her troops, Dov Milstein, named Aharonchik in the book, was shot in the head. Given her poor tactical position, and under heavy fire, Ben-Yehuda decided to withdraw and leave the dying soldier in the field. Much of the book, which is cast explicitly as autobiography, is devoted to Ben-Yehuda's efforts to clear her name; justify her action; deny her peers' and superiors' allegations of failure, incompetence, and irresponsibility; and present her own experience as a young woman for the first time encountering combat, lethal danger, and death, including the loss of close friends. She describes Aharonchik's wound in detail:

> He had a big hole, huge, the size of a fist, in his head, on his forehead, above the left eye, and blood and splinters of broken bones, and tongues of light pink matter, the brain, burst out of this hole onto the face, onto the nose, onto the hands that were still gripping the gun, and the head was slumped over them, and there was a hole almost the same size at the back of the head, nearly reaching the shoulder, behind, and brain at the back, and the blood was streaming as if from a fountain, streaming and streaming down the back, on the neck, on the hand clutching the gun, and the legs were twisted awkwardly upward toward the sky.[43]

This description shows that Aharonchik lacked even the remotest chance of surviving—not with a fist-size hole in his head. Besides horror, the detail and repetition create an effect of precision and reliability. But Ben-Yehuda's focus on the destroyed body goes beyond the rhetoric of her self-defense, or she would not have repeated it when, returning with a British escort, she encountered the body again: "We saw Aharonchik's body through the burning twigs and understood what the smell was. And we began to clear away the twigs. The shining white was his undershirt. Only his undershirt was left on him. All his body was crushed, smashed, the skull fractured, cracked open. The ears, the eyes, the nose, the hands, everything was cut and crushed, and out of its place, evilly, viciously, the stomach was pummeled and scorched" (250).

Ben-Yehuda dwells on the mutilated corpse to make explicit that this death offers no symbolic escape. If in the previous quoted passage the image

of legs pointed toward the sky might suggest a polemic of justice, or an accusation of a divine force, here death occurs in material immediacy. It cannot
be cloaked with heroism, altruism, or any other national salve. It cannot be
handled with protective metaphors of significance, or an afterlife. Violent
death constitutes an immanence that cannot and must not be softened or
made easier to accept. In this sense Ben-Yehuda may be aligning herself with
women poets of her generation who, as Hannan Hever has shown, rejected
the dominant figure in the era's Hebrew poetry, that of the living-dead, and
insisted on the corporeality of death as a way of confronting rather than
camouflaging loss and war's price.[44]

Ben-Yehuda carried the vision of Aharonchik's body for more than thirty
years, when her account in 1948 was composed. Her detailed description
insists that the trauma is not long gone but rather a present horror that
her readers too must witness. For Ben-Yehuda combat crushes all common
sense. Her meetings with death, whether through losing close friends, trying to identify the bodies of soldiers unknown to her, killing people while
looking into their fear-filled eyes, or experiencing her own fear and helplessness in battle, all shatter her grasp on structured reality. Givens become
doubts, and nothing can be taken for "granted" any longer (136). She loses
track of time, and reason collapses. She questions what it means to eat, to
throw a party, to sing, to dress and match colors. Her gaping stare at the
world places everything in question, including by stamping the memory of
Aharonchik's body on her vision of her own, thus diffusing, it would seem,
the distinction between male and female.[45]

The specific female corporeal presence is likewise central in the construction of Ben-Yehuda's autobiographical voice. Early in October 1947 a
fellow officer tried to rape her as she slept. Awake, she knocked him down,
unconscious. As she recounts: "I button up fast, to call for help, but—no.
I can't! He's naked! What could I say? Who's going to help me? Hell, there
is no one" (207–8). While considering her steps, she overhears her male
peers, who assume she is sound asleep, talking about her. Ben-Yehuda had
just been selected to participate in an officers' training course for handling
explosives, a pick opposed by these peers. If a token woman was to be sent,
they wanted it to be "one of their own," meaning from their political party,

and they considered her "untalented, she can't lead, she's ruthlessly ambitious . . . a destructive element . . . cynical" (209).

The attempted rape and the overheard conversation are narrated in immediate sequence, creating a clear link and analogy. Both attacks remain secret: Ben-Yehuda never told anyone about the rape attempt and never confronted her peers with her knowledge of their conversation. But in her writing she directly reproaches them for the latter while blaming herself for the former. More specifically, in her autobiographical text she expresses her pain and mortification at being rejected by her peers but blames herself for the sexual assault. These linked episodes are emblematic of Ben-Yehuda's position within the Palmach as an outcast and near victim. Her gender is a disgrace to be concealed: "I was awfully scared that I was a kvetch, a sissy, because I am a woman, or because I am just snot" (87). Her very presence on the front lines marks her as an aberration of the natural order. In another overheard discussion she recalls: "I once heard . . . them laughing at me. One was saying to the other, I tell you, listen to me, once, when she raised her leg, in a sports exercise, her balls popped out" (274).

The body, weak, vulnerable, and ugly, is the focal point of the Palmach experience Ben-Yehuda paints. Along these lines, months of training and combat do not allow her to bathe often enough. Ben-Yehuda goes into great detail about the eczema and sores that developed on her body, as well as everyone's bodily smells, which at moments of crisis became offensive. It is unsurprising, then, that the two showers recounted in the book border on mystical cleansings. The body Ben-Yehuda depicts is not the young, vital, vigorous, beautiful body preserved of the Palmach soldier in national memory. Ben-Yehuda, from her marginalized and rejected position, employs this weak, irritated, malodorous body to criticize the Palmach, as well as the society that sent its members into combat.[46]

But the body does not figure only in miserable or disintegrating states, such as those of Aharonchik and Ben-Yehuda. It also appears, as in Raab's work, as perfection. Ben-Yehuda met Nino, the living-dead shell-shocked Palmach soldier who calls himself a *muselmann*, at the Tel Aviv café Kassit. Nino, she writes, is so good-looking. Unusually so. Rare. He looks like a movie actor . . . in short sleeves. In the middle of winter—in short sleeves. And that little muscle, the one opposite the tip of the elbow, in it I saw life itself. If I were a sculptor. If I ever become a sculptor. I would try to catch that. An arm, bent at the elbow, leaning on the table, supports the head, oh-so-heavy, with that cloud above, the black one, and the muscle opposite the elbow—alive. Full of life. Maybe that's what they meant in the Bible, "and his muscles were made firm." The name of the sculpture would be: Israel will not surrender. Maybe better still: The Hebrew man does not surrender. Will not surrender. The Hebrew. This is the best: A Hebrew. A Hebrew Youth. One of those Bialik wrote about in *Megilat ha-esh*. Those gorgeous ones that fall into the Black Sea. I could never understand what Bialik meant. How could I have understood. (338)[47]

In the scene at Kassit, Ben-Yehuda too is an object of observation. Nino practically "stares holes" in her back. But she returns the gaze. Nino's figure is compiled of elements borrowed from popular culture, from the Palmach aesthetic of physical fortitude (the short sleeves), from a neoclassical aesthetic, with its emphasis on balance, symmetry, and the ideal human form, and from the Hebrew canon: Jacob's testament to Joseph, which is misquoted here, and Bialik's *Megilat ha-esh*.[48] She imagines the referenced black cloud following not only Nino but also herself from the front line. It marks them both as having experienced combat.

The masculine body represents perfection in its beauty, self-sacrifice, vitality, heroism, and national continuity from the Bible until Bialik, the national poet. From her marginalized position Ben-Yehuda claims to have no way of understanding "what Bialik meant."[49] Yet she imagines how she might sculpt Nino. Her view of Nino accepts the eternal superiority of the masculine within a national context but at the same time grants her the vantage point to construct him—and allows her to cast herself as a subject regarding him. Nino is constructed as a subject that blends the body and the universal national. And, as she observes Nino, Ben-Yehuda herself becomes simultaneously an embodied and a universal national self.[50]

The night she spends with Nino, the sexual intercourse and intimate conversation they share, establishes momentary equality. Their exchange is that of lovers as well as peers in combat. They agree on everything, as if their experience were identical. Reciprocity and intimacy allow Ben-Yehuda to become a representative voice of her generation, just as the corporeal hideousness of war did. Ben-Yehuda's gaze at the masculine body, whether irreparably damaged or perfectly ideal, enables her to construct a feminine subject that can preserve its corporeality, join national discourse, and diffuse this discourse from within. The specific components of her voice reframe a national discourse that aspires to be unquestionably hermetic, monolithic, and whole, challenging its existing androcentric premises and, I would suggest, exposing its cracks.

Before they part Nino, who is convinced he will not survive, asks Ben-Yehuda to promise to write about the soldiers who die. She recounts this request in 1948: "If no one will write about us, exactly what happened, and how it happened, with all the shit and all the truth, it'll be like we died for nothing. This is the only thing I have left, that I care about, that it should not turn out that we died for nothing" (346). Ben-Yehuda fulfills her promise in the book, which is a memorial for her friends who died. Her autobiographical project vitalizes the memory of the casualties of 1948, and offers an alternative to the canonical *Gvilei esh* (Parchments of Fire), the commemorational war anthology published in 1953 by the Israeli Ministry of Defense.[51]

Ben-Yehuda was not the first woman to attempt to deandrocize the national narrative, or at least to renarrate it, allowing for a woman's perspective. In 1953 Anda Pinkerfeld Amir (1902–1981), who had edited *Gvilei esh*, published an epic poem about a mother and daughter, Ada and Rachel, which narrated the heroic sequence of Shoah, survival, escape, illegal immigration to Mandatory Palestine, enlistment in military Jewish efforts, and finally Rachel's death in battle in the Old City of Jerusalem and Ada's enlistment as a nurse to help those injured in combat, as a collective national mother. The poem was based closely on historical events. Pinkerfeld Amir retold the destruction of European Jewry, the Israeli War of Independence, and the founding of the state through heroines. Her narrative is a triumphant ode filled with pathos to the bravery and devotion of the women. It presents wholehearted identification with the national story. This sort of identification and lack of ambivalence and criticism are jumbled in Ben-Yehuda's writing. Rather than providing balanced poetry in meter, Ben-Yehuda, writing three decades later, produced undisciplined prose.

She challenges hegemonic memory and, in so doing, gains her representative voice by recounting the charms and weaknesses of many of her friends, along with the specific circumstances surrounding their death. In telling of others Ben-Yehuda gains what Nancy K. Miller has called "identity through alterity."[52] After Aharonchik's death Ben-Yehuda begs her Palmach superiors to let her version of events be heard. She is then denied this opportunity, but by recounting his death later, she ultimately prevails in telling her story.

Yehudit Kafri: From Splintered Vision to a Kaleidoscope

Yehudit Kafri is a curious case of critical neglect. She has published poetry and prose continuously since the late 1950s, but apart from passing comments, no critical attempt has been made to discuss her work. In 1995 Kafri published her autobiographical book, *Kol ha-kayitz halakhnu yehefim* (All Summer We Went Barefoot), about her childhood in Kibbutz Ein Ha-Horesh, a childhood described as "a kind of perpetual expulsion from Paradise."[53]

Kafri describes her earliest memories as being marked by sin, guilt, and punishment. As a newborn, she was separated from her parents and subsequently spent only a few hours a day with them. The child care worker (*metapelet*) at the children's house was responsible for her health, nourishment, physical growth, clothes, and education. Her parents had no right to intervene, nor did they seek to do so. She recollects her fears associated with sleeping in the children's house, with no adult nearby and no light to cut the pitch-blackness. She also remembers pining for dolls, of which there were just two in the playroom, to be shared among seven girls.

Indeed numerous sociological, psychological, historical, and literary studies, as well as personal writings, have been devoted to collective education in the kibbutz movement, and I will not presume to venture on this well-trodden path.[54] Rather I am interested in the way autobiography has served these authors as adults in confronting their childhood and in the body's place in constructing their opposition, and their formulated subjectivity, in friction with Israeli collectivity. Kafri, as well as Gertz and Zarchi, all relate to the confiscation and invasion of the child's body as an affront to subjectivity.

For Kafri an important such moment occurs in the context of her insistence, in early adolescence, on showering alone. Sarah, the kibbutz child care worker, forgets their agreement and sends a boy in to shower with her: "That feeling that he 'had seen' me, and that this can't be undone. I didn't tell her. I didn't dare to. I turned around. I turned my back, and hurried away. But it stayed. Inside. Like all the other things that cannot be erased. Even though you try your whole life" (92). Being "seen," just as she is enjoying the privacy of her shower, frustrates Kafri's budding attempts to recognize her sexuality, differentiate her bodily identity from that of the group, and construct a subjectivity stemming from both an embodied and a universal self. What she could not say as an adolescent, however, she can say as an adult. As she preserves and retells the moment, she critically turns it back toward the oppressive system and concepts of equal education.

Kol ha-kayitz consists of brief chapters, usually one or two pages long, arranged nonchronologically. The structure plays with the traditional autobiographical self, which is often described as complete, coherent, and unified, even if developed in relation to others. Whereas Ben-Yehuda skirts the convention of a linear progressive narrative by relying on spoken language —laying the ground for her circular repetitions and lengthy digressions in *1948*—Kafri devises a different solution: "For years I wanted to write about my childhood, and did not. . . . My memory did not preserve a sequential story—day after day, year after year. Only fragments of images. Until one day I said to myself: there is the answer! Put the fragments into writing. They will gel into a picture of their own accord. It may not be a complete picture, with many gaps, still—a few major lines will connect, some pieces of the mosaic will be put together, and finally, some sort of a bottom line might emerge" (unmarked page). The decision to relate a fractured story built from independent units and images offers narrative resolution for Kafri, but it also serves another purpose: that of challenging a solid, all-encompassing worldview from Kafri's childhood that left little room for doubts.

In a segment titled "On Truth and Pain" Kafri recalls a book of Chinese folktales that left a lasting imprint on her, one of which told of a girl whose mother had died. When the girl grew up, her father bought her a mirror and told her it was a magic instrument. Whenever she missed her mother, she could look into it and her mother would appear immediately. The girl was overjoyed. One day a wise man came to the family's remote village, and the girl showed him the treasured object that had preserved her mother's face. The man told her it was a mirror, showed her his own unlovely reflection in it, and continued on his way, after which the girl sank into an incurable depression. Kafri concludes:

> I was a little girl, but I already knew a lot about sorrow and truth. Truth was at the bottom of all the uncompromising, disconnected, semisense- less, absolute, tyrannical orders that guided our upbringing, and that we were too young to oppose. . . . That Chinese tale gave me license to be suspicious of the truth. And in the conflict between truth and pain and pity, it forbade the truth to dominate and destroy the little that was nec- essary for the continuation of life. Since then I know that sometimes one must lie in order to protect. And then the truth journeys inward, to the deep hidden zone where emotions and knowledge are fostered, and where poems are born (179).

It is therefore the very dissemination and deferral of absolute truth that enable Kafri's speech—that is, where poems are born.

In *Kol ha-kayitz* Kafri unearths the painful memories of being raised in a children's house on a kibbutz—modeled, as she discovers while writing, on a Prussian orphanage—intertwined with the sensual pleasures of a child- hood spent outdoors, in intimacy with the kibbutz's natural and agricultural landscape, the orange groves and the wildflowers, and with her own initi- ation into language and poetry. These various threads meet in the segment "About Truth and Pain," which casts the various richnesses of her upbringing against the rigid and often cruel, if well meaning, application of collective equal education. Kafri does not tell her parents until she has grown up that one child care worker whipped her with a leather belt.

Her worst memories, however, involve policing of the body. Forced sleep and force-feeding ("Yocheved stops my nose with her fingers. All of a sudden I can't breathe. Instinctively I open my mouth to breathe, and then she shoves in the spoonful of food" [63]); the detested dense black comb that the children call "Hitler" (38); the humiliation when the child care worker calls out, "There goes Yehudit again with that grimace of hers" (31). These are but a few of the instances in which the child's body is invaded and exposed in public, denying its owner's subjectivity. In one stinging section Kafri recalls how she fought Sarah the child care worker, squirming unsuccessfully to prevent her from taking her temperature anally, in the presence of older children not from her own group. The invasion instills control over the child's body. Kafri's autobiographical subject is constructed through the body. It is in explicitly telling and exposing the humiliation that she constructs her embodied subjectivity and begins to inch her way out of it. For a subject wrestling to free itself of an imposed essence, autobiographical narrative offers an initial step toward universal subjectivity. When the well-defined border between embodied and universal subjectivity is collapsed, the vulnerable, oppressed body, through the voice of the full-fledged author, conserves past injuries as it clearly challenges the social and ideological system that oppressed the author as a child. It is thus only in returning to her lowest moments that she can confront her upbringing.

Maintaining open wounds constitutes not only an emotional stand but a moral commitment. Scars of the past connect Kafri's perception of World War II and her personal meeting with Shoah survivors, as a child in Mandatory Palestine, to the present context in which she writes: the 1982 Lebanon war, with the Israel Defense Forces occupying Beirut.[55] As she tells of child survivors who came to the kibbutz after the war, Kafri wonders what children who witnessed the Sabra and Shatila massacre—carried out by Christian forces in a Palestinian refugee camp in Lebanon with tacit approval from Israeli authorities—will remember as adults.[56] The comparison sets off a despondent essay on murderousness and war. Although she raises the question regarding Palestinians, Kafri sustains ambivalence in her references to them. Brought up on a kibbutz under the Hashomer Hatza'ir movement, she probes the ambiguities in the proclaimed ideals of universal equality and brotherly love between nations as she exposes the deep fear of Arabs instilled in the children. All the same she does not hammer her points, instead making her case through subtlety. An Arab house amid the kibbutz orange groves stands "ruined but real, as if someone designed it to be a very accessible symbol of something" (99). Kafri does not define what that "something" is. Her autobiography is more concerned with maintaining her position of friction and conflict with the collective, be it her family, the kibbutz movement, or the national Israeli project, than with replacing their truths with alternatives of her own.

Nurith Gertz: Reconstruction of the Umbilical Cord

Nurith Gertz's *El ma she-namog* (Not from Here), written in collaboration with her mother, Deborah Gertz, challenges an array of concepts: motherhood, authorship and writing, autobiography and biography, memory and imagination, documentary prose and fiction.[57] As noted before, the background entails the Gertz family leaving Kibbutz Ein Ha-Horesh before Nurith's birth and moving to Jerusalem.[58] A second pivotal event is the family's decision to return Nurith to the kibbutz, alone, as a young girl.

The story is ostensibly that of Deborah/Dora, a biology teacher born in Poland who completed her doctorate in agriculture in Italy and immigrated to Mandatory Palestine in 1933, but the voice that narrates and selects, as it quotes the subject's letters and diaries, is Nurith's. Generically the book is a hybrid: a romance that tells of Dora's succession of lovers, dwelling especially on the jilted Lotek; a pioneering narrative about early Zionist settlement in Mandatory Palestine; a post-Shoah memoir about Jewish life in Poland; a mother-daughter narrative; a poststructuralist critique of Zionism. Writing Deborah's life is first presented as a rescue mission that the daughter undertakes to help her mother:

In May 1993, when she turned eighty-seven years old, she got fired. Until that day she had been an editor of a children's science magazine. Every morning she would get up, get dressed, go to the university, sit in her office for four or five hours, and work. When she was fired, we were worried she would decide she'd had enough of life and we suggested she start writing memoirs. What are memoirs? All the stories that for years we had lent half an ear to, that always began like this: "Have I already told you the story about Alessandro (or about Lotek, or about Grandmother Matel's restaurant . . .)?" The answer to that was always "Yes, mother, maybe a thousand times" and the persistent sequence was: "Well, Alessandro would sit with me in the garden, by the well . . ." Now she took it upon herself to sit every morning, and, like Scheherazade, to write all these stories. A chapter a day (14).

Even as the daughter sets up this rescue effort, she rejects and belittles the project. In fact, both daughter and mother are apprehensive about it. The daughter declares a lack of interest in the stories she has heard "maybe a thousand times" but never truly listened to. On the other hand, as she puts it, she cherishes these early memories of mother-daughter intimacy: "These memories from Italy . . . were part of my childhood memories. The Italian student songs mingled with the Russian lullabies I grew up on and Alessandro de Philipes [her mother's classmate at the Italian university she attended] would appear after a few Volga songs, and after all the Yiddish songs. "Tell me about Alessandro now." These stories unfold, one by one in a . . . schoolgirl's notebook, in a style that perhaps demands editing, but does not receive any" (15).

Even in light of the daughter's expressed affinity with this content, which she reputes to have transmitted unfiltered, the memoir's therapeutic value is dubious, at least for Dora. In particular the story compels Dora to revisit a pivotal choice she made as a young woman, to abandon Lotek, her passionate lover in Poland, and link up with Aharonchik, Nurith's father, in what settled into a strained and unrewarding relationship. In recalling Dora translating, from Polish to Hebrew, Lotek's letters to her from the 1930s, Nurith comments: "The last letters are the most difficult. She has to be forced to translate them, and in her diary . . . it says: '. . . This breaks my heart. I've already lived through this. How can I live it again'" (61); "'Why have you sentenced me to live through this twice'" (31).

Likewise it is unclear if the journey to Poland that concludes the story is undertaken in answer to the unstated wishes of the mother, or those of the daughter. Nurith quotes Dora: "'What an antisemitic country that was, Poland, I wouldn't go there even if you killed me. I have no longing for that country'" [. . .] After a few months of these conversations I said to her: 'Alright, Ma. We'll go to Poland.' And it felt right. Why not?" (104). However, upon their arrival, Dora's position becomes clear: "Mother didn't want to go to Poland. But now we are here, and she is in a real state of hysteria. . . . You can tell she's come home" (128). Among other things, these lines leave unclear who exactly is playing the role of "Yiddishe Mama," who will relinquish her own wishes in favor of those of the other.

This dual ownership of story, of memory and of its retelling, constitutes the underlying tension in *El ma she namog*: that of authorship and birth, of unification and differentiation, of ties and severance between mother and daughter. As Nancy K. Miller has observed, telling the life of a parent is an opportunity to recreate the one who created you.[59] Miller, however, was reading memoirs of sons and daughters of deceased parents. *El ma she-namog* is an attempt to hold on to life, or perhaps a daughter's attempt to charm her mother into the desire to live. The mother's voice reverberates in it, and the text becomes an arena of unresolved struggles. Deborah/Dora's presence is so powerful that it nearly suppresses Nurith's own motherhood.[60] Dora's return to the world of her childhood marginalizes her daughters, Nurith and her older sister, Dalit. She substitutes Polish for Hebrew, and beg as they may, her daughters are not granted a translation of her conversations until they have returned from Poland, watching the video documenting the trip. The voyage into the past threatens the daughters' position in their mother's life. It questions her identity as exclusively a mother, both in her daughter's story and in her own. She emerges as having a multifarious identity, a distinct existence, and numerous relations, the most significant of which seems to be that with her own parents, who had lived in Tel Mond and with whom she wants to be buried. Again this tie has a corporeal manifestation, as shown in Nurith's quote from Dora's diary: "Only when my mother died did I feel the umbilical cord that tied us to each other had actually severed. Until then I did not know how much I had been tied to her biologically" (164).

This comment illuminates the whole project as an operation to reconstruct the umbilical cord connecting Dora to her daughter Nurith, Dora to her mother, Nurith to her grandmother and her great-grandmother. The book serves as a verbal manifestation of the cord, or as a narrative in search of the complexities and dynamics underlying the mother-daughter relationship. Their mutual and separate memories meet in the joint search for the mother's past, which is, by extension, the daughter's past. Dora's relation to her own mother, Matel, validates her connection to Nurith.

It might seem that the sequence in *El ma she-namog* could fuse into a processed, conscious, and unbreakable verbal umbilical cord, but it does not. *El ma she-namog* is a book consumed by longing for mothers. Nurith's maternal grandfather, Zvi Zevulun Weinberg, was abandoned by his father as a child, and his mother sent him, along with his younger brother, to live with their grandfather, who refused to accept them, leading to their placement in foster care. When he finally returned to his mother, "and she smothered him with embraces and tears and kisses, he did not feel happiness or love. Only longing. And humiliation" (109).

On their visit to Poland, searching for Dora's childhood home, they are guided through the town of Sovalki by Nahum Edelson, the last Jew left in the place. He too misses his mother: "His mother died and he fell into depression. He had nothing left. She was the closest person to him. Edelson's eyes are teary. He is seventy years old. Cannot eat (cancer, my mother says), leaves us every few minutes (prostate trouble, my mother guesses) alone in a town of goyim, an orphan" (111). Dora's parenthetical commentary curbs the pathos of Edelson's words. Less important than the content of her comments—they obviously carry no relief—is that Nurith can more easily face Edelson's bereavement supported by her mother. Armed with her mother's interpretation, she can handle the fear of becoming an orphan herself.

Dora's presence cannot be taken for granted. This is in part because at the core of the book's longing for mothers, living and dead, lies a sense of betrayal, and an unappeasable rage. These sentiments are linked to Nurith's childhood move to a kibbutz, for which Dora offers two possible explanations: "because there was a war going on (explanation A) and also because my mother worked at two jobs, in the morning and in the evening [she was an editor as well as a teacher] and it was difficult for her (explanation B). And the explanations vary according to need."[61]

> For years I thought that anyone who lived on a kibbutz could only die from a bullet in the heart. "Eternity in a fleeting moment," it said in *Kehiliyatenu* [a group diary produced in 1922 by the founders of Kibbutz Beit Alfa, who belonged to Hashomer Hatza'ir]. I too evidently rose to life in the kibbutz. According to my mother I was one year old, and did not want to eat, and so they sent me to the kibbutz. There, in the kibbutz, on the spacious lawn, opposite the children's house, in the shade of the weeping willows, among the red geraniums, I was left alone in a crib, with no food and no water for twenty-four hours. No one in the family was allowed to approach me. That was the system. After a day and a night, when I had almost collapsed from crying and fatigue, I began to eat. It worked (90).

This episode links Nurith's personal story with the Zionist socialist pioneering narrative. Pioneer values esteem a death if it takes place in violent and national circumstances. Vulnerability of body or soul, let alone that of babies, does not fit the national circle, especially one that venerates youth and its spirit of extremes, as did *Kehiliyatenu*. Nurith's narrative suggests that the ideals adopted by Hashomer Hatza'ir in manifestos such as *Kehiliyatenu* enabled group behavior that endangered the society's vulnerable members, and permitted severe parental betrayal. The attractiveness of this text, accepted as an inspiration in kibbutz life (as Nurith quotes: "Eternity in a fleeting moment," a line glorifying violent death), as well as the agreeable kibbutz landscape, which Nurith cannot possibly remember from infancy—weeping willows, spacious lawns, red geraniums—only magnify the event's grimness.

Dora is the source of this information, and she offers, as we saw, varying explanations for sending Nurith to the kibbutz. These different versions indicate the absence of one true and correct story that one might grasp, attack, or seek comfort in. The same holds for Dora and Aharonchik's initial decision to leave the kibbutz, with possibilities including his case of malaria; her desire to separate him from his lover; his preference to be a manager as opposed to working in the fields; or her possible tiring of socialism or attempts at agriculture. Over and over again, the evasiveness of a solid, comprehensive, and reconstructible truth is raised as the journey continues into the past. The multiple versions question the value of pursuing a bare single truth, or where it might be found, and this multiplicity is what interests Nurith, more than the isolating of a truth. The absence of a single truth has an impact that exceeds family relations, casting light as well on the broader role of the collective.

Against this vagueness Nurith, in her preface, presents *El ma she-namog* as a book documenting only known facts:

> This book is compiled in fact from three books, and maybe more. The first is a book about a ruined Arab house, in the hills near Motza. Once I went in. In distant childhood, maybe earlier than that, and recently I rediscovered it. I had thought that should I ever write a book it would be about the people who had lived in that house, and about what had happened to them. But since I do not know anything about the people who lived in that house, the book did not get written. (9)

The implication here is that everything that did get written in the book has been verified and corroborated. Multiple documents, letters, and oral testimonies quoted in the text support this assumption. But the ruined house does not disappear. Its image becomes a key motif, and is part of the mother-daughter journey from its early stages, when the two travel to Ein Ha-Horesh to meet the people with whom Dora began her life in Mandatory Palestine: "We are trying to reach the Ein Ha-Horesh of January 1933, the mud and the swamps. On the way we stop by the palm tree, in the wadi, there stands the stone house, with its arch, the ruined garden, a few early anemones and rain. And every time that same feeling: I've been here before. This is a familiar place. Maybe during the Mandate. Before childhood memories began" (29).

The house flickers all through the book, but the image crystallizes only at the end. Meanwhile the book's commitment to documentation has been uncertain all along, but it is only when Dora and her daughters, Nurith and her sister, Dalit—who has joined them—reach Ostrov Mazovietski, Grandmother Matel's hometown, that the story shakes itself free of this demand. As their journey nears its end, Dora and her daughters search for the grave of Rabbi Wolfe Ber, Matel's father. His house is gone, even as some of the Jewish graveyard remains, but the search for it provides Nurith with a vision:

> Between the red roofs, on the brick road of Ostrov Mazovietski, I can finally see Rabbi Wolfe's wooden house, from the end of the previous century. . . . And Matel's mother is making jam out of the blueberries she picked with her brothers in the woods. "Come in, come in," I can hear that mother, her voice seductive, sweet. She calls me. No. I do not come yet. But if I did enter that house, I might find a kind of oval china plate hanging above the chest-of-drawers, and on it a picture of a wadi, and beyond it, how wonderful: a palm tree, a few prickly pear bushes, and a ruin with an arched roof. That plate hung on Rabbi Wolfe Ber's wall to remind him of where he should be bound. . . . [Matel] would sit there for hours and look at it, and slowly enter into it, cross the riverbed, go into the ruined house, light the fire in the clay oven, and go out in the garden to pick pomegranates for her mother, who was ill, and they said the fruit of Eretz Yisrael could save her. So I came all the way to Ostrov to find out that I remember the house in the riverbed from there: from Rabbi Wolfe Ber's house. From my grandmother's longings (169).

Gertz here intertwines Zionist longings for a land supposedly ruined and deserted, one that will heal diaspora ailments, with her own Zionist existence in the place where Zionism has now practically succeeded in erasing a previous community. National aspirations blend with private dreams: Matel imagines healing her mother with the fruit of Eretz Yisrael, which grows on a tree planted by an unrecognized Other. Rabbi Wolfe Ber's plate, with the traditional image signifying love of Zion, preserves Zion in its ruins as an aesthetic, emotional, and ideological stance. Nurith, his great-granddaughter, links her present-day existence as an Israeli to this untouchable past, which has a concrete but largely unacknowledged presence in the Israeli landscape, through her grandmother's imagination. However, unlike the materially present Palestinian ruin, Rabbi Wolfe Ber's home can only be summoned in Nurith's mind.[62] It is a missing past, or postmemory, that she draws from the image on the plate, serving as a kind of time-traveling photograph, an "'umbilical' connection to life."[63]

Ruth Ginsburg has observed a dichotomy in Hebrew literature, naming it the "paradox of motherhood," between the monstrous, sexual mother and the silent, asexual, self-sacrificing mother.[64] At first reading Dora and Matel seem to represent opposing ends of this split. But if Matel and Nurith are permitted authorship and imagination, and if the limits of the fictional and the documentary are challenged—along with the strict divisions between biography and autobiography, biography and fiction, diary and memoir, dreams and wakefulness—perhaps the two poles of the "motherhood paradox" can be dissolved as well. Perhaps Dora can be permitted a story; perhaps the absent, silent mother, who sacrifices all for her children, can meet the creative, sexual, present monster, who threatens to annihilate her children.

Here the daughter who writes is reborn, and gives birth to her mother, her grandmother, and her great-grandmother. This inversion of the familial story allows for a revision in the national story. If the binary opposition that defines women in Hebrew literature is upset, women's place in the national discourse can be renegotiated. Women can inch their way out of the silent symbolic place they occupied as embodied subjects in formative canonical texts such as *Kehiliyatenu*. Retold as it is here, the Zionist story allows these formerly silenced voices to be heard as individual and as representative, universal subjects. The embodied mother-daughter story of reconstructing the umbilical cord becomes a national, representative, and universal story. Both family and nation are strewn with questions and gaps, allowing for the emergence of a subversive narrative that permits marginal voices to be heard.

Nurit Zarchi: Cartesian Being and the Management of Pain

At the end of her autobiographical book, *Mishakey bdidut* (Games of Lone-liness), Nurit Zarchi questions her own motivation by asking: "Is there any other way for a person to envision a second chance?" For Zarchi autobi-ography is an attempt "to grasp the moment before it all began, the white moment in which it was as if there still could have been another life" (116). In this book a second chance materializes when a second person emerges as a witness to the autobiographer. This Other's look corroborates Zarchi's vision.

As we saw with Yehudit Kafri, Zarchi's upbringing was marked by the kibbutz mind-set. Zarchi too suffered under an insensitive, and sometimes cruel, child care system: "One of the child care workers hit me . . . intense, hard blows, until once, when the water supply was disconnected and we went to eat in the teenagers' dining room, another worker who witnessed an incident stopped her by threatening to expose her at a kibbutz meeting."[65]

Zarchi recounts two occasions on which she returned as an adult to visit Kibbutz Geva, where she grew up starting at age five: "Both times to permit someone who I wanted, and he agreed, to glimpse back into my childhood, and maybe in his presence to confront it myself" (111). But even this witness cannot help her touch the distant girl that was she. However, in writing she casts us, her readers, as witnesses to that girl's existence, and our retrospec-tive vision of her can perhaps provide a second chance. This construction shows how autobiography allows the Other to be me, and extracts Zarchi from otherness.

Stylistically Zarchi's narrative is characterized by perspective, shadows, darkness, light, and fields of vision. Memory has a visual quality, constitut-ing what eternally flickers in and out of sight. Her vision rests on literary and mythological scaffoldings. Like many other autobiographers, her iden-tity as a reader guides her on the path to memory. If she hadn't read Proust, she claims, she would not have remembered her early childhood home. She quotes the French writer Colette to describe her own mother, and has re-peated meetings with the monstrous mythical dog Cerberus.

Zarchi's prose often borders on poetry, her images expanding and inter-rupting the narrative's direct linear development. Along with her mother and younger sister, she arrives wearing a black mourning dress at the kib-butz, where her mother found work as a teacher following her father's death. This arrival, in 1947, is conceived as the end of a secular pilgrimage, the eucalyptus trees lining the road arching over them like a church vault. En-capsulating her role as pilgrim is Zarchi's revelatory declaration: "At the kibbutz I arrive at the land of the denial of the I. If you don't exist, you don't feel pain is the slogan etched wordlessly across the horizon.[66] I decide to be reborn, a proud and selfless birth in Emek Yizrael [the Jezreel Valley], and in this way I try to exist without taking my self, and my non-self, into account" (27). As she twists the Cartesian dictum, she slits a crack onto the kibbutz worldview. Deference to the collective in order to protect the "I" is read in very personal, utilitarian terms. Rather than being an adoption of altruism, it is a form of survival.

As an adult Zarchi reflects on her childhood kibbutz partly as the out-sider who would pay any price to be accepted, partly as an anthropologist studying a remote society. The kibbutz is referred to as "an order" and "a tribe." "To an outsider," she writes, "[kibbutz society] may seem like Chinese society, whose class structure is difficult to read. But to the locals it is like Indian society, where it is crystal clear that there is no way to change caste, and who may be considered a pariah" (31). Testifying to the system's rigidity, Zarchi's mother joined the kibbutz but remained a second-class member. The family lived on the kibbutz outskirts, in a wooden structure called a "Swedish hut" where other marginal residents were housed. Yet liminality offered Zarchi a vantage point for observation, and common ground with other marginal members, such as the future poet Dahlia Ravikovitch, whose mother also moved to Kibbutz Geva after being widowed. Ravikovitch, older by five years, offered her collection of art postcards to Zarchi, who even-tually began collecting postcards herself. In the text, meeting Ravikovitch and accepting her guidance signal not only Zarchi's particular welcome to the kibbutz but also her anointment into the art world by a future luminary.

Zarchi never joined the kibbutz for various reasons, and her feelings of rejection parallel a sense of early betrayal by her mother, who openly favored her younger sister and was generally unsupportive of Nurit. (As a young child, Nurit had been close to her father.) As in Gertz's narrative, the violence and alienation experienced on the kibbutz echo the mother's rejection. Zarchi writes of her communication with her mother this way: "In the language of my childhood, the water of life and the poisoned water are one and the same" (53). While kibbutz custom held that children spend afternoon until bedtime with their parents, Zarchi avoided this family "quality time," instead walking the kibbutz paths and going to bed on her own. Her sense of impending abandonment is intensified by her mother's suitors:

> I wander by myself along the pathways of the kibbutz while the others go to their parents' rooms. I cannot join Mother. I'm sure she's going to leave me; I know in my heart that I'm leaving her (51).[67]

> Being a social misfit demands a price in the kibbutz: I wasn't even insulted when at the kibbutz meeting it was decided not to approve my application to take the matriculation exams because it was evident from my character and lifestyle that I would not take part in the construction of the country. I wasn't even curious about who it was who had intervened in my favor (109).

As in the other autobiographies read here, the body appears on the one hand to sustain the opposition between the individual and the collective, and between women and nationality, and on the other hand to serve as an instrument of policing the individual by the collective. When Zarchi's mother is away, for example, and she has a boyfriend spend the night in her mother's room, the education committee representative appears at their door the next day: "They were heard," he says to Mother, "one can hear through the walls, you know, what she did with him could be heard" (92–93).

Repeatedly the author seeks to shed her otherness, but these attempts end up laying bare the Other's ferocity. Constrained by her embodied subjectivity, she also invariably tests its limits. In one instance she somehow loses her only pair of shoes—on the traditional kibbutz clothing was collectively owned and distributed—and needs to have them replaced. Afterward, she explains:

> Everyone's sure that I did it on purpose, like the time when I was a little older and the barber from Afula trimmed my hair down to the skull. When I stood at the entrance to the dining hall, the people sitting down froze in astonishment; their eyes followed me as I sat at an empty place at the table, while I tried to pile food on my plate from a serving platter, and to shove it into my mouth.
>
> Though I nearly wanted to die because my ears stuck out, I was considered a rebel in the classic spirit of the kibbutz. Like Madame de Pompadour at the court of Louis XV, but in reverse. I am compelled to become the Other. Who is that? I think of myself as absent islands swept away into an absent sea, while the Other, in contrast to me, is a continuous presence. In order to revive and be saved from nonexistence, I pass a hand over the flame of the Sabbath candle, lingering longer than is feasible. I bite my hand in secret to see whether I feel alive. Meanwhile I observe the faces of the others in order to mimic good behavior. I am the one always making an effort to act according to the rules, while time after time a dark and mysterious factor surfaces and ruins my plans (46).[68]

Here Zarchi has no public voice but only bodily demonstration. She has demonstratively had her hair cut too short. All the same, in narrating an embodied subjectivity experienced as an absence of self, she positions her readers at a point of critical observation. And this observation, or gaze, has the power to redeem her as universally subjective. Because autobiography dissolves the split between observer and observed, allowing the reader to occupy the writer's position, Zarchi can be transformed into a subject— a self—through the act of writing.

What Zarchi describes as her "Copernican revolution" is the discovery of being wanted: of "warmth, affection, attraction, an emotional focus that was not Mother, but the boys from agricultural training, the older boys at school, that someone would want and seek me out" (91). Whereas being a passive object of desire is typically seen to entail lost subjectivity, Zarchi counters this notion through an actively constructed subjectivity based on mutual affection and attraction. In their puritanical adolescence the kibbutz boys and Zarchi are too shy to meet each other's eyes; they avoid physical contact "like a hot iron" (92). Zarchi finds that the timid, desiring gaze of which she becomes a focus does not cancel her being but instead permits it. In other words, she becomes a presence by being desired, and mutuality prevents desire from obliterating her, rendering her an object.[69] Shared desire allows Zarchi to control her story, as the autobiographical narrative itself does.

Prophets and Hedgehogs

RATHER THAN RECAPITULATE my claims in this concluding chapter, I will present a condensed reading of an autobiographical sketch by Ariel Hirschfeld. "Bat kol" (literally: small voice, daughter of a voice, divine voice), a passage from Hirschfeld's *Rishumim shel hitgalut* (Notes on Epiphany), encapsulates the vital presence of contemporary autobiography in Israeli culture.[1] In the following discussion I will cast this passage as representative of my broader view of contemporary Israeli autobiography. "Bat kol" itself depicts an intimate family scene that draws on classic and modern canonical Hebrew texts, as well as on popular Hebrew children's literature, to articulate the broader contexts of Israeli culture, theology, and self-definition. Hirschfeld effectively weaves his narrative from these antecedent texts, which in turn merge with his own.

As we have seen in the works already discussed, autobiographical memory, while individual and personal, is also cultural, literary, and textual. Intertextuality functions in these works as a marker of how narrated lives are saturated by, and grow from, previously narrated lives and texts of varying registers and genres. "Bat kol" is representative of Israeli autobiography, and of autobiography in general, in that it maintains a continuous exchange with memory, personal and collective, intimate and cultural, textual and generic. This exchange has been constructively described by Paul John Eakin, following André Aciman's autobiographical essay, as "mnemonic arbitrage."[2] The financial metaphor for the reflection upon writing memory relates not simply to the past but also to the conscious act of narrating it, "remembering remembering."[3] The traffic of exchange of stocks between markets, with profits sometimes derived from the difference in rates, is applied to the relations between past and narrative present. For Eakin the moment of memory and its identification as such is a moment of epiphany. In Hirschfeld's memoir intertextuality creates such a "mnemonic arbitrage"; the meeting of ancient and new texts holds the "mnemonic exchange" that enables epiphany.

"Bat kol" combines three periods: the narrative present (2005–2006, when the memoir is compiled), the past moment of revelation (1988), and a still earlier moment from Hirschfeld's own childhood, of which he is reminded while watching his son. Alongside this mnemonic exchange, the texts intertwined in the passage add another level of literary and cultural arbitrage, each expanding the revelation from a personal experience to a potentially collective one. This movement, as I have shown throughout this book, is characteristic of Israeli autobiographical writing, in which allusion to other texts both fashions a narrativized remembrance and turns our attention to the craft being plied.

Rishumim is a book framed by mourning. It was written shortly after the death of the author's wife, the novelist, critic, and inspirational teacher Batya Gur. This recent loss meets an earlier one, with which the book also opens: the death during the 1948 war of Ezra Hirschfeld, the author's older brother, when he was eighteen years old, five years before Ariel was born. *Rishumim* opens with a reflection on the construction of the author's self as an offshoot of his lost brother: "Had he not died, I would not be, therefore my very existence is not secure, but rests on death, floats on nonexistence" (15). This threatening "nonexistence" has an opposite meaning in "Bat kol," in which the capacity for willed self-erasure functions as a trigger or gate to revelation—the ability to forget one's own existence both enables and embodies revelation itself.

The opening page of *Rishumim* describes the portrait of Ezra Hirschfeld that hung above his infant brother's cradle. The older brother's death in the war had prompted the birth of the younger. And though Ariel did not get to know Ezra in life, he grew under his smiling gaze. This very personal loss suffered by the Hirschfeld family had grave effects on the author's identity formation. However, the national circumstances that underpin his older brother's death prevent it from being exclusively private, thus framing the memoir in relation to both spheres—the public and the private, the individual and the national—inseparably and at once. The individual-universal voice clearly represents the national, just as the national is the plain on which individual Israeli identities are inscribed, and can formulate themselves.[4]

Rishumim, as its title makes clear, is not a linear narrative (*rishumim* literally denotes sketches but can also refer to "impressions," a connotation that carries a distinct individual perspective, not tied down to "objective facts"). The book consists of short units. The unit in focus here, "Bat kol," is subtitled "A Page from a Diary, Abu Tor, Saturday Night, June 1988." Both title and subtitle unfold an array of cultural contexts: *bat kol* traditionally signifies an intervention of the divine; the subtitle's specified temporal setting, Saturday night, situates the revelation clearly within the Jewish time cycle, with *motzei Shabbat* being the border that separates the holy from the mundane. Just as *bat kol* is a link between the divine and the earthly, so Saturday night is a liminal time of return to the secular—although not traditionally an obvious time of potential revelation, in the way that Friday evening, or twilight as the Sabbath sets in, would be. The Jerusalem neighborhood of Abu Tor likewise represents a meeting of limits. Two neighborhoods in effect share the name: on the Western slope is an affluent Jewish neighborhood, on the eastern slope a deprived Palestinian one. The latter, conquered in 1967, has been annexed to Jewish Jerusalem, but its inhabitants never received full civil rights, and their municipal residential rights are neglected.

Yet another border invoked by the subtitle is the generic one between memoir and diary. The piece is introduced as a diary fragment, suggesting that it is a personal narrative that follows events as they take place, and which lacks the retrospection and hindsight that distinguish autobiography. This fragment is described moreover as "a page from a diary," that is, as a fragment of a whole that will not be exposed to us. The reference to the date complicates matters further, considering that June 1988 precedes the book's compilation in 2005–2006. This time difference is marked within the fragment itself, a gesture that suggests the diary entry has not been quoted without certain changes being made. Indeed, when Hirschfeld describes his son waking in the morning, he adds in parentheses, "(he was at the time two-and-a-half years old)," indicating that the passage was written, or at least edited, after the event (55). The date in the subtitle, June 1988, constitutes yet another time frame—that of the Gregorian calendar, which stands in juxtaposition to the Jewish time cycle implied by *motzei Shabbat*.

Although marked as having been written at night, the passage recollects an early morning scene that occurred when Hirschfeld was still a young parent. It describes a moment of grace, which then engenders in the writer a profound revelation. The moment occurs during the period of calm before young children wake and the day begins—the brief hour when parents are "for themselves," before they resume the responsibilities, chores, and pleasures of parenting. Hirschfeld is sitting for a cigarette and coffee in a dimly lit part of the room, while the children are sleeping in a bright, sunny area of the room. When his son Amitai awakens, the boy is prevented from seeing his father by the variations in light:

> Everything lay in its place, very quiet, illuminated, nearly shining, for the sun streamed in through the window and filled the room. The silence was so complete and the air so pleasant that it seemed as if everything had frozen in its place. Suddenly his face was inscribed with something resembling a question, and with a slight touch of alarm.[5] He glanced aside again and in that high, sweet voice of his asked in the absolute silence: "Am I in the world too?" What had happened to him? Everything was so illuminated and silent and temperate and pleasant that it seemed that all was one, and he himself was lost in it all. . . . [It] seemed that everything existed but him. Nothing made a sound, nothing disturbed, nothing hurt, or itched, or pressed. All around him there was so much world. This is exactly what he asked, "Am I in the world too?" and as soon as his voice was heard, he knew that he too was in the world, and his expression regained its peacefulness, and he went on with his business, that is, he reached out and picked up a toy. (55)

The repeated negations in this passage, emphasizing the absent irritations and disturbances rather affirming comforts and harmony ("nothing," "nothing"), clearly connote a widely quoted midrashic image of the revelation on Mount Sinai, the moment the Torah was received: "Said R. Abbahu in the name of R. Johanan: When God gave the Torah no bird twittered, no fowl flew, no ox lowed, none of the ophanim stirred a wing, the seraphim did not say 'Holy, Holy,' the sea did not roar, the creatures spoke not, the whole world was hushed into breathless silence and the voice went forth: I AM THE LORD THY GOD."[6] Immediately thereafter the midrash deliberates on the exact meaning of the concept of *bat kol*. In the midrash, as in Hirschfeld's memoir, the condition of utter and complete silence is what stages and engenders revelation. The world must be wholly invested in silence and not-being for revelation to break through. Routine must be arrested. Set up by the repeated negations, the booming divine voice can have its full impact. In Hirschfeld's scene the sublime also penetrates into the mundane, before the moment is dissolved back into routine. The rhetoric of emphatic negation recurs in the next paragraph to make clear the reference to revelation: "I did not stir. I did not even inhale smoke from the cigarette" (55). The subsequent use of anaphora further intensifies the moment's emotional force: "I wanted to watch him more and more. I wanted to see how he genuinely was, without me" (56).

There is a moment in which the father could step in and dispel the child's anxiety. But he chooses not to. The child's anxiety is described as fleeting, thus diffusing any possible concern about negligence by a parent seemingly more absorbed in observation than in his child's existential discomfort. The moment of parental holding back also allows the child to assume his own agency—to exist for himself instead of solely as a function of the parent. In exposing these role limits, this moment also touches on the essence of the parent-child relationship, to which we will return when reading the second half of the passage, covering Hirschfeld's own childhood. But before heading in that direction, I want to consider one more reference echoed by Hirschfeld's text, this time to an essay found in his earlier autobiographical collection *Reshimot al makom* (Local Notes).[7]

In chapter 13 of *Reshimot*, "The Present, or He Who Glides on the Wings of the Wind," Hirschfeld contemplates the concept of "present" time as place.[8] The Hebrew word for present, *hoveh*, is simultaneously a verb and a noun, signifying stillness and transience at once, like the person who lying aboard a moving ship is stationary even while he and his craft are carried along by the "wings of the wind"—an image Hirschfeld quotes from a classic medieval poem by Moshe Ibn Ezra.[9] Here too, as in the moment of revelation in

"Bat kol," the ability to hold completely still enables the ascent to a higher, sublime state of being. The denial of self and the attainment of the fullness of being are made here to seem similarly close. The scene of a child left quietly playing alone in the sunlight references a moment in Haim Nachman Bialik's poem "Should an Angel Ask," which explores this same duality.[10] In the opening to Bialik's poem, a lonely, dreaming child plays in a silent, sunlit landscape. The first-person speaker, looking back on his younger self, describes how in the deep silence the child experienced a revelation entailing a split of his self. His soul soared, aspiring to unite with a white cloud, but was not lost. Instead it was salvaged, first by a ray of sun, then by being anchored in a page of Talmud, until finally it was rescued through poetry.

Bialik's poetic speaker observes his earlier self, and although the unifying work of memory implies a subjective continuity with the adult who was the child, the two nevertheless remain distinct: the adult speaks in the present, whereas the child remains silent. In Hirschfeld's "Bat kol" the father and son test the limits of their separate selves ("I wanted to see how he genuinely was, without me").

Returning to Bialik's poem, it is framed as a dialogue with an angel. This exchange with a celestial being presents a striking contrast to the rifts in the child's soul—with the soul being caught, in each of the poem's stanzas, in a new trap (e.g., the white cloud in the sky). The conversation between angel and speaker in the present performance of the poem is juxtaposed with the loneliness and silence that envelop the playing child in the past, and which enable his moment of transcendence. As in Hirschfeld's later essay, silence is here the condition of revelation; speech frustrates it.

In "Bat kol" absolute silence reminds Hirschfeld of an earlier experience. When still a young child, he sat one evening alone on the lawn. Suddenly he noticed a hedgehog coming toward him from out of the dark. The young Ariel tried to coax the animal with "Come, come" but the startled hedgehog escaped. The next evening offered a second opportunity. This time the boy sat still, and the hedgehog passed by within reach of him. The associated feeling of triumph stemmed, he realizes in retrospect, from his capacity to minimize his being to almost nothing—as the world had done when the Torah was given; as he himself later did while observing his son's bewilderment. Reading the two scenes in tandem allows us to see the analogy between the hedgehog and the son, as well as the affinity between the child on the lawn and the remembering father in the early morning quiet. But intertextually the neat division of roles between father and son becomes blurred.

Hirschfeld's account of his encounters with the hedgehog echoes two major texts in Israeli culture. The first is T. Carmi's classic for children, *Shmulikkipod* (Shmulik the Hedgehog), published in 1955, when Ariel Hirschfeld was two years old.[11] The second is Nathan Zach's poem "A Moment" (1960).

Like "Bat kol," *Shmulikkipod* describes a meeting between a boy and a hedgehog. Gadi—named after Carmi's own son—is lying ill and lonely in his bed when he hears a rustling from the window.[12] He looks and sees Shmulik, "a ball with quills and a little head peaking out in front. Come to me— Gadi said to him happily." The illustration shows Gadi stretching out his arms to Shmulik and the hedgehog approaching. That is, a meeting, in the children's story, is immediate: the hedgehog walks up to the boy and touches his hand. This scene, intimately familiar for most Hebrew readers, derives its strength from its perfect fulfillment of a children's literature convention: domesticating and familiarizing the strange and the different while also offering comfort, company, and contact. Despite being different, the two protagonists find common ground: Gadi's hair, which stands on end and thus resembles Shmulik's quills, and a shared favorite food, strawberries. In the course of the story, the boy and the hedgehog grow close and learn to accept their differences but, at its end, go their separate ways.

Hirschfeld's scene echoes this well-loved story. When he first encounters the hedgehog on the lawn, the young Ariel tries to emulate Gadi: "I reached out my arms to him and said: 'Come, come.'" However, in this case, the frightened animal "turned his back on [him] and escaped as fast as he could" (56). The scenario described in T. Carmi's book obviously does not work beyond its fictional bounds. Ariel the child tries to apply literature to life and fails—a failure made to seem harmless because the text in question is a children's book. The next time Ariel and the hedgehog meet, we expect him to take up a different approach, one presumably based on lived experiences with real wild animals rather than on fictional encounters with made-up ones. But in fact what Hirschfeld does is change his reference text, replacing *Shmulikkipod* with Zach's poem "A Moment." It is here that the national context comes to the foreground.

Regarded as seminal to the Israeli canon, "A Moment" formulates the relationship between the poet and the national collective in reference to previous generations of Hebrew poetry. Like its author, the poem represents the poetic generation that came of age after statehood. Few poems have received as much close attention in Israeli criticism, and "A Moment" remains widely quoted and taught.

With this background in mind, when the hedgehog appeared for the second time, the young Hirschfeld sat still "until [he] became an object" (56). The original Hebrew plays here on the root *dmm*, which forms both nouns in the sentence—*dmama* (silence) and *domem* (object, still). The words used to describe the hedgehog's journey across the lawn are a quote from Zach's poem. Here is T. Carmi's translation of the poem (whereby another intertextual link is created through Carmi, the author of *Shmulikkipod* and the translator of "A Moment"):

Nathan Zach / A Moment

Quiet for a moment. Please. I'd like to
say something. He went away and
passed in front of me. I could have
touched the hem of his cloak. I didn't.
Who could have known what I didn't
know.

There was sand stuck to his clothes.
Sprigs were tangled in his beard. He
must have slept on straw the night
before. Who could have known that in
another night he would be hollow as a
bird, hard as a stone.

I could not have known. I don't blame
him. Sometimes I feel him getting up
in his sleep, moonstruck like the sea,
flitting by me, saying to me my son.
My son. I didn't know that you are, to
such an extent, with me.[13]

The poem's widely quoted opening, in which the speaker begs for a moment of silence, using a mix of colloquial and formal language, of understatement and drama, so that he may deliver his announcement or confession, has been read as emblematic of an entire poetic generation.[14] As in the
memoir, silence is presented as the foundation from which poetry and narrative can emerge: be it the speaker's confession, which leads to revelation,
or the experience of otherness and connection in the memoir. Hirschfeld
describes the hedgehog's approach as follows: "When he went away and
passed in front of me I was happy: I had turned to an object in his eyes as
well, he passed very close to my feet and I saw his face extremely close, his
strange expression, his mouth reminiscent of old men of a certain type, his
beady eyes. He went away and passed in front of me. I could have touched
him. I didn't. I felt his utter otherness" (56).

Hirschfeld's memoir offers a humorous take on Zach's poem, with the
momentous figure of the beggar-prophet reincarnated as a hedgehog "reminiscent of old men of a certain type." The indicators of poverty or neglect
in a person ("Sprigs were tangled in his beard. He must have slept on straw
the night before.") are perfectly acceptable in an animal. Hirschfeld's playful
reading of the poem thus eliminates a sense of guilt, which, as Dan Miron
has shown in his impeccable reading of Zach's poem, stems from the speaker's passive refusal to help a beggar who will be dead the next day ("hollow
as a bird, hard as a stone"). In the poem contact with the Other provides an
alternative option for rescue. In the memoir the possible injury caused by
silence is removed—even as a hint of it remains in the initial scene between
father and child.

At the same time, the poem influences our reading of the encounter with
the hedgehog and elevates the moment to one of epiphany and spiritual

ascent. Moreover, it places the personal moment, the singled-out autobiographical memory—boy meeting hedgehog on the lawn—within a collective context.

Of the three possible interpretations Dan Miron offers for "A Moment,"
the first emphasizes its status as "a masterpiece of existential psychology,"
centering on the threats of inauthenticity and bad faith (535); the second
treads the psychoanalytical path, focusing on the speaker's unresolved
Oedipal complex; and the third traces the poem's intricate net of biblical
allusions. For Miron only the third of these readings "fully explains the
fact that the poem is supposed to be a public utterance, a speech in fact, a
veritable declaration." As Miron shows, the biblical subtext explains "why
the speaker had to address a 'public.'"[15] Although Miron universalizes the
"public" in question to "humanity at large," and thus obscures its national
specificity, his reading nevertheless moves the poem beyond the existential
and psychoanalytical registers into those of the public and sociohistorical.
The allusion to Zach's poem in Hirschfeld's memoir has the same effect of
broadening the interpretive frame. It invites the reader to consider it both
as a personal memory and as a moment whose significance derives from a
broader collective context.

In his sweeping introduction to modern Israeli literature, "Locus and Language: Hebrew Cultures in Israel, 1890–1990," Hirschfeld refers to Zach's
poem as a demonstration of the "newness of the language and its archaic res-
onances."[16] Biblical language offers particular fodder for wordplay in Hebrew
poetry, versus in other languages, and need not be quoted directly. Often a
"clang" association with a verse will suffice—that is, when a word's sound
connotes a verse. "Hebrew," writes Hirschfeld in his discussion of this poem,
"acts like a giant organ, producing echoes of echoes at the slightest touch."[17]
Reflecting further on "A Moment," Hirschfeld shows why he would allude
to it when contemplating revelation:

> This is a tale of missed contact: "I could have touched the hem of his
> cloak." And the Hebrew phrase *shulei adarto* (hem of his cloak) evokes the
> Bible itself, though it never appears therein. Zach evokes all those who
> stand in the presence of God (or of God's messengers). The reader does

not know the identity of the "he." Is it a father? Is it God? Undoubtedly both, but more than that: it is the absolute "other," the sublime. And yet, this "other" is inextricably tied in the vocabulary and living memory of ancient Hebrew to two words, *shulei adarto*. Hebrew is felt as an immanent revelation, a medium of sorts for the sublime, transcendent presence. The "he" is, in a sense, language itself.[18]

In the third stanza of "A Moment," according to Hirschfeld's reading, the speaker's "he" is resurrected, not miraculously but within the speaker himself: "'He' exists within the 'I.' The 'I' senses him. The 'he' (father, God, Hebrew) is part of the personality of the living person. Within the poet, within his soul, begins a new, different contact between the sublime 'he' and himself."[19] Thus the ability to feel the "utter otherness" of the hedgehog/ prophet/God/Hebrew-language/child is what makes contact possible. What this reading further suggests is that Hirschfeld's own quiet observation of his waking son, who momentarily *is* "for himself," is not detached but rather wholly connected and engaged. In Hirschfeld's performance of the poem, in his memoir, the contact actually does occur. Thus the memoir is also a corrective, or a healing, reading of the poem.

Like other interpreters of Zach, Hirschfeld reads the "he," or Other, in "A Moment" as a father figure—as is indeed suggested by this mysterious figure's address to the speaker: "my son." In the memoir, as we saw, he describes the hedgehog using the same words that Zach uses to describe the father (or God, or Other). But Hirschfeld makes an additional move by drawing a parallel between the hedgehog and the figure of his son. And in being compared to the hedgehog, the son, in Hirschfeld's autobiographical rereading of Zach, merges in effect with the father figure and becomes associated, consequently, with the motif of revelation. That is, Hirschfeld's revelation may be read as a performance of the closing lines of Zach's poem: "My son. I didn't know that you are, to/such an extent, with me."

In his reading of the poem's biblical connotations, Hirschfeld notes—as have other readers—the allusion to King David's lament over his son Absalom (Samuel 2, 19:5), as well as the cry of Christ on the Cross to his Father ("My God, my God, why hast Thou forsaken me?" Psalm 22:2). Though

Hirschfeld's text does not dismiss the threat of abandonment implied by these allusions, this threat nevertheless wanes in the intimacy of the father-son relationship—or of the Ariel-hedgehog one. Hirschfeld's early morning revelation involves the possibility of a father seeing himself in his son's place. Here the father, who annuls his own self, is with the son—not vice versa. Hirschfeld uses Zach's words but takes them in a new direction.

Unlike the speaker in Zach's poem, Hirschfeld's narrator self-consciously —"authentically," if one follows Dan Miron's existential reading—holds back. The poem opens with his insistence on "Quiet for a moment." This restraint constitutes both the source of the narrator's revelation and its condition of possibility. That is, the narrator's revelation consists precisely in his sudden ability to see his son (or the hedgehog) without the interference of his own self, his own presence. The difference between the Zach and Hirschfeld texts is that, in the latter, the narrator makes a seemingly morally responsible choice, even as the outcome is the same. In Zach's poem this outcome—the nullification of the Other—is masked, whereas in Hirschfeld the choice not to interfere is a choice to nullify the self, rather than the Other.

Hirschfeld's "mnemonic arbitrage," his way of narrating his memoir using different textual and cultural resources—including midrash, modern Hebrew poetry from Bialik to Zach, historical narrative, and children's literature—points to a wider phenomenon in Israeli life writing. At a period marked by the splintering of Israeli society by ethnicity, class, gender, and religion, Israeli autobiography has become increasingly drawn to collective symbols and cultural tropes. The textual conversation with previous texts of different levels, contexts, and forms is recognized as a mark of Hebrew literature. For example, Huda Abu-Much's original research on Anton Shammas's translation of the Palestinian-Israeli author Emile Habibi's fiction from Arabic into Hebrew critically shows that to "domesticate" Habibi's fiction in Hebrew, Shammas weaved traditional Jewish texts and allusions into it.[20]

The personal identities constructed by this practice in Hebrew autobiography could well clear the way to a collective identity that allows for plurality and difference. In this volume the writers I have focused on all adopt a dual position vis-à-vis Israeli society that combines self-fashioned marginality with invocations of authority. Their variegated stories all supply fresh definitions of what it means to be Israeli. These writers' perceived status as relational selves, dependent on national narratives and familiar literary texts, enables them to simultaneously express multiplicity and unity. Their individual stories may therefore harbor an optimistic message for Israeli society. Rather than depicting a state of cultural disintegration, these personal narratives illustrate a deep, continuous involvement in shaping a complex and flexible Israeli national identity that is open to others and shares common languages—and therefore, ultimately, a common life.

NOTES

Introduction: Hebrew Autobiography— Nation, Relation, and Narration

1. See Nancy K. Miller, "Representing Others: Gender and the Subjects of Autobiography," *Differences* 6, no. 1 (1994): 1–27; and Paul John Eakin, "Relational Selves, Relational Lives: Autobiography and the Myth of Autonomy," *How Our Lives Become Stories: Making Selves* (Ithaca, NY: Cornell University Press, 1999), 43–98. A meaningful contribution in this direction is Bart Moore-Gilbert's *Postcolonial Life-Writing: Culture, Politics and Self-Representation* (Abington, UK: Routledge, 2009). Previous instances are few and far apart. See, for example, Robert Sayre, *The Examined Self: Benjamin Franklin, Henry Adams, Henry James* (Princeton, NJ: Princeton University Press, 1964); Paul John Eakin, ed., *American Autobiography: Retrospect and Prospect* (Madison: University of Wisconsin Press, 1991), in which the introduction states that such works have been studied but not as autobiographies. Gershon Shaked contributed to the discussion in the Israeli context: "Matseva le'avot vesiman levanim," in *Tmuna kvutsatit: hebetim be-sifrut yisrael u've-tarbuta*, ed. Malka Shaked and Gideon Tikotsky (Or Yehuda: Dvir, Masa Kritit, 2009), 288–367. But his interest, although both literary and national, does not encompass the actual making of Israeli nationalism in autobiographical discourse. The common ground Shaked finds in the Israeli autobiographies he discusses is the authors' identities as immigrants or children of immigrants, and their strained relationship with the State of Israel.

2. Or, following Benedict Anderson, "imagined communities": *Imagined Communities: Reflections on the Origin and Spread of Nationalism* (London: Verso, 1983).

3. "The nation, like the individual, is the culmination of a long past of endeavors, sacrifice, and devotion." Ernst Renan, "What Is a Nation?," reprinted in Homi K. Bhabha, ed., *Nation and Narration* (London: Routledge, 1990), 19.

4. Gilmore likewise writes: "In this context, we could say that the cultural work performed in the name of autobiography profoundly concerns representations of citizenship and the nation. Autobiography's investment in the representative person allies it to the project of lending substance to the national fantasy of belonging": see Leigh Gilmore, *The Limits of Autobiography: Trauma and Testimony* (Ithaca, NY: Cornell University Press, 2001), 12.

5. Augustine's intensive use of biblical verse creates a web of language both familiar and collective yet distinctly his own—based on tradition as well as innovation. Autobiography, whether within or outside the canonical tradition, has followed this code. Much later, in the eighteenth century, Jean-Jacques Rousseau epitomized the individual-universal duality in his famous autobiographical opening: "My purpose is to display to my kind a portrait in every way true to nature, and the man I shall portray will be myself." See *The Confessions*, trans. J. M. Cohen (London: Penguin Classics, 1953), 17. Rousseau's confessions, although concerned with specific biographical issues—namely his attempt to justify deserting his children at birth and mistreating his partner Therese—were read as a model of modern self-recognition, along with casting the original singular self as universal.

6. See M. A. Guenzberg, *Aviezer* (Vilna: Dvir, 1844), 198–217. Full publication was delayed until the death of certain relatives who would likely have been offended by the book's contents.

7. See Alan Mintz, *Banished from Their Father's Table: Loss of Faith and Hebrew Autobiography* (Bloomington: Indiana University Press, 1989), and Dan Miron, *Bodedim be-moadam* (Tel Aviv: Am Oved, 1987).

8. Moshe Leib Lilienblum, *Hatot neurim* (Jerusalem: Mossad Bialik, Sifriat Dorot, 1970), 84. On p. 106 of the same text, Malal also ties himself to Haskalah fiction through Mendele Mocher Sforim's portrayal of a mother-in-law in *Ha-avot ve-habanim*, as others have noted before me. See Ben Ami Feingold, "Ha-otobiographia ke-sifrut," *Mehkarey yerushalayim be-sifrut ivrit*, 4 (1984): 86–111. For more on these impoverished Haskalah scholars, including their status as child prodigies, their early, confining marriages, and their struggles with faith versus assimilation into modern Europe, see Shmuel Werses, *Megamot ve-tsurot be-sifrut ha-haskalah* (Jerusalem: Magnes Press, 1990), 249–60; David Biale, *Eros and the Jews: From Biblical Israel to Contemporary America* (New York: Basic Books, 1992).

9. For Mendele's styling of the "code" see Gershon Shaked, *Modern Hebrew Fiction* (Bloomington: Indiana University Press, 2000), 12–13.

10. Lilienblum was not the first to frame the Haskalah narrative as an awakening into Zionism—Peretz Smolenskin preceded him in the late 1860s and early 1870s in the journal *Ha-shahar*—but Malal's narrative allowed this ideological shift to be expressed as a life story. For a revisionist view of Haskalah literature and its history, see Amir Banbaji, "The Orient in the Literature of the 'Haskalah': A Levantine Reading in Euchel, Löwisohn and Mapu," *Journal of Levantine Studies* 1 (2011): 93–128.

11. Renan, "What Is a Nation?" 19.

12. Moshe Leib Lilienblum, *Kol kitvey* (Collected Writings), Vol. 4 (Odessa: Moriah Press, 1913), 6.

13. Although Maimon's immediate addressees were non-Jewish German readers, he still describes himself as a member of a community. Maimon does not relate to an imagined community but to a very palpable one, as is apparent whenever he arrives at a new place and can immediately create ties with local Jews by presenting his credentials and demonstrating his vast knowledge. Nevertheless, his story was adopted as a model by Jewish followers, who embedded it in their founding narratives of an imagined community.

14. In her memoir the early Zionist Sarah Azaryahu describes how, on the eve of immigrating to Ottoman Palestine, she sought out Malal at his workplace to receive his blessing, given that he was the Zionist leader whose call she felt she was answering. On entering the office, she was shocked by his unimpressive physical appearance and, more so, by his traditional Jewish garb, and she backed away without introducing herself. See Azaryahu's *Pirkey haim* (Tel Aviv: Newman Books, 1957), 19.

15. For a discussion of Guenzberg's possible proto-Zionism, see Marcus Moseley, *Being for Myself Alone* (Stanford, CA: Stanford University Press, 2006), 365–66, along with footnote 147, p. 577.

16. Miron, *Bodedim be-moadam*, 227.

17. See Mintz, *Banished from Their Father's Table*, 123–202, especially 128.

18. Moseley, *Being for Myself Alone*, 358–59.

19. Scott Ury, "The Generation of 1905 and the Politics of Despair: Alienation, Friendship, Community," in *The Revolution of 1905 and Russia's Jews*, ed. Stefani Hoffman and Ezra Mendelsohn (Philadelphia: University of Pennsylvania Press, 2008), 96–110.

20. See, for example, Yehuda Ya'ari's monumental anthology, *Zikhronot eretz yisrael* (Jerusalem: World Zionist Organization, 1947), and Yaffa Berlowitz, *Lehamtzi eretz lehamtzi am* (Tel Aviv: Hakibbutz Hameuchad, 1996). The intended readership of prestate Palestine memoirs is indicated by the anthology *Divrei po'alot* (1930), which, soon after being published in Hebrew, was published in Yiddish (1931) and English (1932). See Mark A. Raider and Miriam B. Raider-Roth, eds., *The Plough Woman: Records of the Pioneer Women of Palestine* (Waltham, MA: Brandeis University Press, 2002).

21. Mikhail Bakhtin's description of the origins of autobiography and the agora

as the chronotope of autobiography is instructive in this respect and usefully applicable to Hebrew autobiography. See his "Forms of Time and Chronotope in the Novel" (1937–1938), in *The Dialogic Imagination*, ed. Michael Holquist, trans. Caryl Emerson and Michael Holquist (Austin: University of Texas Press, 1981), 130–46.

22. See, for example, Tamar S. Hess, "Henya Pekelman: An Injured Witness of Socialist Zionist Settlement in Mandatory Palestine," *Women's Studies Quarterly* 36, nos. 1–2 (Spring/Summer 2008): 208–13.

23. See Virginia Woolf's wonderful essay "The Lives of the Obscure," *The Common Reader* (London: Hogarth Press, (1951), 146–67.

24. Rachel Katznelson-Shazar, ed., *Divrey poaʻlot* (Tel Aviv: Moeʻtset hapoaʻlot, 1930); Raider and Raider-Roth, *The Plough Woman*; and *Kovetz ha-shomer* (Tel Aviv: Labor Movement Archive, 1937).

25. On the scholarly end, the most comprehensive study of modern Hebrew autobiography to date is Moseley, *Being for Myself Alone*. The scope of Moseley's hugely insightful work is staggering, praised even by Alan Mintz, whose precedent-setting *Banished from Their Father's Table* (1989) Moseley attacks. See Mintz, "Writing about Ourselves: Jewish Autobiography, Modern and Premodern," *JQR* 98, no. 2 (Spring 2008): 272–85. Nevertheless, Moseley's critique of Mintz is a stumbling block. In particular, Moseley's work barely follows Hebrew autobiography into the twentieth century and, moreover, it rejects or discards most theoretical endeavors of the discourse from the last three decades. This is why this study gratefully acknowledges Moseley's contribution but cannot take it as a starting point. Ariel Levinson's forthcoming study of the construction of the self in young men's Hebrew autobiography at the turn of the nineteenth century also promises to be an important contribution to the field.

26. Avner Holtzman, writing in 1999, was the first to note the boom in Israeli autobiography and its tendency to focus on an author's parents. Holtzman listed sixteen autobiographical works, all but one by male authors, and of these, only one by an non-Ashkenazi (A. B. Yehoshua). This allegedly comprehensive list created a slanted and limited vision of the actual multivoiced range of Israeli autobiographies, and overlooked their frequently subversive nature. In addition, the one woman Holtzman does mention, Yehudit Hendel, is noted not for her major contribution to Israeli life writing, *Ha-koakh ha-aher* (Tel Aviv: Hakibbutz Hameuchad, 1984), but for the short story "Namukh, karov la-ritspa." See Avner Holtzman, *Mapat-drakhim: siporet ivrit kayom* (Tel Aviv: Hakibbutz Hameuchad, 2005), 27–31. A further contribution to the field is Nitza Ben-Dov's *Haim ktuvim: aʻl otobiographiot sifrutiyot yisraeʼliot* (Written Lives: On Literary Israeli Autobiographies) (Jerusalem:

Schocken, 2011). This book is aimed at shifting the view created by Holtzman's original survey; a more comprehensive survey is now under way, with support from the Israeli Science Foundation, and I hope to publish its findings in the future.

27. The Sapir Prize, Israel's largest literary award, with prize money equaling about $35,000, is awarded by the national lottery, Mifaʻl Ha-payis.

28. One notable example of an autobiographical best seller counting as popular literature is Yossi Ghinsberg's *Behazara me-tuichi* (*Back from Tuichi*) (Tel Aviv: Zmora-Bitan, 1985), which became essential reading for Israeli backpackers in South America.

29. Amos Oz, *Sipur al ahava ve-hoshech* (Jerusalem: Keter, 2002); English translation by Nicholas de Lange, *A Tale of Love and Darkness* (Orlando: Harcourt Books, 2005). The scholarly journal *Israel* devoted a special issue (vol. 7, 2005) to the memoir, with comments by leading figures. See also Nancy K. Miller: "The Entangled Self: Genre Bondage in the Age of the Memoir," *PMLA* 122, no. 2 (2007): 537–48; and "I Killed My Grandmother: Mary Antin, Amoz Oz, and the Autobiography of a Name," *Biography* 30, no. 3 (2007): 319–41.

30. Yigal Schwartz, *Ma she-roim mi-kan* (Or Yehuda: Zmora-Bitan, 2005), 265–304.

31. Ibid., 288.

32. In a study of Israeli literature of the 1980s, Dror Mishani questions whether the Israeli Ashkenazi cultural domain was ever lost, and suggests that a great rhetorical effort, in which *Sipur* might be read as participating, was invested in its defense and preservation. See Mishani's *Bekhol ha-inyan ha-mizrahi yesh eize absurd* (Tel Aviv: Am Oved, 2006).

33. Yehudit Kafri, *Kol ha-kayitz halakhnu yehefim* (Tel Aviv: Tag, 1997).

34. My translation. The letter can be found in the Oz archive at Ben-Gurion University, notebook 3, p. 514. Oz, incidentally, was touched by the letter and responded with a grateful epistle of his own. I thank Yehudit Kafri for sharing this response with me.

35. The "sweetening" of Israeli literature for international consumption may perhaps constitute a trend. In Dorit Rabinyan's *Strand of a Thousand Pearls* (New York: Random House, 2003), for example, a happy conclusion is substituted for the open Hebrew ending.

36. *Sipur*, 36; my translation.

37. Ibid., 40. Throughout the chapter Oz addresses a male reader, casting his text as a female victim of rape and cannibalistic murder.

38. Bella Brodzki and Celeste Schenck, eds., "Introduction," *Life/Lines: Theoriz-*

ing Women's Autobiography (Ithaca, NY: Cornell University Press, 1988), 1. Nancy K. Miller has problematized representation concepts in autobiography in her "Representing Others."

39. The exclusion of women from the Hebrew canon has also received serious attention. See, for example, Hannah Nave, "Leket pe'a ve-shikheha: ha-haim mi-hutz la-kanon," in *Min, Migdar, Politica*, ed. Dafna N. Izraeli et al. (Tel Aviv: Hakibbutz Hameuchad, 1999), 49–106; Dan Miron, *Imahot meyasdot, ahayot horgot* (Founding Mothers, Stepsisters), (Tel Aviv: Hakibbutz Hameuchad, 1991); Michael Gluzman, *The Politics of Canonicity* (Stanford, CA: Stanford University Press, 2003); Tova Cohen, "Betokh ha-tarbut u-mihutza la," *Sadan* 2 (1997): 69–110; Pnina Shirav, *Ktiva lo tama* (Tel Aviv: Hakibbutz Hameuchad, 1998); Amalia Kahana-Carmon, "Ishto shel Brenner rokhevet shuv," *Moznaim* 59 (1985): 10–15; Yaffa Berlowitz, "Siporet mi-yabeshet avuda," in her *She'ani adama ve-adam* (Tel Aviv: Hakibbutz Hameuchad, 2003), 319–60.

40. Avirama Golan, "Haim ha-sipur shelo hu ha-sipur shelanu," *Ha'aretz*, Books, August 31, 2005, 1, 12. See also Batya Gur, "Ha-tragedia ha-leumit shel av, em u-ven," *Ha'aretz*, Literature and Culture, March 15, 2002, 2, and Nurith Gertz, "Ha-nofim shelo ve-ha-nofim sheli," *Israel*, 7 (2005): 211–17, as well as the *Israel* issue (vol 7., 2005) devoted to *A Tale of Love and Darkness*.

41. Hannan Hever, "'Tnu lo badranim ve-yanuah be-shalom': sifrut yisraelit bi-zman shel kibush," *Alpaim*, 25 (2003): 155–69. For a brief English version see "Israeli Fiction and the Occupation," *Tikkun* 18, no. 1 (January 2003): 63–67.

42. See Werses, *Megamot ve-tsurot*; Mintz, *Banished from Their Father's Table*; Moseley, *Being for Myself Alone*.

43. The manipulation becomes all the more sophisticated because Oz quotes his own earlier fictional works, such as *Michael sheli* (*My Michael*), as now inherently autobiographical. Pursuing such a discussion, however, would lead us astray from our current path.

44. As Homi Bhabha has put it in *Nation and Narration*: "I have lived that moment of the scattering of the people that in other times and places, in the nations of others, becomes a time of gathering . . . gathering the past in a ritual of revival; gathering the present" (291). And: "The emergence of the later phase of the modern nation, from the mid-nineteenth century, is also one of the most sustained periods of mass migration within the West, and colonial expansion in the East. The nation fills the void left in the uprooting of communities and kin, and turns that loss into the language of metaphor. Metaphor, as the etymology of the word suggests, transfers the meaning of home and belonging, across the 'middle passage,' or the central

European steppes, across those distances, and cultural difference, that span the imagined community of the nation-people" (291). Autobiographical writings trace and document this movement.

45. Paul John Eakin, *Living Autobiographically: How We Create Identity in Narrative* (Ithaca, NY: Cornell University Press, 2008), 156.

46. Bakhtin, "Forms of Time and Chronotope."

47. This is so in other national immigrant cultures, such as the United States, as put forward by Robert Sayre: "An American seems to have needed to be an American first and then an autobiographer." See his "Autobiography and the Making of America," in *Autobiography: Essays Theoretical and Critical*, ed. James Olney (Princeton, NJ: Princeton University Press, 1980), 147. A notable Israeli exception to this rule is *Malakh o satan* (Angel or Devil), the 1993 autobiography by Sarah Angel (b. 1959), who served five years in jail on a drug-dealing conviction. Like the Irish-American writer Frank McCourt, Angel made her name in autobiography; she later shifted to fiction.

48. See Eakin, *Living Autobiographically*, 163.

49. Except for Appelfeld and Be'er, the autobiographical writings discussed here have not been translated into English. Kaniuk's *Life on Sandpaper*, about his New York years, has been translated into English, as have some of his novels, but not *Post Mortem*, the book at the heart of this discussion—which has been translated into French. To sufficiently introduce Kaniuk to the non-Hebrew reader, I have translated lengthy quotes from the original.

1. "To Be a Jew among Jews": The Reluctant Israeli Native in Yoram Kaniuk

A section of this chapter was first presented at a conference held in Kaniuk's honor in Cambridge, England, in March 2006 (http://www.oriental.cam.ac.uk /kaniuk/programme.html). I thank Yigal Schwartz for inviting me to that fruitful gathering, and our Cambridge host, the scholar Risa Domb (z"l).

1. Kaniuk's oeuvre consists of approximately eighteen novels, depending on their definition as fiction or life writing, along with children's books. On his relatively recent recognition see Gershon Shaked, "Rashut ha-zea'ka," *Ha-siporet ha-ivrit, 1880–1980* (Tel Aviv and Jerusalem: Hakibbutz Hameuchad and Keter, 1998), 5: 183–205; and Hanna Soker-Schwager, "Hitparkut mekhonat ha-yitsur ha-yelidi: keri'a anti-edipalit bi-ytsirat Yoram Kaniuk," *OT* 1 (2010): 65–99.

2. Risa Domb (z"l) hosted the conference *The World and Works of Yoram Kaniuk*

at Magdalene College, Cambridge, in March 2006. Authors Uzi Weill (b. 1964) and Dvir Zur (b. 1978) wrote a preface and afterword, respectively, for the 2009 Hebrew edition of *The Last Jew*. See *Ha-yehudi ha-aharon* (Tel Aviv: Yedioth Books).

3. See, for example, "Israel Court Grants Author's Request to Register 'without Religion,'" *Ha'aretz*, October 2, 2011, http://www.haaretz.com/print-edition/news /israel-court-grants-author-s-request-to-register-without-religion-1.387571. Yoram Kaniuk, *Tashah* (Tel Aviv: Miskal–Yedioth Ahronoth Books and Chemed Books, 2010); for the English see *1948*, trans. Anthony Berris (New York: New York Review of Books, 2012).

4. Founded in 1941, the Palmach—an acronym for *plugot mahatz* ("striking brigades")—was a Jewish underground prestate military organization. In 1948 it was integrated into the Israel Defense Forces (IDF).

5. Yoram Kaniuk, *Al ha-haim ve-al ha-mavet* (Tel Aviv: Miskal–Yedioth Ahronoth Books and Chemed Books, 2007), 130–33.

6. I was introduced to Kaniuk's writing, and particularly the book *Adam Resurrected*, by Gershon Shaked (z"l) in his *Shoah and Literature* class. On the claim of Expressionism see his "Matseva le'avot ve-siman levanim," in Gershon Shaked, *Tmuna kvutsatit: hebetim be-sifrut yisrael u've-tarbuta*, ed. Malka Shaked and Gideon Tikotsky (Or Yehuda: Dvir, Masa Kritit, 2009), 288–367; and "Rashut ha-zea'ka." Kaniuk is often explicitly crude or provocative. For example, when he writes in *Post Mortem* (Tel Aviv: Hakibbutz Hameuchad and Yedioth Ahronoth, 1992) about his nostalgia for German food—rolls, in this case—which he never ate as a child, he adds: "I blend in the memory the smell of the boy I could have been, roasted, who for a long time I was ashamed that I had not become, in their terrain, in the crematoriums. I was angry at Moshe for not leaving me there to die. And I can smell my own scorched flesh" (77). Although "survivor's guilt," or, in Kaniuk's case, the guilt of someone who wasn't even in Europe, has been commonly portrayed, the severity of his shift from rolls to burnt flesh is without a doubt manipulative, and borders on the pornography of violence.

7. Susan Sontag, "Notes on 'Camp,'" *Against Interpretation and Other Essays*, (New York: Noonday Press, 1966), 274–92; the quotation appears on p. 275. Sontag elaborates in note 7, p. 279: "Camp is a vision of the world in terms of style—but a particular kind of style. It is the love of the exaggerated, the 'off,' of things-being-what-they-are-not." For Soker-Schwager's suggestion see "Hitparkut mekhonat."

8. Sontag, "Notes," 277. Judging by Sontag's later work, and following general developments in the humanities since the essay was written, it is perhaps safe

to assume that Sontag herself would have refined this definition, and may have agreed about the difficulty of secluding any cultural performative phenomenon as apolitical.

9. Ibid., p. 288, note 41, and p. 290, note 52.

10. As implied in an earlier note, critical developments over the last several decades likely render camp itself a political sensibility. As far as Kaniuk is concerned, critics are divided: Uzi Weill's argument is opposite to that of Soker-Schwager. In the preface to *Ha-yehudi ha-aharon* (2009), Weill defines the book as being as distant as possible from artifice. In his view the book is natural, perhaps even "authentic"—although he does not use this word; he does use *truth*, a word Soker-Schwager, like Sontag, would echo. Weill writes: "Every page, every paragraph, every phrase in the book speaks the truth. . . . But what is that truth? . . . It is always the moment of meeting between the book and the reader. Which is why it changes every time you read it" (8). Weill also reads the book as "dreamlike," a quality that contradicts the artifice of camp and could explain why the book can be fantastic and make sense at the same time (9).

11. Dvir Zur, afterword to *Ha-yehudi ha-aharon* (Tel Aviv: Miskal, 2009), 588–89.

12. Ibid., 590

13. Soker-Schwager, "Hitparkut mekhonat," 82.

14. Kaniuk, *Post Mortem*.

15. Yoram Kaniuk, *Ha-berlina'i ha-aharon* (Tel Aviv: Miskal, 2004), 132.

16. Miron, *Bodedim be-moadam*; Shaked, *Modern Hebrew Fiction*; Hannan Hever, *Producing the Modern Hebrew Canon: Nation Building and Minority Discourse* (New York: New York University Press, 2002).

17. Kaniuk blends, and somewhat bungles, historical with personal knowledge, including horrific scenes his mother witnessed as a child in Ottoman-ruled Palestine. He mentions having read her diaries several times.

18. Kaniuk, *Post Mortem*.

19. Until the 1970s Israel's leadership emerged from this immigration wave, with members including the first prime minister, David Ben-Gurion, and the second president, Yitzhak Ben-Zvi.

20. Gershon Shaked, in his reading of *Post Mortem*, stresses the critical view of Zionist projects from both Moshe's perspective and Yoram's after him. Shaked reads the son as identifying with the father against the mother and her Zionist faith, but to frame Moshe as anti-Zionist would deprive both father and son of their fundamentally contradictory position as well as their complexity. See "Matseva

le'avot," 313. Shaked sees Kaniuk's identity as formed by a duality between his father and his mother, the Others in his life (314). This view, however, smoothes over the contradictory position held by his parents, his father's the more visible of the two.

21. In chapter 27 (beginning p. 113) Kaniuk recounts the "important" things Sarah did, including teaching three presumably unteachable illiterate students to read. Kaniuk relates how his mother built these boys' self-esteem in the process (without doing the same for her own children). After statehood she helped create an educational framework for new immigrants in the periphery—the Negev and the Galilee. But anger permeates even this description, according to which his mother never sought validation from outsiders but only at home (115). Acts of generosity toward the collective thus fill the void created by an insufficiently loving home life.

22. As does Haim Gouri's song "Bab-el wad," written to commemorate troops lost in the convoys, which has been remade and preserved in contemporary Israeli popular culture. The relatively recent version by the Biluyim, for example, is available on YouTube. Other War of Independence fronts have become controversial, but the convoys have maintained their iconic heroism, alongside the helplessness of those in the ambushed cars.

23. Gershon Shaked, "Matseva le'avot," 314. See also Soker-Schwager, "Hitparkut mekhonat"; Schwartz, afterword to Yoram Kaniuk, *"Eytim" ve-"Nevelot"* (Tel Aviv: Miskal, 2006).

24. Kaniuk, *Tashah*, 139; 137–142.

25. Yoram Kaniuk, *Ha-yehudi ha-aharon* (Tel Aviv: Am Oved and Hakibbutz Hameuchad, 1982).

26. In *Of Life and Death* Kaniuk hallucinatorily returns to the moment of waiting to be shot as in Goya's painting *The Third of May 1808*, viewing himself as the revolutionary with the stigmata facing death. This is how he recapitulates his feelings from 1948: "I see the French shooting squadron executing the Spanish defenders of Madrid, and one of them, the dark one in the middle, he's the largest of them all and his hair the most disheveled, and on one of his palms is the mark of the nail of the messiah on the cross, he spreads his hands on an imaginary cross and I see the amazing man and in front of him one of the shooters, his rifle nearly touches the man, they will all be executed now, but the man in white is already dead, even though he is still living his last eternal moment and feeling it in his body, the man in white is running in my blood, someone comes to wipe the sweat from my face and my right hand is bleeding, the man in the painting will die now, he's in a dying

process, he is that second that is within me, then as now, in Jerusalem and now, the stammering moment between something and something, Goya, between life and death" (90–91). That helpless moment of imminent death is the birthplace of his future suffering.

27. This last of these, *Tashah*, exceeds the scope of this book.

28. *Post Mortem*, 111–12; *Al ha-haim ve-al ha-mavet* (Of Life and Death) (Tel Aviv: Miskal–Yedioth Ahronoth Books and Hemed Books, 2007), 14–15. In *Post Mortem* Kaniuk writes he could never remember the boy's name, and notes his American-sounding nickname. In *Of Life and Death* he is named Trumpeldor, the son of the teacher Damva'esh ["blood and fire"] (14); his nickname is "Trumple"—which would sound American in Hebrew—and he addresses Yoram directly, before he dives, with what in Hebrew is an imperfect rhyme, "For Yoram, who will conquer a cloud," and cries, *"Al ha-haim ve'al ha-mavet!"* (15) Literally "On life and death," the exclamation of derring-do, prevalent in Hebrew slang until the 1970s, may be more accurately translated as "Come what may!" The name Damva'esh comes from the slogan "In blood and fire Judea fell, in blood and fire Judea shall rise," a slogan adopted by the first prestate military organization, Hashomer (founded in 1909), and taken from the hymn of the right-wing Beitar movement (1903). Yosef Trumpeldor (1880–1920) was one of the heroic martyrs of early Jewish Zionist settlement in Palestine.

29. For example, a painful mother-son classroom scene depicted in *Post Mortem*, and discussed later in the main text, also concludes the story "Adama harukha" (Scorched Earth), in Kaniuk's first Hebrew book, *Ha-yored lemata* (Tel Aviv: Schocken, 1963), 180–88. Similarly the plot of "Vultures" is repeated in *Ha-yehudi ha-aharon*, 32–33, as in other works. The blurring of fiction and autobiography is perpetuated by readers, such as Tzvi Dror in a historical survey of the Harel Brigade. Dror quotes from the story "Vultures" as if it were a testimony of the battle over Nebi Samuel. Tzvi Dror, *Harel* (Bnei Brak: Hakibbutz Hameuchad, 2005).

30. I follow Philippe Lejeune's 1975 definition of autobiography: "Retrospective prose narrative written by a real person concerning his own existence, where the focus is his individual life, in particular the story of his personality." See Philippe Lejeune, *On Autobiography* (Minneapolis: University of Minnesota Press, 1989), 4.

31. In *Of Life and Death* fantasy and memory merge when Kaniuk is hospitalized for removal of a cancerous growth from his intestine, and the operation becomes three operations, and he has to be connected to a ventilator for three weeks. Kaniuk relates his emergence from anesthesia and return from "nowhere" (42). In Kaniuk's

hallucinations, incorporating an array of national and other figures, the Yiddish and Hebrew author Mendele Mocher Sforim is a blind train driver who drives Kaniuk out of the hospital. In another a Palestinian writer from Lebanon tells Kaniuk that he had killed his uncle in a battle in 1948. The young man knows this because his dead uncle had identified Kaniuk as the shooter to him (49). In a third, a delegation of French journalists has come to interview Kaniuk, but he cannot meet them because he is hanging, locked, from a chandelier.

The book comprises a cultural catalog, mostly covering popular films, musicals, and songs from the 1950s. But *Of Life and Death* is first and foremost a patient's report of survival, and of the associated humiliations. Just as Kaniuk is unrelenting in his exposure of his parents' ailing bodies, he is explicit in describing his own medical procedures. For this reason reading *Of Life and Death* in bits and pieces may be recommended, in particular from p. 72 on. In a scene capturing the gamut of emotions, two women discuss their dating life as they wash Kaniuk in a tub but suddenly cut their dialogue short when they realize that "this Yoram can hear" (96).

32. This assessment applies in particular to the anecdotes in *Life on Sandpaper*, trans. Anthony Berris (Urbana-Champaign, IL: Dalkey Archive Press, 2011), but see also *Tashah*, when Kaniuk is shot in the eye during the battle over the Palestinian village of Castel; his eye pops into his hand and is placed back and bandaged on the spot (55).

33. On related scandals associated with autobiography, see Paul John Eakin, *Living Autobiographically: How We Create Identity in Narrative* (Ithaca, NY: Cornell University Press, 2008), especially p. 20.

34. Philippe Lejeune, "The Autobiographical Pact," *On Autobiography*, trans. Katherine Leary, foreword by Paul John Eakin (Minneapolis: University of Minnesota Press, 1989), 4. See also Nancy K. Miller, "The Entangled Self: Genre Bondage in the Age of the Memoir," *PMLA* 122, no. 2 (2007): 537–48.

35. See Paul John Eakin, "Introduction: Mapping the Ethics of Life Writing," in *The Ethics of Life Writing*, ed. Paul John Eakin (Ithaca, NY: Cornell University Press, 2004), 1–16.

36. Paul de Man, "Autobiography as De-facement," *MLN* 94, no. 5 (1979): 919–23.

37. See Miller, "The Entangled Self," and Eakin, *Living Autobiographically*, 17–22.

38. Paul John Eakin, *Fictions in Autobiography: Studies in the Art of Self-Invention* (Princeton, NJ: Princeton University Press, 1985), 3.

39. Paul John Eakin, ed., *The Ethics of Life Writing* (Ithaca, NY: Cornell University Press, 2004).

40. On the relationship among autobiography, testimony, and the demand for truth, see Leigh Gilmore, *The Limits of Autobiography: Trauma and Testimony* (Ithaca, NY: Cornell University Press, 2001), 6–7.

41. Judith Butler, "Imitation and Gender Insubordination" (1990), in *The Judith Butler Reader*, ed. Sara Salih with Judith Butler (Malden, MA: Blackwell Publishers, 2004), 119–37.

42. Eakin, *The Ethics of Life Writing*.

43. Eakin, "Introduction: Mapping the Ethics of Life Writing"; Nancy K. Miller, "The Ethics of Betrayal: The Diary of a Memoirist," in *The Ethics of Life Writing*, ed. Paul John Eakin (Ithaca, NY: Cornell University Press, 2004), 147–160, and others in this collection.

44. W. K. Wimsatt Jr. and M. C. Beardsley, "The Intentional Fallacy," *Sewanee Review* 54, no. 3 (July–September 1946): 468–88.

45. Eakin, *Living Autobiographically*, 156.

46. De Man, "De-facement."

47. Moshe too is described as a "corpse" while still alive.

48. Quotation marks are missing in the Hebrew original, and I have refrained from adding them.

49. Erich Kästner's books were translated early on into Hebrew, and Kaniuk read them as a child. *Emil and the Detectives* was published in German in 1929, and first appeared in Hebrew translation in 1935.

50. The story about the Little Fugue recording is repeated in *Tashah* (131–36), and a fictional version appears in chapter 9 of Kaniuk's 1966 novel *Himo melekh yerushalayim* (Himmo, King of Jerusalem) when Assa disrupts a dancing scene and plays the Little Fugue repeatedly until his peers seize the record and throw it out the window. See *Himo melekh yerushalayim* (Tel Aviv: Am Oved, 1966), 102–6.

51. Additional such portrayals of "home" are numerous. In *Ha-berlina'i ha-aharon* Kaniuk relates his brand of madeleine experience. Walking into a pastry shop, he casually chooses a cake and writes that "its taste had been hidden in me before I touched it" (30). In *Post Mortem*, when the young Kaniuk is enamored of his mother's Catholic German friend Tanya, and yearns for the unfamiliar songs she sings, his mother says the longing comes "from Moshe's German dreams which I had weaved into my Eretz Yisraeli soul, which despite all of my efforts, I felt a stranger in already then" (133).

52. This scene also figures in Kaniuk's latest addition to his autobiographical project, *Tashah* (2010). In this work Kaniuk is not sent to rest at home but rather re-

assigned to another unit, whose armored vehicle needs an escort to travel from Tel Aviv to pick up the dignitary Abba Eban and back. During this stay at home, however, Kaniuk does not sit still but rather covers his walls and ceiling with paintings. When he returns from the war, the paintings terrify him and he whitewashes them (19–23). In 1948, which centers on the war experience, his parents become united and conflict free, with plural verbs uniting Sarah and Moshe as his "parents": "My mother and father, so they later said, understood and did not ask. They didn't even know I'd come from Jerusalem" (22).

53. I could not find a translation for this derogatory term for Arab, as obscene as *kike* or *nigger* in English, so I left it transliterated.

54. This and the earlier quotations are taken from pp. 47–48 of *Tashah*.

55. Ibid., 48.

56. Ibid., 49.

57. In *Al ha-haim ve-al ha-mavet* the teacher B is identified as "the teacher Blich" (138).

58. When *Adam ben kelev* (*Adam Resurrected*) was published in 1969, Moshe reciprocated the gesture by recognizing the basis of his son's fiction in his own family stories, although stories he had never told his son: "There was a book about a clown who became a dog. Moshe, who did not read what was written in the present, almost favored the book which was published almost a year before he got his stroke. He sat with me and tried telling me something about the book, and suddenly blushed and nearly barked: 'My father had an uncle, a Christian, he had a German shepherd, and there was a woman, probably his first sickly wife, who fell in love with the dog, crawled in his kennel and slept with it. In the book you gave me, the woman says: "He was the first dog of my life," that was what she said'" (*Post* Mortem, 52).

59. See Hannan Hever, *Ha-sipur ve-ha-le'um* (The Narrative and the Nation) (Tel Aviv: Resling, 2007), 61–75; or, in English: Hannan Hever, "Yitzhak Shami: Ethnicity as an Unresolved Conflict," *Shofar* 24, no. 2 (Winter 2006): 120–39.

60. Kaniuk, *Ha-berlina'i ha-aharon*, 154.

61. For a recording of the song, see the Zemereshet database of Hebrew songs: http://www.zemereshet.co.il/song.asp?id=716.

62. Marianne Hirsch, *Family Frames: Photography, Memory, and Postmemory* (Cambridge: Harvard University Press, 1997).

63. Ibid., 22.

64. This resembles the structure of Kaniuk's previous volume in his autobio-

graphical project, covering his American years, *Haim al niyar zkhukhit* (*Life on Sandpaper*, translated as *I Did It My Way*). In *Life* this structure gestures toward the jazz idiom that permeates the book, giving each shifting voice its solo, and sometimes allowing them to join together.

65. Solomon Maimon, *Hayey Shlomo Maimon, katuv beyedey atsmo*, trans. Y. L. Barukh (Tel Aviv: Miskal—Yedioth Ahronoth Books and Chemed Books, 2009).

66. Ibid., 8.

67. Clark Murray, Maimon's translator into English, quotes these lines in his preface to *Solomon Maimon: An Autobiography* (Urbana: University of Illinois Press, 2001), xxxii. See also Michael Stanislawski, who describes Maimon as "a quixotic and rather unruly Polish Jew who made his way to Berlin and to the forefront of the German philosophical world": *Autobiographical Jews: Essays in Jewish Self-Fashioning* (Seattle: University of Washington Press, 2004), 56. For the Eliot quotations see George Eliot, *Daniel Deronda* (New York: Penguin, 1988), 436, then 435.

68. See Avner Holtzman, *El ha-kera she-ba-lev* (Jerusalem: Bialik Institute, 1995), 161; Michah Yosef Berdichevsky, *Mahanayim*, Dorot Series (Jerusalem: Mossad Bialik, 1971), chapter 8.

69. See Sander L. Gilman, *Jewish Self-Hatred: Anti-Semitism and the Hidden Language of the Jews* (Baltimore: Johns Hopkins University Press, 1986), 125–26; Liliane Weissberg, "1792–93—Solomon Maimon Writes His *Lebensgeschichte* (Autobiography), A Reflection on His Life in the (Polish) East and the (German) West," in *The Yale Companion to Jewish Writing and Thought in German Culture, 1096–1996*, ed. Sander L. Gilman and Jack Zipes (New Haven: Yale University Press, 1997), 108–15.

2. "I Have a Pain in My Mother": Natan Zach and Haim Be'er

Gary epigraph translated from the French by John Markham Beach (London: Michael Joseph, 1962), 261.

Jacques Derrida quotes his mother's distorted speech after she suffered a stroke: "Circumfession," in *Jacques Derrida*, trans. Geoffrey Bennington (Chicago: University of Chicago Press, 1991), 23. She is referring to her own mother, Derrida's grandmother, but she expresses his pain and the shift that illness, old age, and dependence have created in their lives, positioning her as a sore organ in his body. He cannot separate himself from this pain because, as her aphasic expression clearly connotes, his mother is his body, and the relationship that began with him being a part of her body has now turned sadly askew. This theme returns in the poem Zach includes in his "Beintayim," which I will return to later.

1. Yoram Kaniuk, *Post Mortem* (Tel Aviv: Hakibbutz Hameuchad and Yedioth Ahronoth, 1992), 24.

2. Natan Zach, *Mot immi* (My Mother's Death) (Tel Aviv: Hakibbutz Hameuchad, 1997), 57.

3. Haim Be'er, *Havalim* (Tel Aviv: Am Oved, 1998); English translation: *The Pure Element of Time* (*Havalim*), trans. Barbara Harshav (Hanover, NH: University Press of New England, 2003).

4. James Olney, ed., *Autobiography: Essays Theoretical and Critical* (Princeton, NJ: Princeton University Press, 1980).

5. For more about Zach's position within his generation, see Hamutal Tsamir, *Beshem ha-nof* (Jerusalem and Beer Sheva: Keter and the Heksherim Center at Ben-Gurion University, 2006), 59–89, and Michael Gluzman, "'To Endow Suffering with Elegance': Dahlia Ravikovitch and the Poetry of the State Generation," *Prooftexts* 28, no. 3 (2008): 282–309.

6. According to Jewish law, Judaism is passed on matrilineally. Given the national ethnocentricity of Israeli society, Jews have a clear advantage, one that is legally anchored and culturally fortified.

7. This section was first presented at the MLA Annual Convention in Philadelphia on December 27, 2009. I would like to thank my copanelists, Professors Nancy K. Miller and Nili Gold, for their comments. In the original Hebrew, the English translation of the title is "Death of My Mother"; I have opted for my own translation here, which I think better serves the text.

8. Zach, *Mot immi*, 5.

9. For Saint Augustine see *The Confessions*, Book XI:1 (New York: Airmont Publishing Company, 1969), 209. I have quoted from Derrida in "Circumfession," in *Jacques Derrida*, trans. Geoffrey Bennington (Chicago: University of Chicago Press, 1991), 8.

10. Sometimes, as Brenner does in the second volume of his complete works: *Breakdown and Bereavement* (Tel Aviv: Hakibbutz Hameuchad, 1978), the author states that the found life writings are too fragmented to bring to print as they are and therefore must be published as part of a novel. See Menachem Brinker, *Ad ha-simta ha-tverianit* (Tel Aviv: Am Oved, 1990).

11. Section 3 of the book has three such instances: "Once, beyond despair, I reproached her for the mound of used toilet paper which accumulated by the toilet. . . . Another time she said: It's you. You want to see me in my degradation. Another time I found her slapping her one hand with the other and scolding it: It's no good

what you are doing. It's wrong. You are going to wind up being taken out of your home for it" (9).

12. See Tsamir, *Be-shem ha-nof*, 59–89.

13. See p. 103 of Zach, *Mot immi*, for the Luftwaffe reference.

14. Zach's mother asks him for pills that would facilitate her exit, thereby relieving her pain. (He is unable to deliver them but soon after her death procures some for himself.) Eventually, when no other hospital would care for her, she was moved to the Italian hospital in Haifa, managed by Italian Franciscan nuns. Zach's poem "Il Figlio della Signora della Camera 9"—in *Kol ha-shirim ve-shirim hadashim* (Tel Aviv: Hakibbutz Hameuchad, 2008), 2:321; *Anti-mehikon* (Tel Aviv: Hakibbutz Hameuchad, 1984), 43—relates to this point with a note naming the time and place of its writing, "Haifa, the Italian Hospital, 18.12.82," although Zach would distance himself from the term *experience* (as discussed later in the main text). A telling dating discrepancy marks the poem. In the memoir Zach expresses his hope that his mother will make it to her eightieth birthday, but she disappoints him, dying a few days before his own birthday. Yet the poem has his mother dying December 18, five days *after* his actual birthday. This is an excessively detail-focused reading—a poem is not a legal document—but the attempt to frame it as a document, and the error in the date in *My Mother's Death*, highlights Zach's tense relationship with memoir, autobiography, and exposure. Ruth Kartun-Blum discusses this poem and other autobiographical poems relating to Zach's mother in her essay on the Christian foundations of Zach's poetics. See *Hirhurim al psichopatologia be-shirat Natan Zach* (Tel Aviv: Hakibbutz Hameuchad, 2009), 48–56.

15. On creating a self see Paul John Eakin, *Living Autobiographically: How We Create Identity in Narrative* (Ithaca, NY: Cornell University Press, 2008).

16. Detailed readings of fairy tale collections, such as Ruth B. Bottigheimer's reading of the Brothers Grimm, may expose a given editorial imprint and its ideological worldview; however, this entails careful comparison of versions and editions and yields less decisive findings when it comes to fairy tales. See her *Grimms' Bad Girls and Bold Boys: The Moral and Social Vision of the Tales* (New Haven: Yale University Press, 1989).

17. The daily newspaper *Davar* reported the two women's murder and Heinrich Scher's suicide on January 7, 1960.

18. Zach's description of his other paternal uncle's family also diverges from the story of the dwarfs: his aunt Betty's aggression toward her husband, Inshel (Yehiel), is aimed at distancing Inshel from his son, her favorite child. Uncle Inshel himself

dies of a broken heart one month after his son Rolf is killed by a bomb explosion on a Haifa bus in 1948 (*Mot immi*, 101). The intensity of responses to these events also diverges from the tired indifference in the dwarfs' story. In an autobiographical poem of the same period Zach concludes: "It was a problem of love. / The rest could be overcome." (*Kol ha-shirim*, vol. 2, 293; my rough translation)

19. Zach spoke bluntly of the atmosphere in his childhood home in a *Ha'aretz* interview with Dalia Karpel: "I'm the Candyman Melting in the Rain," March 11, 2010, http://www.haaretz.com/i-m-the-candyman-melting-in-the-rain-1.264665.

20. Zach, *Mot immi*, 71. Notably the image of the chin, protruding like the handle of a broken dish, repeats itself in his poem "Il Figlio della Signora della Camera 9."

21. The poem opens the cycle "Beintayim," published in Zach's collection *Anti-mehikon*, 39–52. Shimon Sandbank reads this fragment as a key to Zach's work; see his review of Zach's collected works, *Kol ha-shirim ve-shirim hadashim*, in *Ha'aretz*, February 25, 2009, http://www.haaretz.co.il/misc/article-print-page/1.1247509.

The Hebrew for "fear not" (line 7)—the whole line reads "And hold her cold hand and say fear not"—is *al tir'i* (אַל תִּירְאִי), do not fear, high language with biblical allusions—often used by God and the prophets. Likewise, in the Bible three of eleven feminine appearances relate to the mothering of sons (and, notably, not daughters) (see Genesis 21:17; Genesis 35:17; Samuel I, 4:20) and nearby death, including that of a mother. In Zach's poem the grown son says these words to his mother, acknowledging perhaps that he has not been a balm to her, and that just as the biblical Benjamin and Ichabod could not help their respective mothers, who died after their birth, he cannot help his mother. Each biblical mother marks her son by naming him so that he will carry the circumstances of his birth and her death within him, his name depicting their symbiotic, although failed, relationship. Zach's poem, with its biblical connotations, illuminates the mother's experience rather than the son's pain and perspective.

22. In Zach's March 10, 2011, interview with *Ha'aretz*, he recalls the Christmas tree in his childhood home in Berlin. As noted, Ruth Kartun-Blum, in her interpretation of the cycle, highlights the Christian setting of "Il Figlio della Signora della Camera 9," which she reads as mirroring the Pietà, in which the Virgin holds the dead Jesus. Here the son kneels at his mother's bed, and the language used to describe him is ascribed to the Italian nuns, the "focalizers" of the poem, watching one "master" at his mother's deathbed. The Hebrew word *adon*, unlike *ish* or *gever* (man) or *ben* (son), connotes the foreignness of the speaker, as well as the Christian frame—because *Adon*, capitalized, denotes the Lord; specifically, in a Christian context, *Adon* is Christ (*Dominus*). The choice of the word *adon* also echoes the

foreignness of the Hebrew language in the mouths of the Italian or possibly Palestinian nun-nurses, and registers their respectful distance toward the patient's "native" son.

23. *Selected Poems and Prose of Paul Celan*, trans. John Felstiner (New York: W. W. Norton, 2001), 277.

24. Roland Barthes, *Camera Lucida: Reflections on Photography*, trans. Richard Howard (New York: Hill & Wang, 1981), 109.

25. Jacques Derrida, *The Ear of the Other* (New York: Schocken Books, 1985). See Nancy K. Miller, "Representing Others: Gender and the Subjects of Autobiography," *Differences* 6, no. 1 (1994): 1–27.

26. Zach, *Mot immi*, 59. The next few sections in Zach's book quote directly from Dr. Christian Barnard's *Good Life Good Death: A Doctor's Case for Euthanasia and Suicide* (Prentice Hall, 1980).

27. Miller, "Representing Others," 12. See also Paul de Man, "Autobiography as De-facement," *MLN* 94, no. 5 (1979): 919–23.

28. Zach, *Mishana le-shana*, 122.

29. Ibid., 125.

30. See particularly Hannan Hever, *Pit'om mare'e ha-milhama* (Tel Aviv: Hakibbutz Hameuchad, 2001), and also Dan Miron, *Mul ha-ah ha-shotek* (Jerusalem: Keter, 1992).

31. Haim Be'er, *Halomoteyhem ha-hadashim* (Tel Aviv: Am Oved Books, 2014), 122–23. In Hebrew the adjective for "fresh" is *haim*, echoing the author's first name, while Be'er means "well" in Hebrew, spelled with the letters bet, aleph, resh, an acronym for *ben* Avraham Rakhlevsky—the son of Avraham Rakhlevsky. The Hebrew title, *Havalim*, can also literally mean "rope."

32. Haim Be'er, "Seder ha-dorot" (The Order of Generations), in *Sha'ashu'im Yom Yom* (Day-to-Day Delights) (Tel Aviv: Am Oved Publishers, 1970), 48.

33. Unless stated otherwise, quotations are from the English edition, *The Pure Element of Time* (2003). When needed, the Hebrew version, *Havalim* (1998), will be noted.

34. Be'er, *Havalim*, 17.

35. See p. 170 in *The Pure Element of Time* (p. 204 in *Havalim*) for bar mitzvah dinner.

36. The verse to follow also appears on p. 182 (and see p. 216 in *Havalim*): "Turn out the light. / Tomorrow is a day to work. / Mary-Mary black or white, / Not me and not some foreign jerk." And after a pause, he concludes his reprimand with an eternal pair of words: "Brothel of Bastards."

37. See p. 40 in *Havalim*. Lineage as a definer of narrative identity and ability marks a scene in which the young Haim meets Agnon, whom he does not yet recognize, in a bookstore. Agnon questions the boy about his family tree, and Haim responds by tracing it back seven generations. But Agnon chides him that a person should know his family tree back to Adam and Eve.

38. Another memorable story told by Be'er's grandmother is of an encounter between a family ancestor and a frightened, cold escapee from the 1812 Napoleonic-Russian battlefield, perhaps the emperor himself. The forebear points the soldier in the right direction, and they trade coats to prevent the soldier from being identified. The Napoleonic cloak is subsequently made into a curtain cover (*parochet*) for the Torah Ark, which is then donated to the Hurba Synagogue in the Jewish quarter of Old Jerusalem; the cloak itself is preserved in a Haifa museum. Be'er doubts his grandmother's story until he sees the artifact on display at the museum. In "Batei Ungarin," included in his first poetry volume, *Sha'ashu'im Yom Yom* (1970), he records a different version of the story. Named for his grandmother's Orthodox Jewish neighborhood in Jerusalem, the poem depicts Grandmother Hannah intimately telling his uncle Zechariah about "the seventy rubles which one of her forefathers gave the drunk Cossacks in the Russian winter of 1812 for Napoleon's imperial cloak, and about the curtain made of it, in gold and gilded green for the synagogue in Mishkenot Sha'ananim, a precious vessel" (50).

39. *Havalim*, 79.

40. Romain Gary, *Promise at Dawn*, trans. John Markham Beach (London: M. Joseph, 1962), 7.

41. *Havalim*, 84–85.

42. Dov Yosef (Bernard Joseph, 1899–1980) was the Israeli minister of rationing and supply, who headed the notorious austerity policy of 1949–1959.

43. Regarding the line "As Nabokov confesses," the writer referred not to the "story teller" but to the "fictionist": "The man in me revolts against the fictionist." *Speak, Memory* (New York: Universal Library; Grosset and Dunlap, 1951), chapter 5, 58. Be'er universalizes this point—his man becomes a person; by replacing "fictionist" with "story teller" he highlights the craft of fiction and the art of narration instead of dwelling on the revolving door between life and fiction.

44. *Havalim*, 330.

45. Here I have altered Harshav's translation for accuracy. The original (in italics) reads: ". . . which accompanied me during the two years since I *started groping for what Ruhama Weber declared to me—that one day I would make some resurrection—* suddenly grew dark." This scene occurs in the first chapter of the second part of the

book, when Ruhama Weber listens to the mother tell about her *Shvartz Yor* (Yiddish for "black years" and referring to her time with her first husband) and Ruhama tries to stop her, saying: "The child must not hear such things . . . this child should be outside, with children his own age."

"On the contrary, let him hear." Mother ignored the neighbor's reprimand, turned to me, and said: "I'm telling you that on purpose. You have to know everything. Maybe someday you'll make something of it." (64)

46. See Haim Be'er, *Feathers*, trans. Hillel Halkin (Hanover, NH: University Press of New England, 2004), 16–18. Another parallel scene is that of her death (pp. 57–58 in *Feathers*).

47. The "obvious choice" reference appears on p. 109 in *Havalim*.

48. *Havalim*, 126–27.

49. For the fictional scene of the blessing of the son, see *Feathers*, 120–25.

50. Eakin, *Living Autobiographically*, 163–64.

51. Six years younger than Amos Oz, Be'er grew up on the same streets as his literary counterpart, and frequented the same bookshops and library. It is striking to compare Be'er's vision of the city and its landscape to Oz's, between 1948 and 1967. Oz's Jerusalem is a suffocating small town, vulnerable and in perpetual danger, whereas Be'er's Jerusalem is a land of adventure and surprise. There are no Palestinian figures in his story, but he marks the traces of the Nakba in the landscape. Thus, when he accompanies his father to pay their annual apartment rent, he notes that the owners of the Sansour Building, in the heart of Jerusalem, where the lawyer's office is located, are now exiles across the border. In his childhood wanderings he habitually winds up at the border. Beyond it is not heterotopia but the bustle of an urban hub that is his mother's forebears' town, where he longs to go (*Havalim*, 290).

52. The post-bomb white flakes of plaster are also embedded in *Feathers*, chapter 9, p. 147.

53. *Havalim*, 164. "Quicksand" is my departure from Harshav's translation, which says "demanding"; she seems to have mistaken טובעניות for תובעניות. Instead of "search for their *path*," Harshav has "search for their *undermining*."

54. My changes to Barbara Harshav's translation for correctness are set here in italics: "The preference for the one memory and its persistent cultivation by *diligent* repetition, which *cloaked it with* words and led to a *certain* crystallization of it, and especially to an artistic shaping, might be what blocked the earlier, vivid but shapeless memory and prevented it from floating up. And who would guarantee me that that memory itself, *from the moment* that *it* surfaced at long last, even before the flesh of the words was closed *over* it, won't ward off what now wants to *erupt from*

those internal places that never know peace. And the hand wants to hold onto those *obscure* things that no longer have shape but essence, as they were back then in *their initial* vibrations, an eternal and direct present—that hand will return empty."

55. For a subtle discussion of narrative identities see Eakin, *Living Autobiographically.*

56. Hannan Hever, review of *Havalim,* "Mar'e le'atsmo etsba meshuleshet," *Ha'aretz,* Books, September 23, 1998, 1–2. For anecdotes as a self-contained genre see also Catherine Gallagher and Stephen Greenblatt, "Counterhistory and the Anecdote," *Practicing New Historicism* (Chicago: University of Chicago Press, 2000), 49–74. For a discussion of linear narrative, meaning, and sequential history, see Hayden White, "The Value of Narrativity," in *On Narrative,* ed. W. J. T. Mitchell (Chicago: University of Chicago Press, 1980) 1–23.

57. Although Be'er credits his mother and grandmother for his becoming an author, he also notes that his father could apparently recite Pushkin and Lermontov by heart and had written commendable short fiction and poetry in Russian, according to a friend from his hometown, but that he had abandoned the language because "they, the Bolsheviks" had murdered his brothers in the cellars of Lubyanka Prison for counterrevolutionary Zionism" (*Havalim,* 179). This "writing gene" is not registered in the story as a possible source for Be'er's own path.

58. Lest we ignore the irrational weight here, the story keeps reminding us that this event took place on the very day on which the Hebrew University of Jerusalem was founded, as a venue of rationality.

59. Gary, *Promise at Dawn,* 262.

3. Languages of Immigration: Shimon Ballas and Aharon Appelfeld

1. See Gershon Shaked's response to *The Story of a Life:* "Ha-briha min ha-yisrael-iyut" (The Escape from Israeliness), *Ha'aretz,* Books, April 20, 1999.

2. Shimon Ballas, *Be-guf rishon* (Tel Aviv: Hakibbutz Hameuchad, 2009), 113. An early version of this chapter was presented in winter 2009 at a celebration honoring the author and the book's publication at the Van Leer Jerusalem Institute. For further analysis of Ballas, see Ariel Sheetrit, "Beginning Again: The Boundaries of Self-Invention in Shimon Ballas's *Be-guf gishon,*" *Auto/Biography Studies* 28, no. 1 (Summer 2013): 2–35.

3. Aharon Appelfeld with Meir Appelfeld, *Od hayom gadol* (Jerusalem: Keter and Yad Ben Zvi, 2001); English: *A Table for One,* trans. Aloma Halter (Jerusalem: Toby Press, 2005), 71.

4. Ballas, *Be-guf rishon*, 97.

5. Ibid.

6. Shimrit Peled's article has finally done just this, but it was written nearly thirty-five years after the novel was published. See her "Naphil muvas be-nof hasar tslalim: mizrahiyut, ashkenaziyut u-merhav baroman hayisraeli le-ahar milhcmet 1967" ("Mizrahiness," "Ashkenaziness," and Space in the Israeli Novel after the 1967 War), *Teoria u-vikoret* 29 (2006): 149–72.

7. Ballas, *Be-guf rishon*, 113. The Hebrew here is "edot ha-mizrah." I have chosen "Sephardic" for lack of an English equivalent that would contain the term's political implications. In Israel, demonstrating the political valence of ethnic categorization, Jewish immigrants of all Arab and Middle Eastern origins have been grouped together as *edot ha-mizrah*. No equivalent term exists for Ashkenazi Jews. In recent decades *Mizrahi* has been accepted as the parallel for *Ashkenazi*, permitting the difference between "East" and "West" to be marked without the condescending, degrading, folkloric connotations of *edot*. In addition, a limited number of speakers such as Ballas have domesticated the hyphenated "Arab-Jewish" identity, which allows for a specific identity marker.

8. Ballas, *Be-guf rishon*.

9. On the "autobiographical pact," discussed earlier, see Phillippe Lejeune, *On Autobiography* (Minneapolis: University of Minnesota Press, 1989).

10. Shimon Ballas, *Ve-hu aher* (Tel Aviv: Zmora-Bitan, 1991); English translation: *Outcast*, trans. Ammiel Alcalay and Oz Shelach (San Francisco: City Lights, 2007).

11. Virginia Woolf, "The Lives of the Obscure," *The Common Reader* (London: Hogarth Press, 1951), 146–67.

12. See Nancy K. Miller, "Representing Others: Gender and the Subjects of Autobiography," *Differences* 6 no. 1 (1994): 1–27.

13. Paul John Eakin, *How Our Lives Become Stories: Making Selves* (Ithaca, NY: Cornell University Press, 1999), 49.

14. Erich Kästner, *When I Was a Boy*, trans. Isabel and Florence McHugh (New York: Franklin Watts Inc., 1959).

15. This resembles but is less confrontational and offensive than chapter 5 of Amos Oz's *A Tale of Love and Darkness*.

16. Shimon Ballas, *Ba-ir ha-tahtit* (Tel Aviv: Tarmil, 1979).

17. Ballas's memory fails him here, as memory tends to do: the article was published late in fall 1969, and the invasion occurred a year before that—in August 1968.

18. Svetlana Boym, "On Diasporic Intimacy," *The Future of Nostalgia* (New York: Basic Books, 2001), 251–58.

19. Shimon Ballas *Ash'ab me-Baghdad* (Tel Aviv: Am Oved, 1970).

20. Ibid., 119–20.

21. The germs of this section were presented at several conferences, including that of the American Association for Jewish Studies in Washington, DC, in December 2005, and in Karlstad, Sweden, in June 2006. Yigal Schwartz has recently added meaningful contributions to the view of Appelfeld's position in Israeli literature and to the relationship between fiction and autobiography in Appelfeld's work. See his *Ma'amin beli knesiya* (A Believer without a Church) (Or Yehuda: Kinneret, Zmora-Bitan, Dvir, 2009), chapters 2 and 4.

22. Aharon Appelfeld, *Sipur Haim* (Jerusalem: Keter, 1998); English translation: *The Story of a Life: A Memoir* (New York: Schocken, 2004). "Linda H. Peterson . . . demonstrates . . . that English autobiographers from Bunyan to Gosse believed themselves to be participating in a distinctive generic tradition." Paul John Eakin, introduction to Lejeune, *On Autobiography*, viii.

23. See Emily Miller Budick, *Aharon Appelfeld's Fiction: Acknowledging the Holocaust* (Bloomington: Indiana University Press, 2005), 153–79. For a careful and detailed comparison between autobiographical and fictional presentations of the same scene in Appelfeld's work, see Schwartz, *Ma'amin beli knesiya*, 53–100.

24. Appelfeld, *The Story of a Life*, 42.

25. Appelfeld, *A Table for One*, 53.

26. Ibid., 35 (*Od hayom gadol*, 44). Aloma Halter accurately translates as follows: "By raising the immigrant from an anonymous individual to that of a suffering man, I was in the avant-garde, allowing readers to experience immigrants as sensitive people" (35). *Avant-garde*, however, does not carry the loaded ideological connotations of the Hebrew term *halutz* (pioneer or scout). For further revisionary discussion of Israeli culture in the 1950s, see Gali Drucker Bar-Am's important PhD dissertation, "'*Ich bin dayn shtoib?*' [Am I Your Dust?]: Representations of the Israeli Experience in Yiddish Prose in Israel, 1948–1968" (in Hebrew), Hebrew University of Jerusalem, 2013.

27. In a personal essay from 1979, "Edut" (Testimony), Appelfeld writes: "Those who chose to make aliya to Eretz Yisrael strove to heal not only their body." The essay appears in the Appelfeld collection *Masot be-guf rishon* (Jerusalem: Jewish Agency, 1979), 18.

28. *A Table for One*, 105. If a reader were to follow *The Story of a Life* as a source of

information about the author's life, he or she would conclude, from passages such as the following, that Appelfeld's father did not survive: "I'd already seen many dead people in the ghetto and in the camp, and I knew that a dead person doesn't get back up on his feet and is eventually put in a pit. Yet I still didn't grasp death as an end. I continued to expect my parents to come and collect me" (52).

29. Gershon Shaked, *Ein makom aher* (There's No Other Place) (Tel Aviv: Hakibbutz Hameuchad, 1988).

30. Shaked, *Ha'aretz*, April 20, 1999.

31. Appelfeld, *The Story of a Life*, 198.

32. Appelfeld, *A Table for One*, 9 (*Od hayom gadol*, 14). The English translation is altered slightly from that by Aloma Halter; quoted by Schwartz in *Ma'amin beli knesiya*, 153.

33. Appelfeld, *A Table for One*, 87.

34. Ibid.

35. Eakin, *Living Autobiographically*, 67.

36. About Appelfeld as an Israeli writer, see also Schwartz, *Ma'amin beli knesiya*, 137–58.

37. An unpublished lecture I thank Amia Lieblich for sharing with me.

38. For example, the Sinai war of 1956 appears in Appelfeld's memoirs as colossally boring. Stationed in a trench in Motza, expecting a Jordanian army that never arrives, Appelfeld avoids political issues. He writes in *A Table*: "One soldier who couldn't take this long drawn-out waiting period actually deserted" (29; *Od hayom gadol*, 36). In 1963 Appelfeld spent a month of reserve duty on Mount Scopus, which he examines in the same book: "I was certain that these spiritual hills would enrich me and that I would return completely changed. I was wrong. . . . Over the years I had grown accustomed to tough periods of training, but to be shut up for an entire month with three soldiers who spend most of their time cursing life and cursing army reserve duty is far harder than any exhausting training under the relentless sun" (54).

39. For Appelfeld, in *The Story*: "From the very outset, I felt that literature does not provide a suitable basis for sociological analysis. True literature engages what is concealed in fate and hidden in the human soul; it exists in the metaphysical realms" (149).

40. Ballas, *Be-guf rishon*, 100.

4. Gendered Margins: Narrative Strategies, Embodied Selves, and Subversion in Women's Autobiography

An earlier version of this chapter was published in *Prooftexts* 27, no. 1 (2007): 151–87.

1. Sidonie Smith, *Subjectivity, Identity, and the Body: Women's Autobiographical Practices in the Twentieth Century* (Bloomington: Indiana University Press, 1993), 20. See also James Olney, "Autobiography and the Cultural Moment: A Thematic, Historical, and Bibliographical Introduction," in *Autobiography: Essays Theoretical and Critical*, ed. James Olney (Princeton, NJ: Princeton University Press, 1980), 13–17.

2. Following Antonio Damasio's formulations, Paul John Eakin has recently suggested that the term *embodied self* is a redundancy—since the "self" is inherently "embodied" and the sense or "feeling" experience of the body defines the self: see his *Living Autobiographically: How We Create Identity in Narrative* (Ithaca, NY: Cornell University Press, 2008). However, viewing gender within a historical-cultural context, I still find the term to be meaningful.

3. Elizabeth Grosz, *Volatile Bodies: Toward a Corporeal Feminism* (Bloomington: Indiana University Press, 1994), vii.

4. Smith, *Subjectivity*, 6. And on p. 9 of the same text: "Yet the individual self could endure as a concept of beingness only if, despite the specificities of individual experience, despite the multiplication of differences among people, the legend continued to bear universal marks. This self has to move freely toward its cultural positioning as universal subject but retain a threshold of particulars."

5. Ibid., 11. See also Hélène Cixous, "Sorties: Out and Out: Attacks/Ways Out/ Forays," in *The Newly Born Woman*, ed. Hélène Cixous and Catherine Clément (Minneapolis: University of Minnesota Press, 1988), 63–132.

6. Smith, *Subjectivity*, 15.

7. Carolyn Heilbrun, *Writing a Woman's Life* (New York: Ballantine Books, 1988), 17.

8. Shoshana Felman, *What Does a Woman Want? Reading and Sexual Difference* (Baltimore: Johns Hopkins University Press, 1993), 156.

9. It would seem that while women need to write themselves out of silenced embodied subjectivity, men invest their unruly corporeal subjectivity in a universal subjectivity. Relevant examples might include Aharon Appelfeld's pre-army examination in *The Story of a Life* (see chapter 3); or Yoram Kaniuk's description of Jews

lynching an Arab man in Tel Aviv, and of his parents' ailing bodies, in *Post Mortem* (see discussion in chapter 1). Other applicable cases are Haim Be'er's father's exposed penis on his son's school trip, and his mother's decision not to take her own life when she gets her period, along with her realization of potential motherhood, in *Havalim* (see chapter 2). Michael Gluzman's contribution to studying the male body in modern Hebrew literature has been comparatively the most significant and continuous. See his *Ha-guf ha-zioni* (The Zionist Body) (Bnei Brak: Hakibbutz Hameuchad, 2007).

10. Nurith Gertz and Deborah Gertz, *El ma she-namog* (Tel Aviv: Am Oved Publishers, 1997), 32.

11. The final subversive scene of Alona Frankel's *Yalda* (Tel Aviv: Mapa, 2004), awarded the 2005 Sapir Prize, is particularly noteworthy. For discussions of women, the Shoah, and autobiography, see Carol Rittner and John K. Roth, eds., *Different Voices: Women and the Holocaust* (St. Paul: Paragon House, 1993); Dalia Ofer and Lenore J. Weitzman, eds., *Women in the Holocaust* (New Haven: Yale University Press, 1998). I thank Manuela Consonni for pointing out both of these texts to me. For further recent discussions of Israeli women's autobiography, see Orly Lubin, "Bein mitbah ha-poalim lakafe ha-hungari: otobiographia shel isha ironit," *Tarbut demokratit* 10 (2006): 357–94; Margalit Shilo, "Prati ke-tsiburi: Itta Yelin ve-Yehudit Harari kotvot otobiographia," *Katedra* 118 (2006); Yael Ben-Zvi Morad, "Be-guf rishon nashi" (First Person Feminine: Contemporary Hebrew Autobiographies by Women), PhD diss., Ben-Gurion University, 2014.

12. *Shdemot* 4 (1995).

13. Periodically the radio show was threatened with cancellation and Ben-Yehuda's salary targeted for cutting, but an intervention by the Israeli Journalists' Association and then prime minister Ariel Sharon, a personal friend, removed the threat.

14. Amos Oz mentions Israel Zarchi in *A Tale of Love and Darkness* as the devoted friend who bought three copies of his father's first book: "I did not tell anyone except, many years later, his daughter Nurit Zarchi, who did not seem overly impressed by what I had told her." Amos Oz, *A Tale of Love and Darkness*, trans. Nicholas de Lange (Orlando: Harcourt Books, 2005), 135.

15. Orly Lubin, *Isha koret isha* (Haifa and Or Yehuda: Haifa University and Zmora-Bitan, 2003), 15–61.

16. For an illuminating discussion of autobiography, women's bodies, and the nation in the 1940s, see Orly Lubin, "Ha-emet she-bein misgarot ha-emet: oto-

biographia, edut, guf ve-atar," in *Aderet le-Binyamin*, Vol. 1, ed. Ziva Ben-Porat (Tel Aviv: Hakibbutz Hameuchad and Tel Aviv University, 1999), 133–49.

17. See Hamutal Tsamir, *Be-shem ha-nof* (Jerusalem and Beer Sheva: Keter and the Heksherim Center at Ben-Gurion University, 2006); Chana Kronfeld, *On the Margins of Modernism: Decentering Literary Dynamics* (Berkeley: University of California Press, 1996); Barbara E. Mann, "Framing the Native: Esther Raab's Visual Poetics," *Israel Studies* 4 no. 1 (1999): 234–57; Hannan Hever, "Hamtsa'at ha-yelidiyut be-shirat Esther Raab," *Mi-reshit: shalosh masot al shira ivrit yelidit* (From the Beginning: Three Essays on Nativist Hebrew Poetry) (Tel Aviv: Keshev Publishing House, 2008), 9–34.

18. Esther Raab, *Gan she-harav* (A Garden in Ruins) (Tel Aviv: Tarmil, 1983); and *Kol ha-proza* (Collected Prose) (Hod Ha-Sharon: Astrolog, 2001). Raab's poetry has been the subject of elaborate critical discussion, with directly pertinent discussions including Mann, "Framing the Native," and Hever, "Hamtsa'at ha-yelidiyut be-shirat Esther Raab." For other central contributions in recent decades, see Dan Miron, *Imahot meyasdot, ahayot horgot* (Tel Aviv: Hakibbutz Hameuchad, 1991); Michael Gluzman, *The Politics of Canonicity: Lines of Resistance in Modernist Hebrew Poetry* (Stanford, CA: Stanford University Press, 2003); Dana Olmert, *Bitnua't safa ikeshet* (Haifa: Haifa University Press, 2012); Kronfeld, *On the Margins of Modernism*; and Tsamir, *Be-shem ha-nof*.

19. Yehuda Raab, as narrated to his son, Benjamin Ben-Ezer (Raab) (1956), *Ha-telem ha-rishon: zikhronot, 1862–1930* (Jerusalem: World Zionist Federation, 1988), 20.

20. See Daniel Boyarin, *Unheroic Conduct: The Rise of Heterosexuality and the Invention of the Jewish Man* (Berkeley: University of California Press, 1997); David Biale, *Eros and the Jews: From Biblical Israel to Contemporary America* (New York: Basic Books, 1992); Gluzman, *Ha-guf ha-zioni*.

21. All quotations from this paragraph come from Raab, *Kol ha-proza*, 67; see also 31.

22. For an English translation see Shirley Kaufman, Galit Hasan-Rokem, and Tamar Hess, eds., *The Defiant Muse: Hebrew Feminist Poems from Antiquity to the Present* (New York: Feminist Press, 1999), 93.

23. See Hever, *Mi-reshit*, 20.

24. Ehud Ben-Ezer suggests that Yehuda Raab's financial straits that year, during which he sold the family home and moved to a smaller, less centrally located one in the moshava, may explain his decision not to send his daughter to school. Perhaps he could not afford the tuition and his pride compelled him to use the mixed classes as an excuse. Whatever the reason, Esther Raab was hurt, angered, and frustrated

by the development, as her adolescent diary clearly shows (see *Kol ha-proza*, 158). However unnerving, the experience did not shake Raab's admiration for her father.

25. Raab uses the English word here, in transliteration.

26. Raab, *Gan she-harav*.

27. Rachel Yanait Ben-Zvi, *Anu olim* (Tel Aviv: Am Oved, 1959).

28. Ziona Rabau describes the scene of her own birth in the Palestinian village of Ein-Sini'a—as Orly Lubin has shown—where her parents immigrated in 1906, to mark the limits of her family's existence in the village. See Lubin, "Bein mitbah ha-poalim la-kafe ha-hungari, 357–94, especially 369–70. See also Ziona Rabau, *Ani tel-avivit* (Tel Aviv: Tarmil, 1984), 19–21. For a fuller discussion of Yanait's book, see Tamar Hess, *Heik ha-em shel zikhronot* (Or Yehuda: Masa Kritit, 2014). This book also accounts for Hayuta Busel, who writes of her daughter's birth in Degania as a formative moment for the kibbutz. Likewise Zehava Uri describes Rivka Yatzkar giving birth in Degania during World War I, under dire conditions, as an indicator of socialist settler women's solidarity.

29. Adriana X. Tatum offers a subtle and illuminating reading of this passage in reference to the linguistic and cultural environment in which Raab was raised, and the concepts of nativeness she develops. See her "Paris or Jerusalem? The Multilingualism of Esther Raab," *Prooftexts* 26 no, 1–2 (2006): 6–28.

30. Ibid.

31. Yehuda Raab, *Ha-telem ha-rishon* (Jerusalem: World Zionist Organization, 1988), 144.

32. Lubin, "Bein mitbah ha-poalim la-kafe ha-hungari."

33. Shlomo Grodzensky, "Mi-Yisrael ad Yisrael" (From Israel to Israel), *Amot* 1, no. 1 (1962): 371–72.

34. Esther Raab, *Amot* 1, no. 2 (1962): 96.

35. Tsamir, *Be-shem ha-nof*, 96.

36. Hever, *Mi-reshit*, 14.

37. Ibid., 17–18.

38. This discussion skips over the so-called Palmach generation, and major authors such as Moshe Shamir (b. 1921), S. Yizhar (b. 1916), Haim Gouri (b. 1923)—in his prose—and Hanoch Bartov (b. 1926). Biographically both Kaniuk (b. 1930) and Netiva Ben-Yehuda (b. 1928) could be part of this generation, and both served in the Palmach. The seven years that separate Ben-Yehuda from Shamir and the nine that separate Kaniuk from Shamir enabled them to serve as young soldiers in the 1948 war but not to develop as Palmach generation writers.

39. Ehud Ben-Ezer notes that this segment was first published in 1969 and blends

two periods. Raab's first poems were published in *Hedim* in 1922, but she hadn't moved back to Tel Aviv from Cairo until 1925. The orchard scene then must have occurred in Petah Tikva before 1921, when she was first married.

40. See Hamutal Tsamir's reading of Raab's poem "Al ma'arumaikh hogeg yom lavan," in her *Be-shem ha-nof*.

41. See Dan Miron, "Illu nikhtav bi-zmano," *Siman kri'a* 16–17 (1983): 519–21.

42. Yael Feldman, *No Room of Their Own: Gender and Nation in Israeli Women's Fiction* (New York: Columbia University Press, 1999), 177–91. See especially her discussion of the idiosyncratic gender-bending terms Ben-Yehuda creates, *nekevim* and *zekharot*, on pp. 185–88.

43. Netiva Ben-Yehuda, *1948—Bein ha-sefirot: roman al hathalat ha-milhama* (Jerusalem: Keter, 1981), 231. The translation is, unless stated otherwise, mine. This sort of detailed description is not common practice among autobiographical authors of Ben-Yehuda's generation, even decades after the war. General Raphael Eitan, for example, when faced with the memory of his friends' mutilated bodies, writes: "The bodies were brutally crushed. I can't describe the details": Raphael Eitan with Dov Goldstein, *Raphul: sipur shel hayal* (Ma'ariv: Tel Aviv, 1985), 37.

44. As Hever has shown, the living-dead metaphor not only symbolically sanctified death in violent national circumstances, it also relegated women to the margins of Israeli culture: Hannan Hever, *Pit'om mare'e ha-milhama* (Tel Aviv: Hakibbutz Hameuchad, 2001), 50, 194–99. In Ben-Yehuda's retrospective narrative, the living-dead are not the dead who haunt the living but instead the living—the soldiers who have survived combat—who go on with their lives as if they were dead.

45. As for the official IDF memorial website, it records Milstein's death as having happened in defense against a direct attack on Ramot Naftali, the settlement and base from which Ben-Yehuda and her group had set out that morning, and not in an ill-planned exercise: http://www.izkor.mod.gov.il/izkor86.asp?t=88942.

46. Yitzhak Rabin also describes the Palmach troops' exhaustion as so overpowering that they could not keep their eyes open long enough to hear Ben-Gurion announce the state's establishment on the radio. But throughout his narrative of the 1948 war, although he counts the casualties and the wounded, he refrains from describing bodies and bodily injuries. See Yitzhak Rabin with Dov Goldstein, *Pinkas sherut* (Tel Aviv: Sifirat Ma'ariv, 1979), 49. Raphael Eitan mentions lack of food, but recounts that the Palmach troops stole enough from the kibbutz storage rooms to make up for it: see Eitan, *Raphul*, 12.

47. Haim Nachman Bialik began writing his long narrative poem *Megilat ha-*

esh (Scroll of Fire), subtitled "A Legend of the Destruction," during the June 1905 *Potemkin* battleship mutiny in Odessa, casting it as a "Hurban" story, or one referencing the destruction of the Temple (Babylonian Talmud, tractate Gitin, p. 57b). In Bialik's version, following the Temple's destruction, four hundred young people are taken prisoner and abandoned on an island. The women march blindly into a ravine, where a deep black river is rushing. All but one of the men, who does not jump, dive to their deaths. This is the scene to which Ben-Yehuda refers. *Megilat ha-esh* is concerned with preserving the "sacred flame" of the Temple in the hearts of the survivors. Traditional criticism has noted the blurred and mystifying vision that this poem evokes of youth and beauty, love, individuality, self-sacrifice and self-destruction, redemption, and national spiritual survival. See Ya'akov Fichman, *Megilat ha-esh*, in *Bialik: yetsirato le-sugeiha bi-r'i ha-bikoret*, ed. Gershon Shaked (Jerusalem: Mossad Bialik, 1974), 314–16; Hamutal Bar-Yosef, *Magaim shel decadence* (Jerusalem: Mossad Bialik, 1997), 127–28.

48. Regarding the misquoting: Genesis 49:24 refers to Joseph's arms, not his muscles.

49. Generations of readers have found *Megilat ha-esh* to be an obscure poem, yet the accepted reading stresses individual responsibility and devotion to the national cause at all costs.

50. Smith, *Subjectivity*, 5–17.

51. Nurit Zarchi reflects on *Gvilei esh*, which includes personal writings, letters, and literary work: "I know all of *Gvilei esh* by heart, all the letters those boys that fell wrote to their sweethearts. I recite them more than any other literature that I will ever read. I follow their conflicts, the books they've read, the red sunsets they saw over the Jerusalem hills during cease-fire, and the heartaches they suffered because of a delayed letter, a lost kiss, a moment before it was all lost." *Mishakey bdidut* (Tel Aviv: Yedioth Aharonot Sifrey Hemed, 1999), 95.

52. "Autobiography—identity through alterity—is also writing against death twice: the other's death and one's own. Every autobiography, we might say, is also an autothanatography." Nancy K. Miller, "Representing Others: Gender and the Subjects of Autobiography," *Differences* 6, no. 1 (1994): 12.

53. Yehudit Kafri, *Kol ha-kayitz halakhnu yehefim* (Tel Aviv: Tag, 1997), 21, originally published in *Shdemot* 4 (1995).

54. One might return to Bruno Bettelheim's *The Children of the Dream* (London: Macmillan, 1969), or consider a more recent comprehensive addition to this discourse, Yehezkel Dar, ed., *Hinuch be-kibbutz mishtane* (Jerusalem: Magnes Press,

1998). See also Tal Tamir, *Lina meshutefet: kvutsa ve-kibbutz ba-toda'a ha-yisraelit*, exhibition catalog (Tel Aviv: Tel Aviv Museum of Art, 2005).

55. Kafri, *Kol ha-kayitz*, 28.

56. At Ein-Ha-Horesh the Shoah was a dominant presence to which most founders, including Kafri's parents, had lost their families. After the war the survivors who joined the kibbutz, the poet Abba Kovner among them, carried testimony and memory with them. I thank the anonymous *Prooftexts* reader who brought this point to my attention.

57. Because the authors share a surname, I will refer to them by their first names.

58. As with Kafri, force-feeding is central to Gertz's memories of Ein Ha-Horesh. See also Zarchi's *Mishakey bdidut*, 52.

59. Nancy K. Miller, *Bequest and Betrayal: Memoirs of a Parent's Death* (New York: Oxford University Press, 1996), ix–xiii.

60. Nurith's mothering emerges in relation to her maternal grandfather, Zvi Zevulun Weinberg, a teacher and author who never achieved recognition, and his jokes, which Nurith tells her daughter: "Years later I would pinch her and ask what city had Joshua conquered, and she would say 'Ai' and it was still funny" (*El ma she-namog*, 127). The joke has a physical dimension that links the grandfather's world of Jewish learning, and the trivia stemming from it, to a bodily sensation that can be transferred over generations. The body's material presence figures repeatedly in framing family relations.

61. Also, on p. 91 of *El ma she-namog*: "According to [family] lore, when my father was asked, 'How much does she weigh,' he said, 'As much as she weighs is too much.' Maybe that is why I did not want to eat and had to be sent to the kibbutz."

62. I thank Zohar Weiman-Kelman for this insight.

63. Marianne Hirsch, *Family Frames: Photography, Narrative and Postmemory* (Cambridge, MA: Harvard University Press, 1997), 23. Hirsch explains: "Postmemory characterizes the experience of those who grew up dominated by narratives that preceded their birth, whose own belated stories are evacuated by the stories of the previous generation shaped by traumatic events that can neither be understood nor recreated" (22).

64. Ruth Ginsburg, "The 'Jewish Mother' Turned Monster: Representations of Motherhood by Hebrew Women Novelists, 1881–1993," *Women's Studies International Forum* 20, nos. 5–6 (1997): 631–38.

65. *Mishakey bdidut*, 53; English translation (not yet complete): Lisa Katz, *World Literature Today* (September–December 2004), 36, http://www.poetryinternational

web.net/pi/site/cou_article/item/3085/Girl-Inside-Girl-Inside-Girl-Inside-Girl/en. Unless stated otherwise, the translation is mine.

66. The Hebrew translation for "if you don't exist, you don't feel pain" reads "*im einkha kayam einkha koev*" (27), echoing the Hebrew version of Descartes (*ani hoshev mashma ani kayam*) in sound (*hoshev vs. koev*) and in structure.

67. Katz, *World Literature Today*, 37.

68. Ibid., 36.

69. Zarchi's concepts of reciprocity and love resemble Hélène Cixous's formulations in her reading of Shakespeare's *Antony and Cleopatra*, in "Sorties," *The Newly Born Woman*, trans. Betsy Wing (Minneapolis: University of Minnesota Press, 1986), 122–30.

5. Conclusion: Prophets and Hedgehogs

1. Ariel Hirschfeld, *Rishumim shel hitgalut* (Notes on Epiphany) (Tel Aviv: Xargol Books, 2006).

2. André Aciman, "Arbitrage," *The New Yorker*, July 10, 2000.

3. Paul John Eakin, *Living Autobiographically: How We Create Identity in Narrative* (Ithaca, NY: Cornell University Press, 2008), 163.

4. See Hannan Hever, *Producing the Modern Hebrew Canon: Nation Building and Minority Discourse* (New York: New York University Press, 2002).

5. The Hebrew word for "inscribed" is *nirsham* (written, registered), derived from the same root as *rishumim*.

6. *Midrash Rabbah*, Exodus (Yithro) XXIX.9, trans. S. M. Lehrman (London: Soncino Press, 1951), 344.

7. Ariel Hirschfeld, *Reshimot al makom* (Tel Aviv: Am Oved, 2000). I thank Galit Hasan-Rokem, who suggested this connection to me.

8. Ibid., 78–81.

9. For the "stillness and transience" reference, see ibid., 79.

10. *Should an Angel Ask*

> "Child, where is your soul?"
> Look for it angel—wander through the world!
> You'll find a peaceful village, forest-walled,
> capped by an azure heaven's wide expanse,
> and in its midst one single, lonely cloud.
> There, summer afternoons, a child would play,

a solitary, gentle, dreaming child.
Angel, I was that child. And once,
when silence draped upon the drowsy world,
and drew the child's eyes up toward the sky
toward that single being, pure, distinct,
then like a dove that from its dove-cote flies,
his soul went after the enchanting cloud.

Did it melt away?

"There is a sun in the world, my angel!
My soul was saved by mercy of its rays.
A golden beam caught up my small white moth,
in whose bright light it glimmered a long while. . . . (52).

See Haim Nachman Bialik, *Selected Poems*, Bilingual Edition, trans. Ruth Nevo (Jerusalem: Dvir and Jerusalem Post, 1981), 52–55.

11. *Shmulikkipod* was written and illustrated by a pseudonymous "Kush," an acronym combining "Carmi" and "Shoshana." Shoshana Hyman, a sculptor and the book's illustrator, was the biographical Gadi's mother and Carmi's then wife.

12. In this way, as Yael Tamir has observed—and I thank her for this observation—both Carmi and Hirschfeld in their way sign Philippe Lejeune's "autobiographical pact" by using their sons' names: Gadi and Amitai.

13. T. Carmi, ed. and trans., *The Penguin Book of Hebrew Verse* (Harmondsworth: Penguin Books, 1981), 576.

14. See the extended discussion in Dan Miron, *The Prophetic Mode in Modern Hebrew Poetry* (New Milford, CT: Toby Press, 2010).

15. Ibid., 541.

16. David Biale, ed., *Cultures of the Jews: A New History* (New York: Schocken Books, 2002), 1034.

17. Ibid., 1034.

18. Ibid., 1035.

19. Ibid.

20. Huda Abu-Much, "Emile Habibi be-ivrit" (Emile Habibi in Hebrew), PhD diss., Hebrew University of Jerusalem, 2013. For a pathbreaking discussion of Arabic and Hebrew in Palestine and Israel, see Lital Levy's *Poetic Trespass: Writing between Hebrew and Arabic in Israel/Palestine* (Princeton, NJ: Princeton University Press, 2014).

CREDITS

Aharon Appelfeld, excerpts from *A Table for One* reprinted by permission of Toby Press.

Aharon Appelfeld, excerpts from *The Story of a Life: A Memoir*, translation copyright © 2004 by Schocken Books, a division of Random House, Inc. Used by permission of Schocken Books, an imprint of the Knopf Doubleday Publishing Group, a division of Penguin Random House LLC. All rights reserved. Any third party use of this material, outside of this publication, is prohibited. Interested parties must apply directly to Penguin Random House LLC for permission.

Shimon Ballas, excerpts from *Ash'ab me-Bagdad* reprinted by permission of the author.

Shimon Ballas, excerpts from *Be-guf rishon* reprinted by permission of Hakibbutz Hameuchad.

Haim Be'er, excerpts from *Sha'ashu'im Yom Yom* reprinted by permission of the author.

Nurith Gertz, excerpts from *El ma she-namog* reprinted by permission of the author.

Yoram Kaniuk, excerpts from *Post Mortem* © 1992 by Hakibbutz Hameuchad and Yedioth Ahronoth. Reprinted by permission of Yedioth Ahronoth.

Esther Raab, excerpts from *Kol ha-proza* reprinted by permission of Astrolog Publishing.

Natan Zach, "A Moment," translated by T. Carmi, from *The Penguin Book of Hebrew Verse*, p. 576, edited by T. Carmi (Allen Lane, 1981). Copyright © T. Carmi, 1981. Reproduced by permission of Penguin Books Ltd.

Natan Zach, excerpts from *Mot immi* reprinted by permission of the author.

Nurit Zarchi, excerpts from *Mishakey bdidut* © 1999 by Yedioth Ahronoth Sifrey Hemed. Reprinted by permission of Yedioth Ahronoth.